DANGER ZONE
A DETAILED EXPLORATION OF KISS' CRAZY CRAZY NIGHTS!

JULIAN GILL

BOCA RATON PUBLIC LIBRARY
BOCA RATON, FLORIDA

ISBN13: 978-0-9997765-0-6

Revision: 09/19/2018 06:55:10 PM

Copyright © 2018 by Julian Gill / KissFAQ.com
Cover artwork © 2017 by Nils Brekke Svensson

All rights reserved. No part of this book may be reproduced or transmitted in any form or by any means, electronic or mechanical, including photocopying, recording, or by any information storage and retrieval system, without explicit permission in writing from the copyright owner. Scans/photographs of artwork and/or items of collector's interest are provided for illustrative purposes only under U.S. code TITLE 17, CHAPTER 1, § 107, "Limitations on exclusive rights: Fair use." No claim over the copyright of any of the original artwork or designs, or any quoted works and lyric excerpts, is made.

If Life Is a Radio, Turn Up to Ten

Table of Contents

Foreword 9

Album Overview 11

Introduction... 15

"Crazy Nights" Album Refocused 19

Collecting "Crazy Nights"....................................... 49

Song Stories... 51

Christopher K. Lendt... 65

Phil Ashley 83

Diane Warren 101

Adam Mitchell 107

Bruce Turgon 125

Tom Kelly 129

Gary Corbett.. 145

Bruce Kulick 189

Ron Nevison 219

On Tour: Crazy Nights.. 231

The Video... 309

The "Crazy" Reviews... 313

The "Crazy" Quotes 317

Foreword

Celebrating the history of KISS on an album-by-album basis can be a daunting task. Some recorded efforts, such as "Dressed to Kill" — and the inevitable transition into the "Alive!" period — nearly write themselves. Others, notably "Rock And Roll Over" or "Love Gun," are almost pointless endeavors, due to the limited number of people directly involved in the projects; in addition to the amount of time that has passed since their creation — making participant's memories hazy at best. Albums, be they the 1978 solo releases, or "The Elder," provided a greater challenge. Inevitably, regardless of personal feelings and subjective analysis, both of those projects fell short of the mark, particularly with the amount of effort made by the band members in their creation. Both of those projects had numerous parties involved, many of whom were available to assist with the investigation. That made a detailed exploration, decades later, a worthwhile exercise. Of all of the unmasked KISS albums, 1983–1997, only "Crazy Nights" saw the band truly stepping into the proverbial "danger zone" and reaching for higher aspirations, musically and commercially.

As was the case with oft maligned "The Elder" — and to a lesser extent the 1978 solo albums — KISS' "Crazy Nights" album was a "failure." It did not provide the expected, and much needed hits in the U.S., nor did it lead to a massive SRO two year tour. It certainly didn't resurrect the fortunes of the band, which to that point had stagnated both in the stores and on the road. Outside of the U.K. the album missed the bull's-eye by a wide margin; but like "The Elder," the relative failure was not from a lack of creative energy and effort by the band. There was more than enough passion, creativity,

and attention to detail during the creative process. What was missing was a little bit of luck, and perhaps timing.

Even in failure, the "Crazy Nights" era served as a critical catalyst that would ultimately see the band surrender to their past, and to a certain extent embrace it. In many ways it would have been inevitable, as much as they had tried to jettison the 70s during the mid-1980s. By the end of the tour, the trend of loading the set with 1980's songs had been reversed and classics like "Strutter," "Calling Dr. Love," and oft maligned "I Was Made for Lovin' You" started returning in concert — the reaction of the KISS Army was clear for those performing on stage to witness. In the years that followed, 1990–1994, the band's sets grew to substantial length, packed full of the songs the fans really wanted to hear. And the endgame was clear...

"Here in the danger zone, it's a jagged edge we climb
But if you take it like stone, and stand on your own
You can make the grade in time"

("My Way" — Stanley/Child/Turgon)

Album Overview

U.S. Release Details:
Mercury/PolyGram 832-626-1/2/4 (USA, 9/21/87)
Mercury 558-861-2 (USA, 9/1/98 - Remaster)
Casablanca/UMe B0020467-01 (LP/digital reissue, 9/2/2014)

Tracks:

A1. Crazy Crazy Nights •
(3:45) — Paul Stanley / Adam Mitchell
A2. I'll Fight Hell to Hold You
(4:10) — Paul Stanley / Adam Mitchell / Bruce Kulick
A3. Bang Bang You
(3:53) — Paul Stanley / Desmond Child
A4. No, No, No
(4:19) — Gene Simmons / Bruce Kulick / Eric Carr
A5. Hell or High Water
(3:28) — Gene Simmons / Bruce Kulick
A6. My Way
(3:58) — Paul Stanley / Desmond Child / Bruce Turgon

B1. When Your Walls Come Down
(3:25) — Paul Stanley / Adam Mitchell / Bruce Kulick
B2. Reason to Live •
(3:59) — Paul Stanley / Desmond Child
B3. Good Girl Gone Bad
(4:35) — Gene Simmons / Davitt Sigerson / Peter Diggins
B4. Turn on the Night •
(3:19) — Paul Stanley / Diane Warren
B5. Thief in the Night
(4:05) — Gene Simmons / Mitch Weissman

Album Details:
Produced by Ron Nevison. Recorded at One on One Recording Studios, Canoga Park, CA, Rumbo Recorders, Canoga Park, CA, and Can-Am Recorders, Tarzana, CA; March–June 1987. Recording assistants: Toby Wright, Julian Stoll, and Jeff Poe. Mixed at Can-Am Recorders by Ron Nevison, June–July 1987.

Players:
Bruce Kulick — bass on "Hell or High Water;" all guitars on "No, No, No"
Phil Ashley and Paul Stanley — keyboards
Tom Kelly — backing vocals

Chart Action:
Chart peak (USA): #18 (10/31/87) with 34 weeks on Billboard's Top-200 charts — marking the band's highest U.S. album charting since 1979. Other countries: UK #4; Norway #8; Sweden #11; Switzerland #14; Canada #20; Japan #21; Australia #24; Germany #44; Holland #44.

56	52	54	10	ECHO AND THE BUNNYMEN SIRE 25597/WARNER BROS. (8.98) (CD)	ECHO AND THE BUNNYMEN
㊸	NEW▶		1	KISS MERCURY 832 626-1/POLYGRAM (CD)	CRAZY NIGHTS
58	49	36	11	HANK WILLIAMS JR. WARNER/CURB 25593 WARNER BROS. (8.98) (CD)	BORN TO BOOGIE

10/10/87	10/17/87	10/24/87	10/31/87	11/7/87	11/14/87	11/21/87
57	24	19	**18**	20	19	21
11/28/87	12/5/87	12/12/87	12/19/87	12/26/87	1/2/88	1/9/88
24	25	27	30	31	31	31
1/16/88	1/23/88	1/30/88	2/6/88	2/13/88	2/20/88	2/27/88
32	34	38	39	44	48	52
3/5/88	3/12/88	3/19/88	3/26/88	4/2/88	4/9/88	4/16/88
55	58	69	70	77	84	98
4/23/88	4/30/88	5/7/88	5/14/88	5/21/88	5/28/88	6/4/88
115	126	142	153	171	186	x

RIAA/Sales:
"Crazy Nights" was certified Gold by the RIAA on Nov. 17, 1987, and Platinum on Feb. 18, 1988. In the U.S., the album has sold over 104,000 copies since the SoundScan® era commenced in 1991. The album was also certified Gold by the CRIA (Canada) for sales of 50,000 copies on Sept. 30, 1987 and Platinum (100,000) on Nov. 18, 1987; and both Silver (60,000) and Gold (100,000) in the U.K. Sales in Finland sales exceeded 25,000 copies.

Danger Zone | 13

Supporting Singles:
• Crazy Crazy Nights / No, No, No (Mercury 888-796)

Chart peak (USA): #65 (10/31/87) with 7 weeks on the Billboard Hot 100 chart. Other countries: UK #4; Norway #7; Holland #28; Belgium #31; Australia #34.

9/26/87	10/3/87	10/10/87	10/17/87	10/24/87	10/31/87	11/7/87
94	87	80	71	74	** 65 **	97

Billboard Album Rock Tracks:

9/19/87	9/26/87	10/3/87	10/10/87	10/17/87	10/24/87	10/31/87
42	40	** 37 **	39	42	47	X

Cashbox:

9/26/87	10/3/87	10/10/87	10/17/87	10/24/87	10/31/87	11/7/87
89	83	83	80	** 79 **	88	94

• Reason to Live / Thief in the Night (Mercury 870-022)

Chart peak (USA): #64 (1/30/88) with 12 weeks on the Billboard Hot 100 chart. Other countries: UK #33; Holland #89.

12/5/87	12/12/87	12/19/87	12/26/87	1/2/88	1/9/88	1/16/88
98	87	80	68	68	68	68

1/23/88	1/30/88	2/6/88	2/13/88	2/20/88	2/27/88	
67	** 64 **	86	86	93	X	

Billboard Mainstream Rock Tracks:

12/12/87	12/19/87	12/26/87	1/2/88	1/9/88	1/16/88	1/23/88
39	38	** 34 **	34	35	35	38

Cashbox:

12/12/87	12/19/87	12/26/87	1/16/88	1/23/88	1/30/88	2/6/88
89	87	85	** 82 **	86	99	X

** The single didn't chart the weeks of Jan. 2–9.

• Turn on the Night / Hell or High Water (Mercury 870-215)

Chart peak (USA): Did not chart. Other countries: UK #41.

Performed Live:
Following the trend established during touring support of the previous four albums, 55% of the "Crazy Nights" album's tracks were performed live during the opening month of the supporting tour. Songs included the title track, "Bang Bang You," "No, No, No," "Hell or High Water," "When Your Walls Come Down," and "Reason to Live." Decades later, "Crazy Crazy Nights" made a surprising return to the band's set list for the 2010 "Sonic Boom over Europe" tour, being performed sporadically afterwards...

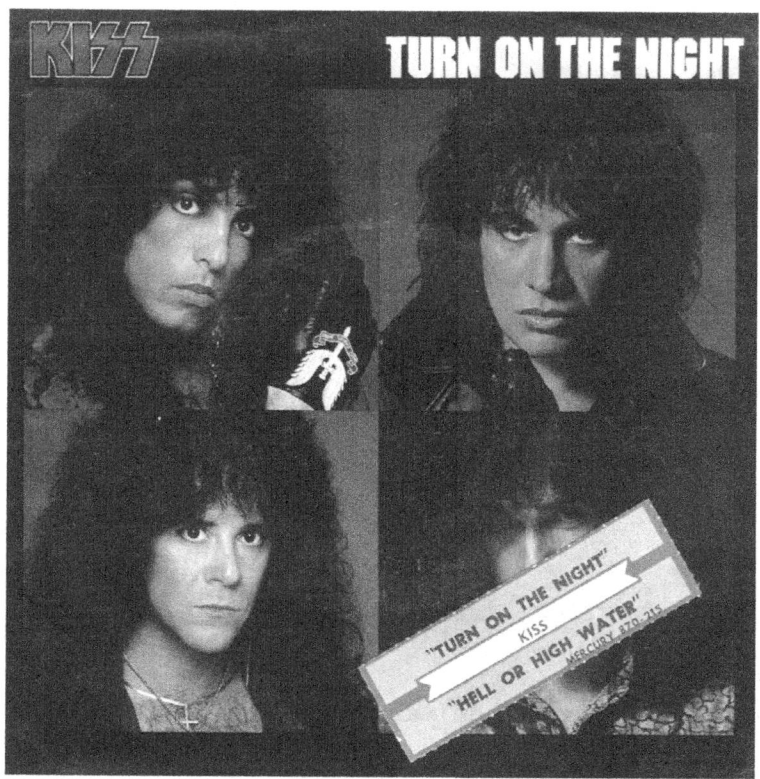

Introduction

By the summer 1986, Paul Stanley was already considering the direction of the next KISS album. The previous album, "Asylum," had only crept to gold status, and Paul was watching as bands, which had once opened for KISS, particularly Bon Jovi, exceed expectations with vastly successful commercial albums. KISS's efforts were simply not good enough, for that sort of breakthrough, and Paul wanted an emphatic album that reinvigorated their career. Rather than continuing to the produce themselves, he felt that an external guiding hand could only help the band with the production, quality control over the material, and provide a fresh perspective to help gain the desired airplay. He also knew a hot producer who he thought could help the band attain its goals: Ron Nevison (who had also been considered for Paul's 1978 solo album). Ron's musical background and track-record was enviable and he was also on a hot streak in the 1980s producing platinum albums for Chicago, Heart, Led Zeppelin, Bad Company, The Babys, Meat Loaf, and Ozzy Osbourne. More importantly, it was the transformation and rebirth of 1970s rock act, Heart, who had their career turned around with their 1985 self-titled album that included the mega hits "These Dreams" and "What About Love" that made him stand out. Paul held initial discussions with Ron in the fall of 1985 while KISS was in London to film videos for the "Asylum" album. Over the Christmas/New Year's holidays 1986, the two shared a rental in Aspen to hang out and get to know one another better.

Ron was brought in with one particular goal in mind: To produce a KISS album that could sonically compete with the sort of pop/metal material burning up the charts and filling MTV's high-rotation playlist. Prior to working with KISS he'd done exactly that with Ozzy Osbourne's "The Ultimate Sin,"

but the obvious lessons that might have been learned from that artist's album may have been missed with the enthusiasm for KISS's project. In the studio, the sessions were much the same as had become the norm in recent years. Gene arrived with dozens of song ideas and demos, which he left Nevison to sort through, while Paul arrived with a much smaller select group of already highly refined songs — many of which had been deliberately written using a keyboard instead of guitar. Paul also felt that with all of his other projects, Gene's material was more a result of other people's efforts with him simply adding a few basic ideas for the requisite credit. As a result, and due to the relationship they had already built, Ron favored Paul's material, which became the natural focus of the album and mission statement. Gene had been reticent about engaging an external producer in the first place, so took something of a back seat during the project — even if he was more involved than he had been during the previous two albums. He also was not sold on the idea of moving away from KISS's core ethos in search of commercial pop success. Gene and Paul's relationship, which was approaching something of a nadir, was challenged during the sessions, with Paul accusing him of not being fully invested in the band. Gene would respond by buying Paul the Porsche that features in the "Reason to Live" video.

The album's basic tracks were recorded at One on One Recording Studios in Canoga Park, CA, which had a drum room Nevison particularly liked. However, the majority of the album would be recorded at Daryl Dragon's Rumbo Recorders due to its Neve board and comfortable and laid back environment. While the resulting sonics of the album color opinions, Ron tried to bring out Bruce's guitar in a new way, presenting them in the foreground like a lead vocal as a dynamic balance to the underlying keyboards and synthesizers. While certainly not as aggressive as later featured on "Revenge," Bruce is nonetheless very proud of the work that he did on the album. Bruce would also play a

lot of the rhythm guitar in order to allow Paul to focus on the vocals. In hindsight, few participants would argue against the key used for several songs being taken down a step. In the search for textures, Ron also had Eric use drum pads during the sessions. Keyboards would also feature strongly, but while Paul's material had taken on a definite commercial slant, Gene's stronger basic rock sensibilities were used for counterbalance, though Paul wasn't particularly amused to discover that "Thief In The Night" was a Creatures era leftover that had already been recorded/released. With songs such as "No, No, No," and its scorching guitar introduction, were used to keep the album from moving too far away from KISS's core. Bruce's confidence — and his maturing as a songwriter — was evident with material such as "Hell or High Water," one of his four co-writes on the album. Born during the "Asylum" tour, Bruce saw Gene as the only person who could help him realize the piece. However, he would also write with Paul, with the resulting "When Your Walls Come Down" steering clear of becoming too commercial. Throughout the process Nevison thought they had the material, such as the title-track, power ballad "Reason to Live," or power pop vehicle, "Turn on the Night," to generate the hits Paul desired.

It wasn't to be, and while the album proved to be a hit in the U.K., it certainly didn't live up to expectations elsewhere. The "Danger Zone" is about celebrating the 30th anniversary of another KISS attempt at reinvention; through a series of interviews with those intimately involved (available and willing) in the album's writing, recording, and resulting tour.

18 | Crazy Crazy Nights

"Crazy Nights" Album Refocused

KISS wanted, and more importantly desperately needed, a massive hit album following the respectable, but hardly stellar sales figures of "Lick It Up," "Animalize," and "Asylum." With the loss of original band members — and a period with a rapid succession of lead guitarists — the band had finally become a stable unit again; though one still definitively led by the vision of Paul Stanley and Gene Simmons. While earning two Gold (and one Platinum) albums in the U.S. may have served to rehabilitate the band's fortunes, it was still a far cry from the level of success the band had enjoyed during their heyday. It was time to take the band to a level similar to that which other competing bands were enjoying. Bands were recognizing the importance of getting singles played on contemporary hit radio (CHR), essentially the rebranded radio powerhouses that rotated top-40 music that was actually selling. It changed the dynamics of how they thought about their albums, even if they wanted to rock on traditional album oriented rock (AOR) stations that played a broader selection of singles. On Apr. 12, 1986 the band came off the road at the end of the "Asylum" tour. With all of the other projects that Gene was involved with, and other issues, it made sense to write-off the majority of 1986 to prepare for the next album. With the band's top producer of choice not immediately available, it made sense to wait and spend additional time writing and refining the material that would be used on the album. In the meantime, the band members headed off on their own to work on a variety of projects...

On April 30, the second Keel album produced by Gene, "The Final Frontier," was released shipping 150,000 copies. Even with contributions by Michael Des Barres, Gregg Giuffria,

Joan Jett, and Jaime St. James; and an "oddly limp cover" (Billboard, 4/19/86) of Patti Smith's "Because the Night," the album couldn't chart higher than #53 on the U.S. Billboard Top-200 charts. By June Gene was back in the studio, producing an album for Black 'N' Blue. Having opened for KISS during the "Asylum" tour, Gene took the helm for the band's third studio album. In addition to producing, Gene would co-write three of the album's songs and brought both Peter Criss and Ron Keel into the sessions to provide backing vocals, and Marc Ferrari on guitar, on "Best in the West." Jamie St. James recalled, "I actually got Peter Criss to come into the studio to sing on the Nasty Nasty record, and Gene and Peter hadn't talked in years, years and years... Peter was actually scared to come in, but I talked him into it, and of course, once he gets to the studio, not much singing happened. Him and Gene just sat and talked and went on and on for hours. But it was kind of cool to see those guys unite and think, hey, I got those guys back together again a little bit... His voice is in there. He's solo not just backgrounds" (Popoff, Martin - Hardradio). With record label Geffen concerned at the lack of a radio single, one track recorded for the album, the Gene co-written "Promise the Moon," was dropped in favor of the Jonathan Cain penned "I'll Be There for You." The demo of "Promise the Moon" was released on Gene's "Vault" in 2018. Oddly, it would be "I Want It All (I Want It Now)" issued to radio as the first single from the album. A remixed version of "I'll Be There for You" followed. Disappointingly, following released on Sept. 8, the album only scraped to #110 on the U.S. Billboard Top-200 before sinking without a trace.

Gene also had a very full schedule with a plethora of non-musical activities. After studying acting for two years with Alice Spivak, Gene was keen to continue putting some of his new found skills to the test. By May filming had commenced on the Gary Sherman directed film, "Wanted: Dead or Alive," a modern-day sequel to the 1958 Steve McQueen TV western with the same title. Starring Rutger Hauer, playing the great-

grandson of the original bounty hunter — albeit as a former intelligence agency operative — the cast also included TV show Benson's Robert Guillaume. Gene, as the antagonist, played a cookie-cutter sadistic middle-eastern terrorist (Malak Al Rahim) who works his way through Southern California slashing throats and blowing up cars, boats, and movie theaters. Released on January 16, 1987 the film would ultimately gross $7.5 million at the box office and remain notable for Gene's "grenade in the" mouth screen-exit. "Never Too Young to Die," a movie with Gene cast in a major role and starring John Stamos and Vanity, came out on June 13, 1986. It should be noted, however, that his work on the movie had been completed in October 1985, immediately prior to the "Asylum" tour rehearsals commencing. Gene recalled, "I was offered two parts in 'Never Too Young to Die:' the role of Marine commander and a hermaphrodite. ... That'll teach me to read scripts before accepting roles. ... I had to shave and wax my chest, wear a prosthetic set of boobs and all sorts of other indignities — respectfully, to those that enjoy that sort of thing" (Hollywood Reporter, 11/4/15). PR summed up the film's plot perfectly: "A preppie turns James Bondish hero, thwarting a gang of psycho crazies bent on poisoning the water supply of a big city." Gene wasn't playing the hero, and was instead cast as the hermaphrodite rock star Velvet von Ragnar who blackmails Los Angeles by poisoning its water supply. Reviews to the limited release weren't particularly kind, with one commenting that the movie, "... should never have been made... Don't fret. They will lose so much money on this one they won't be able to raise the price of a cup of coffee, let alone [the] funds for a sequel" (Louisville Courier-Journal, 6/14/86). Others simply called it "idiotic," with the acting described as, "Somewhere between the truly inept and laughable" (Shreveport Times, 6/14/86).

The general consensus was savage: "The whole movie is like a chase into a sewer; you get the definite illusion of floundering

through offal, with bombs going off all around you. 'Never Too Young to Die' isn't just bad. It's aggressively bad: bad with a vengeance" (Los Angeles Times, 6/17/86). Firmly in the B-movie category, the $4.7 million film was hindered by accusations by producer Steve Paul that network television had refused to air promotional clips provided for promotion on the grounds that they were too violent or sensuous (in the case of Vanity's scenes). In the second week of release an independent commercial was issued to try and save the film, which had a limited promotional budget of $700,000. Unsurprisingly, the movie was a flop more readily seen in drive-ins rather than cinemas, though it did include the notorious musical scene where Gene co-opted some of Jayne County's "It Takes A Man Like Me To Be A Woman Like Me" while wearing a Lynda Carter cast-off costume from her "Encore" TV program. Gene also used the opportunity to bring in a band he was producing, Keel, for a cameo. It's not clear whether the move aided or hindered their career.

Gene also appeared as the character radio DJ "Nuke" in "Trick or Treat" released October 24, 1986. With wider distribution the supernatural horror film also featured Ozzy Osbourne playing the cameo role of a televangelist denouncing heavy metal music as evil and corrupting. Gene Simmons' teamed up with writer/director Gary Sherman in the winter of 1986 to work on turning the popular underground comic series "Jon Sable, Freelance" into a television series. The two had worked together on the "Wanted: Dead or Alive" film earlier in the year. Jon Sable, was described as "A former Olympian, war veteran and African game hunter who lives in Manhattan and splits his time between mercenary assignments and writing children's books" (Variety) under the name Nicholas Fleming. Almost a more interesting Clark Kent, or a Walker Texas Ranger meets Death Wish vigilante type character hybrid. One can immediately notice some similarities between Sable and Doc Savage, the Man of Bronze. A first for Gene, he played the role of a hero when the pilot episode

was filmed and the development of his acting skills could only benefit from trying different types of character-types. According to Dale Sherman, "The finished product was shown to the networks and ABC took great interest in it. Bringing [Gary] Sherman in to discuss the series that was to follow, ABC requested only one major revision: Gene Simmons had to go" (Dale Sherman, "Black Diamond"). According to an interview Sherman did shortly before the series was canceled, he explained that Gene was anxious for the pilot to go to series, but that ABC did not like him in the role and said that they would not be interested in the series if he were to remain part of the project.

Gene was replaced by Louis Van Bergen and the series did go into production debuting on Saturday, November 7, 1987. Unfortunately, it only survived for 7 episodes and was cancelled in early January 1988. The pilot also featured Rene Russo as Sable's love interest Eden Kendell, Ken Page as the blind sidekick Joe "Cheesecake" Tyson, Holly Fulger as Mike Blackman, Marge Kotlisky as Cynthia, and Lara Flynn Boyle, later of Twin Peaks fame, playing a kidnap victim (it was her first acting role). Gene later suggested that, "Within a week of filming, I found out they intended to turn Jon Sable into a weekly adventure TV series. I had assumed it was going to be a few TV movies of the week. I wanted to stay in the band and in my off time, I wanted to act. The reality was becoming clearer — it looked as if it just wouldn't work into my schedule. I also wasn't very good in the part. They paid me off and I left the project. They hired another actor & Sable saw the light of day on ABC for six episodes" ("Sex, Money, KISS"). Regardless, this was not the last connection that Gene Simmons had with the Sable concept, one which he has apparently continued to find endearing. Executive producer Richard Rosetti recalled, "Simmons discovered he wasn't up to the regimen of a television shooting schedule" (Wilmington Morning News, 10/24/87). That ABC ordered the series into production in February 1987 suggests more that

there would have been a direct conflict with KISS' recording schedule confirming Gene's assertion.

Eric Carr, during this period, took the opportunity to start working with other bands with his newly formed Streetgang Productions. The first act that he'd work with Hari-Kari, an all-female thrash band. The band went nowhere, except into the hands of another developer, when Eric couldn't give them all the attention they needed due to his KISS commitments. In June 1986 the various artists "Hear 'N Aid" project finally saw the album release following a series of delays. While KISS hadn't participated in the "Stars" single recording, they did donate the "Asylum" era B-side, a 1984 live version of "Heaven's On Fire," for use on the album. While Paul Stanley was rumored to be cutting a solo album (Billboard, 6/21/86) any work he did in the studio was seemingly restricted to preparation for the next KISS album. Paul also became involved in some film projects when he took a small role in the teen gymnastics film "American Anthem." However, like his role in "Young Doctors in Love" in 1981, his work ended up on the cutting room floor though he would attend the film's premiere party at the Palladium in New York City on June 23, 1986. The sub-$4 million grossing film made many critics "Worst of 1986" lists, so Paul likely dodged a bullet.

Paul also, "Took a small role as himself in the parody documentary, 'The Return of Bruno,' starring Bruce Willis" (Dale Sherman, "Black Diamond") for HBO. Gene Simmons, and some other artists such as Jon Bon Jovi, also appeared in this comedy music-documentary which saw Willis playing Bruno Randolini, as an unknown rock 'n roller. Paul's visibility was certainly less than Gene's at the time though he wasn't invisible. On August 22, he (and Bruce Kulick) joined other members of Mötley Crüe, RATT, Heaven, and Autograph at the Roxy in Hollywood to perform as part of the Party Ninjas (Billboard, 9/6/86). Songs included "Highway to Hell," "Touch Too Much," "Rock And Roll," "Whole Lotta Love," and Free's

"All Right Now." He attended Mick Jones' MTV Video Music Awards after-party at the Manhattan Hard Rock Cafe on Sept. 5. It would be during this event that Paul told the press present that he had shelved plans to record a second solo album in order to focus on KISS (Billboard, 9/20/86).

Rumors also abounded in late-1986/early-1987 about whom Paul Stanley was going to produce, with Guns 'N' Roses being high on that list. While Paul is reported to not have been particularly keen on the idea of working with Guns 'N Roses, due to their personal reputations, the band also had a poor opinion of Paul. According to Slash, "Paul Stanley came down to one of our shows and hung out where we hung out. I'm looking at this guy watching what we do. He's a nice guy, but he didn't have a clue as to what we were doing. Everyone gets the basic idea: They're a rock 'n' roll band. But they don't get the formula" (LA Times, 6/6/86). Paul recalled, "Immediately after my interactions with the band, I started to hear lots of stories Slash was saying behind my back — he called me gay, made fun of my clothes, all sorts of things designed to give himself some sort of rock credibility at my expense. This was years before his top hat, sunglasses, and dangling cigarette became a cartoon costume that he would continue to milk with the best of us for decades. I didn't wind up being involved with G'n'R's album. No surprise there" ("Face The Music"). Names like Jet Boy, Cher, and Poison were also regularly brandied around as acts Paul was considering working with. Even Paul commented, "Poison is the first band that I will work with... the guys are great, and we're all very much from the same place" (Rock Scene Spotlights #2).

Paul was staying visible and certainly cultivating relationships with other bands. On June 20, 1987, he was flown into Dallas to join Poison on stage at the Texxas Jam for a cover of "Strutter," the last song in their set. By this time, Paul had clearly adopted his "Crazy Nights" dress sense... The band's

performance was filmed, and Paul featured in the video for the band's final single from the album, "I Won't Forget You." Poison also covered "Rock and Roll All Nite," a song they had often performed as an encore in concert, for the "Less Than Zero" movie soundtrack (released Nov. 16). Both would have been overtly conscious decisions by the young band. Paul, who was interviewed at the event, stated, "I love popping up at events like this... I've never had the chance to play Texxas Jam with KISS, but I've heard so much about it over the years. It's lived up to what I expected. The fans are crazy" (Hit Parader, 1/88). Whatever the case, by mid-1987 the timelines for possible participation in Poison's second album had diverged, with KISS scheduled to be out on tour, until mid-1988. Poison instead used Tom Werman for "Open Up And Say ... Ahh!," an album that ultimately attained 5x Platinum certification in the U.S. At the 1987 "Monsters of Rock" festival at Donington on August 22, Paul joined Bruce Dickenson and Dee Snider on headliner, Bon Jovi's, encore cover of "Travellin' Band" and "We're An American Band." Gene, who was also present, opted to not participate. Paul had also joined the band on stage on August 7, at the Meadowlands Arena, for "Travellin' Band" with Mötley Crüe's Tommy Lee.

For Paul the most important project remained KISS. For him it was a sacrifice he would make versus gaining personal recognition in other areas. By the summer 1986, Paul Stanley was already considering the direction of the next KISS album. The previous album, "Asylum," had only crept to gold status, and Paul was watching as bands, many of which had once opened for KISS, exceed expectations with vastly successful commercial albums. Bands like Mötley Crüe and Bon Jovi, both of whom had opened for KISS just a couple of years earlier, were at the top of the rock world. Both of those groups enjoyed extremely successful albums in 1987 with "Girls, Girls, Girls" and "Slippery When Wet" (technically released in 1986) selling four and twelve million copies

respectively. He perceived that KISS's efforts were simply not good enough, for that sort of breakthrough, and Paul wanted an emphatic album that reinvigorated their career while making a defining statement. He was "Emphatic about coming out with a 'great album,' something that would light the fire under their career again. Paul's vision wasn't like the grandiose thinking that had been responsible for (Music From) 'The Elder,' but he did want something big and important. And it would require a top producer with name recognition who would give KISS entree to working with top songwriters and getting radio airplay at key stations. In short they needed a guru" (CK Lendt, "KISS & Sell"). And in the form of a guru that did not include names such as Eddie Kramer or Bob Ezrin. Rather than continuing to the produce themselves, he felt that an external guiding hand could only help the band with the production, quality control over the material, and provide a fresh perspective to help gain the desired airplay. He also knew a hot producer who he thought could help the band attain its goals: Ron Nevison (who had previously been considered for Paul's 1978 solo album).

Nevison's musical background was enviable. He was also in the midst of a very hot streak in the 1980s, producing Platinum certified albums for Chicago, Heart, Led Zeppelin, Bad Company, The Who, Meatloaf, and Ozzy Osbourne. More importantly it was the transformation and rebirth of Heart who had their flagging career turned around with their 1985 self-titled album that included the mega hits "These Dreams" and "What About Love." More so than his work with Ozzy, it was the parallels with fellow 70s rockers Heart that made him an appealing prospect. Paul conducted initial discussions with Ron in the fall of 1985 while KISS was in London to film videos for the "Asylum" album. Ultimately, Ron was brought in with one particular goal in mind: To produce a KISS album that could sonically compete with the sort of pop/metal material burning up the charts and filling MTV's high-rotation playlist. If Ron could turn around Heart's career and make a hot

record for Ozzy Osbourne, with the "Shot In The Dark" single hitting #68 on the Billboard singles charts, then surely he was a perfect selection for KISS. However, with Ozzy Osbourne's "The Ultimate Sin," there may have been some obvious warning signs missed with the overriding enthusiasm for KISS project. While the album was certified Gold and Platinum in April 1986, it would take an additional 8 years to reach 2x Platinum despite a strong initial charting (hitting #6 on the Billboard Top 100 album charts). Even with the controversy attached to Ozzy's name recognition a high charting album didn't necessarily equate to mega sales experienced by other bands. While KISS' recovery had certainly left then in a better position than they had been a few years earlier, they were still not able to fill larger venues on a consistent basis and album sales were stuck with sales figures for albums between 500,000 and 1,000,000 copies. Officially, "Asylum" had only been certified Gold, a marked downshift from the Platinum+ of its predecessor. Touring could also be described as stagnant at best, close enough to a break-even proposition in some cases.

Paul particularly liked Nevison's work with bands he liked such as The Babys and Bad Company. As a result, Paul pushed hard for Ron's involvement: "Ron's probably one of the few, really like one of two or three real producers. Most producers are clowns. Producers are like managers. You don't need a degree or a license. So, any yo-yo who decides today he's a producer is a producer. Most of the time, we've always kept away from them. Because, my philosophy been, I don't know what you've done. I've done 20 albums, y'know you may have had a hit record last year, but what did you do two years ago? There's not a lot of guys who hold a consistent track record. Ron's always been great. When he was an engineer, he was great, whether it was working on Zeppelin or Bad Company, or the Who, or producing Heart or Ozzy. He's one of the few legit people that are worth checking out. And, I've always wanted to work with him" (KISS Explorer, 1988). In fact, Ron

had been first choice to produce Paul's 1978 solo album. Gene was certainly not enthusiastic about the idea. According to Gene, "When we started working on 'Crazy Nights,' we looked for someone else to pull the cart — another person to help guide the band... So we hooked up with a producer named Ron Nevison, who Paul had wanted to work with for a while, although I never did" ("KISStory").

Ron, however, was busy working with Joe Cocker, Survivor and finishing up work on Heart's "Bad Animals" album in 1986. Gene, who was wrapped up in his own projects, acquiesced to Paul's plan to wait for Ron to become available. Paul and Ron would meet up in Aspen, CO, in December 1986, to plan out the album and get to know one another. According to CK Lendt, there was concern in the business office at the time that the band's finances were in a very unhealthy position. The break from recording and touring resulted in the band taking a gamble on the album being a major success, rather than keeping the money train ticking over however slowly with a fast studio/tour turn-around. The risk would be worth it if everything worked out as planned. For Paul, the plan was simple: "I wanted an album of 10 — of, if we were lucky enough, 11 — songs that upheld a certain quality we've strived for. The idea this time was, 'Let's take longer, really give ourselves as much variation as possible, then decide what we wanted to do.' This time, I don't think we wanted to have to limit what we do based on other people's ideas of who we are or should be" (Detroit Free Press, 1/15/88). Who dares wins...

Unfortunately, it was always going to be the material that counted, not who produced it, even by Paul's admission. Gene was ultimately able to sell himself on the concept of bringing in an external producer to help bring a new perspective to the material. If he had any doubts he didn't publicly mention them at the time and was instead busy producing E-Z-O's album. During late-1986 "E-Z-O" had met

Gene Simmons on a visit to New York. Having already essentially taken their music as far as they could in their native Japan with two releases, "War" (1985) and "Prey" (1986), the band were keen to break into the larger American market with their unique style of music. "I wanted to work with the band after I heard one riff," remembers Gene, "I said, 'anybody that can come up with a classic riff like that is good.' They had 'powerful,' they had 'mysterious,' they had 'fast.' They are as good, or better, than most musicians I have worked with" (Geffen Press Release, 1987). Not only would Gene co-produce the band's first English-language album with Val Garay, but also as a non-English speaking immigrant, he worked with lead singer Masaki to help him with his English and pronunciation. Gene also brought in co-writers such as Adam Mitchell and Jamie St. James to work with the band on their material. KISS had other administrative details to deal with during 1987: Peter Criss. Since leaving KISS in 1980, Peter had not sold his share of the KISS Company, and as a result was supposed to be receiving royalties on albums on which he didn't play. In an agreement reached on February 3, 1987, Peter finally sold his share in the KISS Company, including the rights for the use of his "Cat" makeup. In some ways this would be the biggest mistake Peter could ever have made, because even though the band had been unable to pay him the monies he was due, he was giving up a very valuable asset for a single lump payment. Lawyers had been negotiating the separation from the partnership for months, and "eventually, an agreement was reached. Peter would get a one-time cash payout as the settlement of his interest in KISS" (CK Lendt, "KISS & Sell").

By March, recording of the "Crazy Nights" album commenced, with the working title "Who Dares Wins." It was perhaps the perfect motto to sum up the gamble being taken. Eric Carr had suggested "Who Dares Wins" was little more than a cool unofficial title, though it survived long enough to appear on some Japanese advertisements for the album.

According to Eric, "During a photo session our wardrobe girl had this commando patch lying around with 'Who Dares Wins' on it, and I said, 'Hey, what a great idea for an album title!' Then she brought it over to Paul who said the same thing. We ended up not using it because it didn't look good in print, and it sounded as if no one would understand it" (KISS Fire). However, one must wonder whether it was abandoned because W.A.S.P., who had opened for the band during their previous tour, had already used the phrase on the cover of their 1985 album "The Last Command." Another title that the band apparently played with was "Condomnation," but "The record company weren't too keen with the PMRC and all" (Kerrang #155). However, Paul later questioned the seriousness of the title in the first place: "Well, 'Condomnation' was never really the title. It was just a thought that passed through our minds and gave everyone a chuckle. But we always bounce a lot of ideas around before we get something everybody likes" (Hit Parader, 1/88).

In the studio, the sessions were much the same as had become the norm in recent years. Gene arrived with dozens of song ideas and demos, which he left Nevison to sort through, while Paul arrived with a much smaller select group of already highly refined songs — many of which had been deliberately written using a keyboard instead of guitar. Paul also felt that with all of his other projects, Gene's material was more a result of other people's efforts; with him simply adding a few basic ideas for the requisite writing credit. As a result, and due to the relationship they had already built, Ron favored Paul's material; which became the natural focus of the album and mission statement. Gene had been reticent about engaging an external producer in the first place, so took something of a back seat during the project — though he was certainly more invested in the project than he had been during the previous two albums. He also was not completely persuaded on the idea of moving away from KISS's core ethos in search of commercial pop success. Gene

and Paul's relationship, which was approaching something of a nadir, was challenged during the sessions, with Paul accusing him of not being fully committed to the band, with all of his external projects continuing to distract his focus and creative energies. Ron and Paul worked well together and the material that Paul was working on was in a similar vein to that which both Heart and Ozzy had released. With songs like "Crazy Crazy Nights," "My Way," and "Reason To Live" already in forms that closely resembled their album versions, all that was required was to recruit a keyboardist. That role would be filled by Phil Ashley, a session player extraordinaire who had regularly worked with Paul the previous two years at Electric Lady Studios in New York City.

During early 1987 Paul mentioned in some interviews that he was writing material for the next KISS album on keyboards. For many fans this was a portent of doom, and Paul was understandably defensive concerning their use: "We've added keyboards to KISS' sound, but we're still a rock 'n' roll band pure and simple! If we add keyboards, it's not because we're taking away guitars. It's because we're adding keyboards. They are there to augment the guitars, never at the price of guitars" (Creem Collector's Series, Vol. 2 #1). One of these tracks was "Crazy Crazy Nights," a song intended to be the album's lead-off single long before the band had even entered the studio. Written with Adam Mitchell, Paul was fond of the song though in hindsight he would prefer more guitars and less prominent keyboards. He commented, "It's a really good song, but I'm not terribly fond of its sound on the album. There are some songs that I think are absolute crap, but 'Crazy...' isn't one of them" (Classic Rock, 11/2001). The album's basic tracks were recorded at One on One Recording Studios in Canoga Park, CA, which had a drum isolation room Nevison that particularly liked. However, the majority of the album would be recorded at Daryl Dragon's Rumbo Recorders due to its Neve board and comfortable and laid back environment.

While the resulting sonics of the album color critical opinions, Ron tried to bring out Bruce's guitar in a new way — presenting them more in the foreground, like a lead vocal, as a dynamic balance to the underlying keyboards and synthesizers. While certainly not as aggressive as later featured on "Revenge," Bruce is nonetheless very proud of the work that he did on the album. He also performed a lot of the rhythm guitar in order to allow Paul to focus on the vocals. In hindsight, few participants would argue against the key used for several songs being taken down a step. In the search for textures, Ron also had Eric use drum pads during the sessions. While Paul's material had taken on a definite commercial slant, Gene's stronger basic rock sensibilities were used as a counterbalance. However, Paul certainly wasn't particularly amused to discover that "Thief In The Night" was a "Creatures" era leftover that had already been recorded/released on a Simmons produced album. According to Gene, the band recorded this song simply because he had always liked it and nothing more. The long ignored anthem "It's My Life" was also considered for use on the album.

During the recording of the album, "Paul finally had enough and read his trusted comrade the riot act. 'We were in the parking lot one day, and I said to Gene, Look — you're off doing all these other things while still reaping the benefits of this band, and I'm getting screwed. It's not fair for me to put in this kind of time, while somebody else who is supposed to be my partner, is not.' And Gene looked at me and said, 'that's fair.' I could have used Gene's input. But my attitude at that point was that I certainly wasn't going to listen to a guy who's off managing cabaret singers, and producing five bands, while I was trying to make an album" ("KISStory"). Gene's peripheral role in the band during this time gave more scope for involvement by Eric and Bruce. On the album Bruce received four co-writing credits, two each with Paul and Gene. Eric got one, and nearly had other material included. Paul was working with numerous external co-writers

including Desmond Child, Adam Mitchell, and Diane Warren, many of whom were providing hit material working with competing bands. "Turn on the Night" was written with Diane Warren, and was Paul's first collaboration with the then-rising Los Angeles songwriter (who had just earned her first #1 hit with Starship's "Nothing Gonna Stop Us Now"). Adam Mitchell earned three co-writes, notably on the title track and "I'll Fight Hell to Hold You" which was written in New York and based on a title by Paul. Bruce Kulick was responsible for the main riff, while Adam Mitchell would assist in the overall writing of the piece.

Desmond Child was partially responsible for three songs: "Bang Bang You," "The classic story of boys and their toys" (HP 1/88), which was more Spinal Tap-ish than even Gene had managed to that point, "My Way," and the exquisite "Reason to Live." This latter song would not only be the second single released off "Crazy Nights," but was the album's obligatory power-ballad. Paul recalled, "I remember calling up Gene and playing it to him down the phone... I played the song to Gene and obviously the bomb had gone off at the other end. He was speechless" (Kerrang #155). Paul was defensive about the inclusion of such power ballads on KISS albums, a situation that had first started with "I Still Love You" in 1982. He commented, "If a band was to be honest they would tell you that at that time the only hope for airplay was a ballad. Somehow to make it more palatable they got labeled power ballads. A ballad is a ballad" (Box Set Liners). There are some similarities between the song and Foreigner's "I Wanna Know What Love Is" from the Agent Provocateur album (1984). Songs such as "No, No, No," and its scorching guitar introduction, were used to keep the album from moving too far away from KISS's core while keeping up with the guitar hero wizardry present in most bands around that time. Bruce's confidence — and his maturing as a songwriter — was evident with material such as "Hell or High Water," one of his four co-writes on the album. Born during the

"Asylum" tour, Bruce saw Gene as the only person who could help him realize the piece. However, he would also write with Paul for the album, with the resulting "When Your Walls Come Down" steering clear of becoming too commercial sounding. Throughout the process Nevison thought they had the material, such as the title-track, power ballad "Reason to Live," or power pop vehicle, "Turn on the Night," to generate the hits Paul desired.

Ironically, "My Way," the third of the Desmond Child co-writes also included a credit for Bruce Turgon, who had been the bassist in the band Black Sheep, with vocalist Lou Gramm (later of Foreigner). They'd toured with KISS during the "Alive!" tour of late-1975. By early June the album was completed and it was mixed at Can-Am Recorders by Ron, before being turned over to PolyGram in July. For Bruce, at least, the experience working with Ron wasn't negative: "Working with Ron Nevison on 'Crazy Nights' was different for me. I'm used to having Gene and Paul produce because we did 'Asylum' and I played a solo on 'Animalize' for 'Lonely Is the Hunter.' All my other sessions before KISS had a producer, so having Ron Nevison with KISS was like working in one of those situations again" (Kerrang #251). At the end of the process, what mattered the most was both Gene and Paul seemed reasonably happy with the finished product (at the time). For fans, though then and in hindsight, there was a question of the material that was considered for use on the album, but discarded for one reason or another.

For many fans there has long been the question about why one of the earliest compositions, one they perceive to have been one of Paul's strongest creative efforts during this period, "Sword and Stone," was excluded from the album. Even Bruce Kulick was under the impression that it was simply a matter that producer Ron Nevison not liking it, but still felt that a great song had been omitted. He recalled, "I just felt really bad that Ron Nevison didn't like the song

'cause then it would have been on 'Crazy Nights.' But I couldn't control that. And the demo that is out there in bootleg form is pretty good. We did it at Electric Lady with Eric Carr and it's a full-blown KISS track practically. I actually came up with that riff backstage on tour early on, 'Asylum' I think. That's what happens. Paul didn't mind as much, I felt pretty bad about that" (KISS Kollector). Slightly defensively, Ron's opinion on any Kulick disappointment is simple if not somewhat dismissive: "Yeah, that's probably because he's one of the writers, and writers always think that." But, of course! The song was written by Paul, Desmond Child, and Bruce, and grew out of riff that Bruce had brought to Paul, and many fans see it more in the sort of anthemic vein expected of KISS, the rallying point often missing during the period as the band's tone was softened.

Looking back across the memory void of the decades, the explanation is probably even more simplistic than the producer's personal tastes, which no doubt played a part in the process of deciding what material to pursue from the songs he was presented with for consideration. In late 1986 the song was included among several Paul circulated for publishing opportunities with other acts. Loverboy's guitarist was interested, and Billboard reported that band considered it for their next studio album. Clearly though, "Wildside" had material with collaborations with a bit more market cachet that Paul Stanley in 1986/7, namely "Notorious," a co-write with Jon Bon Jovi and Richie Sambora, or "Hometown Hero" written with Bryan Adams.

The connection with a band such as Bon Jovi, who were in the midst of their commercial ascendency, was perhaps enough to make the song unnecessary. Paul's flirtation with Bon Jovi was overt. On Aug. 6, 1987, Paul joined the band on stage, along with members of Mötley Crüe (Vince, Tommy, and Mick), for a performance of "Travellin' Band" to close their set at their East Rutherford, NJ show. On Aug. 13, he'd be

back on stage at the same venue, this time with Bon Jovi's David Bryan, for an encore performance of "Jailhouse Rock" during Mötley Crüe's show. Days later, he, Gene, and CK Lendt were in London during the "Monsters of Rock" tour and flew with the band to the festival site. He'd again join the band, for their encores of "Travelin' Band" and "We're an American Band," along with Bruce Dickinson and Dee Snider. Ultimately, when Loverboy's guitarist, Paul Dean, was recording his first solo album with producer Bruce Fairbairn kept the song for his "Hard Core" album — in its brief review Billboard, noted the song as one of the album's best tracks; it's hardly surprising that it was also the first single from the album (reaching #27 on Billboard's Album Rock Track charts) supported with a video. Going solo provided Dean the opportunity to pursue material that was "much tougher, less pop-oriented" (Billboard, 9/26/87) than the previous Loverboy album had been, in conjunction with the demise of the band. Competed in the fall of 1987, the recording wouldn't be issued until 1988.

The song was also recorded by German band "Bonfire" and included on the 1989 "Shocker" soundtrack. With the question of the song's use by Loverboy/Paul Dean, "not liking it" may simply have been a case of not recording a song that could turn up on other artist's efforts in competition with a KISS version. Fans can surely correlate this situation with what later happened with another Paul Stanley song from the period, "Hide Your Heart," which was similarly ignored by the band in 1987. Similarly, it was offered and taken up by far too many other artists, in a perfect storm of that interest absolutely sabotaging any chance of commercial success for a critically impressive composition. Another unused track was the riff-laden "Dial 'L' For Love," written by Eric Carr, Gene Simmons, and Adam Mitchell. It was assumed that the song had not been fully recorded, for "Crazy Nights," but the release of an exquisite vocal version on Gene Simmons' "Vault" suggests otherwise. Eric has commented that the

song was not good enough (at that point) to make it onto the album, and that it was really still being developed. As the primary writer of the song, Eric had taken it to Gene and Adam for polishing. Gene has commented: "Eric and I co-wrote a song called 'Dial L for Love,' a real fine tune. If it won't be on a KISS record it'll be on somebody's record" (Rock Scene Spotlights #2). A rough demo of the song that does not include completed vocals, was included on Eric Carr's "Unfinished Business" and it was suggested that Eric (at least from his perspective) would sing the song.

Another song that was recorded for the album and omitted at a late stage was "Are You Always This Hot," written by Gene and Adam which recycled the title of a song that Adam had written in 1981 — his original (and completely different) demo had been featured in the theatrical release of the Robin Williams' movie, "The World According to Garp." As a fast-paced rocker, it's not surprising that there was perhaps only room from "No, No, No." Some other songs mentioned at the time that either weren't developed or used included: "Boomerang," "'X' Marks The Spot," "Scratch And Sniff," "What Goes Up," "Hunger For Love," "Dirty Blonde," and "No Mercy" (Simmons/Kulick) which never got past the song-writing stage (at the time). "Boomerang," was later used on "Hot in the Shade." Another song omitted, which had been included on Paul's demo tape for the album was "Time Traveler," written with Desmond Child. Those titles mentioned are just a sample of the some 40 odd songs that Gene and Paul had demoed themselves, and which were in varying stages of completeness.

Like Paul, even Gene brought in some new co-writers: Davitt Sigerson and Peter Diggins. Davitt, a music producer and executive, was a friend of Gene's while Peter was Davitt's song-writing partner whom Gene never met. Prior to writing with Gene, Davitt had recorded solo material and written songs which were recorded by the Jim Vallance related band

Prism. He had also written material for Jeff Paris, Eddie Money, and Loverboy, and had co-written with Desmond Child. Their creation, "Good Girl Gone Bad," was based on something obvious out of Gene's community college experience: "A young lady who Gene went to college with, a girl who started out the demure virgin, all coy and unclaimed ... then met up with 'The Tongue!' The only sad thing about the tale is that when she finally did give way it was in the back seat of a car and with someone else, a friend of Gene's in fact" (Kerrang #155). Eric Carr had material rejected from the album and had to be satisfied with the co-writing credit for "No, No, No." Originally titled "Assume the Position," then "Down on All Fours," one can wonder whether those titles came from Gene's list of possible song titles! Regardless, the song started out with a Bruce riff that he and Eric developed into an idea that Gene jumped on to complete. This would be one of Bruce's favorite tracks on the album because "It's the fastest, ferocious thing, and it features me a lot" (KISS Fire, 1.3). Being a fast-paced rocker, it is hardly surprising, in hindsight, that "Are You Always This Hot," was bumped from the album so that there was only one of that sort of song on the album.

Like its predecessor, Paul was intimately involved in the artistic design of the album's cover. He brought the concept of using a broken mirror design to art director Dennis Woloch, who found it cliché. While not original, it did at least tie back to Paul's guitar designs of the late-1970s. Failing to talk Paul out of the idea, Dennis got to work on the idea with the instruction to feature all four of the band members equally on the cover design. Working with photographer Walter Wick the two proceeded to break numerous mirrors, array band photographs around a staging area so that they reflected on the shards of mirror, and then photograph the whole thing from above. Initial efforts were problematic, with many of the mirror shards being too small and resulting in too many repetitions of an image. Essentially it was too

cluttered and small for Paul's liking. He wanted his face bigger. As a result, the concept was watered down into something that was more generic as the shards got larger to provide the desired result. With multiple repetitions of the band's logo and album titles on the corners the striking cover harkened back to the design of "Rock And Roll Over."

More problematic was the rear cover. One would expect four band member photographs, arranged in a 2x2 grid, to be a cake walk. Certainly the photographer captured the personality of the band members, particularly with Bruce caressing his "banana" ESP guitar, which had been so central to the music contained on the album. Eric appeared playful, which Gene lasciviously thrusting his bass in a phallic manner. Paul was clearly posing for the millions of female fans he hoped would buy the album, though his exposed blue bikini brief would provide decades of juvenile humor for his male fans. Dead center on the rear cover was the band's Chikara symbol that had been used on 1974's "Hotter than Hell" album. Perhaps it was invoked for what it meant in the Japanese language, though it is possible that Eric Carr had discovered that the Japanese pronunciation of the character was similar to his name. By August the band were gearing up for their inevitable tour and the release of the album.

On August 8 the band performed a free show, albeit for less than 3,000 fans, at the Olympic Auditorium, Los Angeles, to film segments for their "Crazy Crazy Nights" video. Directed by Jean Pellerin and Doug Freel, the video was released early in September. During the four-hour shooting, "A comedian was brought on during breaks, but he was promptly booed off the stage" (KISS Fire, 1.3), though with the temperature rising in the auditorium Paul and Gene did hand out drinks to some of the fans. In addition to performing "Crazy Crazy Nights," the band also played "Cold Gin," "Lick It Up," "Whole Lotta Love," and "Detroit Rock City." The band also filmed a performance of "Crazy Crazy Nights" in Los Angeles for

broadcast on the British television show, "Top of the Pops." The clip aired on October 23.

CK Lendt recalled, "As the release date approached, KISS' precarious financial situation was becoming a factor. Cash was drying up. Some of the suppliers and studios would have to wait to get paid until the group got the final installment of their advance from PolyGram when the album was completed. KISS needed a blockbuster record to get the massive radio airplay, something they had had for only a couple of singles in their history. With heavy airplay, sold-out arenas would follow on tour. It was a tall order" (CK Lendt, KISS & Sell). However, even with the "Crazy Crazy Nights" video gaining reasonable traction on MTV, the supporting single proved a dud and only reached #65 on the U.S. singles charts. However, it would become a smash summer hit in Britain reaching #4. While the single wouldn't hit anywhere else, it did manage top-40 appearances in Australia and Holland, and reached #7 in Norway. The single also became the band's first promotional CD single to be issued in that format in the U.S. It was also the first of the band's singles available as a commercial CD single in European markets.

"Crazy Nights" was released on September 21, 1987 and debuted on the Billboard Top-200 album charts at a disappointing #57 entry point the following week. Slowly, it proved reasonably popular and eventually climbed to #18 on the U.S. charts, consistently remaining in the top-40 until February 1988. In Britain success continued with the album reaching #4, the best KISS album position attained since "Lick It Up" had reached #7 four years earlier. Once the initial touring cycle was completed, the album completely dropped off the U.S. charts in May 1988 following a 34 week run. This performance wasn't better enough than the previous albums to justify how the band had approached the album, even if worldwide sales had seen a modest bump. Promotional efforts for the album included Gene and Paul appearing at

the launch of the Frederick's of Hollywood Bra Museum in Hollywood where they donated a 36D bra thrown on stage during the previous tour. In November, while the band finished their rehearsals for the tour in Los Angeles, "Reason to Live," was released as the second single off the album. It was accompanied by a video directed by Marty Callner and featured Eloise Broady, April 1988 Playboy's playmate of the month that Paul was "absolutely crazy about" (KISS Online/"Paul Speaks") at the time. That single managed to reach one position better than its predecessor, though a paltry #64 on the singles charts was hardly going to ignite the album sales the band needed. Again, the single fared somewhat better in the U.K. reaching a nearly respectable #33, undoubtedly due to the strength of the name power engendered by the success of the "Crazy Crazy Nights" single earlier in the year. In other markets the single failed to chart at all.

The "Crazy Nights" tour kicked off in Jackson, MS on November 15 with White Lion in the opening slot until Ted Nugent became available. The set list underwent a revamp with "Detroit Rock City" being switched from opener to closer. Songs from the album that were rehearsed for the tour included "Crazy Crazy Nights," "Bang Bang You," "No, No, No," "My Way," "Reason To Live," "When Your Walls Come Down," and "Hell Or High Water." Only "My Way" wouldn't make an appearance in the set though "When Your Walls Come Down" and "Hell or High Water" were only performed sporadically during the tour. With the album stalled in the charts, the concerts were mediocre with the attendance varying — just as had been the case on the previous few tours. What had been planned to be a bombastic and grand tour was quickly scaled down to reduce expenditures. With a final shot at getting the album moving in the U.S. the band filmed parts of a show at Worcester, MA, on January 27. The footage was used in a Marty Callner directed video for the dynamic "Turn on the Night." During

February the song was released as the album's final single, backed with "Hell or High Water." It only charted in Britain (#41).

The tour meandered on in the U.S. until it became clear that the album was not going to be the savior that had been hoped for. On February 15, 1988, Gene was arrested following a concert in Columbus, Georgia after dropping his pants on stage to "adjust his equipment." He was charged the following day for breach of the city's anti-lewdness ordnance. Amusingly, "police read Simmons his rights after the regular performance. But allowed him to return to the stage for an encore" (Columbus Ledger-Enquirer, 2/16/88). This sadly, would be one of the more notable events occurring during the tour. It seemed that KISS could not compete with the success of other acts, contemporary or not. Bands such as Def Leppard were ripping up the world with their "Hysteria" album and the "reformed" Aerosmith were riding high in concert and on MTV with their "Permanent Vacation" album.
More than the touring, the inadequate ticket sales, and the stagnant record sales, the "Crazy Nights" period saw the KISS financial business finally collapse when investments made as tax shelters collapsed leaving the band owing millions with no assets with which to pay.

One of the ramifications of this decision occurred on March 3, 1988, when the management team of Glickman/Marks, whom they'd so recently thanked on the Crazy Night's liner notes ("without whom we'd be broke"), were unceremoniously fired. Eric took his synth/traditional drum solo to a new level on the tour and Bruce became more comfortable on stage; and much more active in his performance role. Eric's drums for the tour continued their evolution in scale, and he plastered the Chikara symbol on every surface he could! While the U.S. tour ground to a halt in San Diego on April 2, 1988, the band took two weeks off before returning to Japan for the first time in 10 years.

Playing 7 dates in 9 days, the popularity of the band in Japan seemed as strong as ever and the band play an extended set. More importantly, within the context of the band's future, some neglected gems from the band's catalog were added back into the set, notably "Strutter" and "Calling Dr. Love." It demonstrated that the band was starting the move backwards to the past and the glory of their heyday. On June 26, 1988, during the downtime between the Japanese and European tours, Gene and Paul appeared with Ace Frehley at the Limelight club in New York to play an encore. They played the classic and first song that they'd ever played together in 1972, "Deuce." It wasn't all "happy families" again with one member of the crowd reporting that Gene had walked on stage and demanded a bass from John Regan. John refused insisting that Gene hadn't been polite.

While the mini reunion started a whole new set of rumors off about a reunion, one was not about to happen — it would be a regular rumor for the next few years. In August the band played their first club gigs in 15 years appearing at the Ritz in New York City over two nights to warm up for the forthcoming tour. One show was broadcast by WNEW-102.7 Radio from a sweltering and packed venue. What those who managed to get into the show got was a shock to the system as KISS powered through a massive set list with little rapping or solos. This was music, short and sweet, and once again had a KISS show starting out with the traditional "Deuce," no wonder a result of Ace's introducing that song at the Limelight in its historical context as opener rather than closer. Of these club gigs Bruce recalled, "I liked it, but it was a little odd for the other guys. I think they all realized the value of it, we showed that we could play without the smoke and big lights. So in that way it was cool as well. I don't think you will see the makeup version of the band do that" (Scream #46). Following their arrival in England, the band played a so-called surprise show at London's Marquee Club, becoming the first band to play at that classic club's new venue on August 16.

Four days later KISS played at the massive Monsters of Rock festival at Castle Donington. They had been offered the chance to play in 1982, but had been too busy with work on the "Creatures of the Night" album. Now they appeared third to last, opening for David Lee Roth and Iron Maiden. In August, PolyGram, sensing that video may becoming a cash cow released a third KISS video, "Crazy Nights." The video was a compilation of the three music videos from the album. It reached #15 on the video charts, but took until 1991 to receive Gold certification from the RIAA. Its performance hardly measured up to the earlier successes of "Animalize Live Uncensored" and "Exposed" videos.

Bruce recalled, "The Monsters of Rock shows were really exciting. In some ways I'm very nervous for either one of those kinds of shows. In a small club they can see you better, and maybe notice the mistakes a little quicker. When we talk of the big ones it is very exciting to play for so many people. In some ways that's less personal, but it's also very nerve wrecking. So many things could go wrong in a big place. Either way, the band always gave a thousand percent" (Scream #46). Playing to over 90,000 people wasn't something that happened to KISS every year, though the day was mired with the death of two fans, Alan Dick and Landon Siggers. During the band's visit to the U.K. Paul finished work on some new songs at British studios. After that the band headed off to Germany to tour mainland Europe before returning to several U.K. cities in later September, with Australian band Kings of the Sun opening. On October 3, 1988 the European tour concluded at King's Hall, Belfast, Northern Ireland. Apart from the large summer festivals that the band played, the "Crazy Nights" also saw the band visit Iceland. The band returned to the US to work on a project that had already been in progress since the summer — a new compilation.

For some it was too easy to blame the relative lack of success of "Crazy Nights" on the production of Ron Nevison. However, to do so would be completely unjust even though the sound of the album was sonically sanitized and may have had rather too many keyboards that did more than "augment" the guitars. Listening to the sonics of albums like Ozzy's "The Ultimate Sin" (1986) or Heart's self-titled 1985 album, it would be clear that the sort of music Ron was producing fit in with the sort of material that was proving popular in the late 1980s. There really wasn't too much difference, except that other acts were getting radio play and selling out large venues. The sound was polished and was different from what the KISS sound usually was, still it was KISS. Much of that sound came from Nevison the engineer who Gene said "that much of Ron's contribution had been in the engineering area, getting the right sounds for the guitars and drums and mixing them properly" (CK Lendt, KISS & Sell). Bruce Kulick concurred with this feeling stating, "The sound of 'Crazy Nights' is the way Ron Nevison produces rock bands. In some ways the album is very polished, but in another way the guitars is very featured. I was happy about it on that level, but I don't think the band sounded extremely powerful on that album" (Scream #46).

"What a difference a day makes," as the saying goes, "or something like that." Or just a year... The Gods of rock 'n roll are capricious at best, if not outright malicious. Or senile at worst, playing games with the lives of musicians on a whim, drunkenly reveling in the mayhem. Many a tale of woe is there of brilliant albums that never made any impact within popular culture; or conversely mediocre creations that commercially batted far above their weight and surprised even the most accurate of critics. How many times has the excuse, "They were ahead of their time," been used as a sop to explain a perception of failure? Or, "It was the right album — at the wrong time." At a time when KISS was facing numerous hurdles — be financially related such as declining

revenues, IRS tax-shelter rule changes, or former members and producers wanting their royalty monies — the decision to delay the recording of a new album by nearly a year would prove costly. It would also be the most unfortunate of bands that would choose to release an album around the same time as Def Leppard's "Hysteria," Aerosmith's "Permanent Vacation," and even INXS' "Kick." Add the July 1987 release of "Appetite for Destruction" by Guns N' Roses and Whitesnake's self-titled album which continued their steam-roller attack on the airwaves, and these albums have combined for sales of 50 million in the U.S. alone. Fortunately, KISS fared somewhat better than Twisted Sister's "Love Is for Suckers," but like Alice Cooper and unlike Aerosmith they had not successfully reinvented themselves for a new generation.

While hindsight is indeed 20/20, had the band simply entered the studios in June for an Oct. 1986 release, then the competition would not have been as dire as it was a year later, though that month wasn't devoid of quality releases. Billy Idol released "Whiplash Smile," but as direct competitors with KISS releases were somewhat lacking unless one was into Metal Church, Slayer, Iggy Pop, Stryper or Krokus. The same was the case for November, though Yngwie did release "Trilogy" and Cheap Trick "The Doctor." Ultimately, revisionism or "what ifs" have no place in an evaluation of the album's fortunes. Ron delivered exactly what the band wanted at the time: A KISS album that sounded like Bon Jovi — commercial, non-dangerous, slick. Like "The Elder," the album was something completely opposite to what the band was really about. The problem was that the material the band decided to record could not compete with the sorts of material that was being released by Bon Jovi, Def Leppard, and Mötley Crüe. The listening public was also unable to separate what was expected from KISS with what was being presented. It wasn't to be, and while the album proved to be

a hit in the U.K. it certainly didn't live up to expectations elsewhere.

"Who Dares Wins," indeed ...

Collecting Crazy Nights

Few collectibles of note exist from this release era of this album. Singles for "Crazy Crazy Nights," "Reason to Live," and "Turn on the Night" was the last released on 7" vinyl in Japan. Additionally, a picture disc version of the album was issued in high quantities. The common version with band picture on the B-side sells for around $25 in the clear vinyl protective cover that should have an album detail sticker. A rarer European "Monsters of Rock" version which has a different B-side image of the band advertising the summer festivals KISS would play sells for around $50. Poster sleeve singles were released in the UK for "Crazy Crazy Nights" and "Turn on the Night," though these are usually available for $15-20. Additionally, the rich UK release schedule from the album included 12" picture discs for the three singles issued off the album. The "Crazy Crazy Nights" single would add "Lick It Up" and "Uh! All Night"; "Reason To Live" would add "Who Wants To Be Lonely" and "Thrills In The Night"; and "Turn On The Night" would add "King Of The Mountain" and "Any Way You Slice It" in addition to the common B-sides from the 7" version of each single. These would also be available as regular 12" singles with picture sleeves. None of these sell for more than $10-12 for the regular singles and $15-20 for the picture discs.

Promotional 12" singles for the three album singles would be released in the USA with the same song on each side. All three of the 7" singles in the U.S. featured picture sleeves, but even with these they and the promotional versions seldom sell for more than $5. In the U.S. "Crazy Crazy Nights" would be the first KISS track released on a promotional CD-single (CDP-05), but this still doesn't help value with it being available for around $15. The CD should come in a regular 5" CD jewel case with cover insert. No country would release a

CD single for "Crazy Crazy Nights" as a regular release, however as the format took off CD versions of "Reason to Live" and "Turn on the Night" were available in 5" slipcases. These sell for around $10. The "Reason To Live" CD-single included three additional songs, "Thief In The Night," "Tears Are Falling," and "Crazy Crazy Nights," while "Turn On The Night" includes "Hell Or High Water," Heaven's On Fire," and "I Love It Loud." Japan would release their first KISS CD-single, for "Turn on the Night" and "Hell or High Water" (PolyStar P10R-30001).

Song Stories

Crazy Crazy Nights

During early 1987 Paul mentioned in some interviews that he was writing material for the next KISS album utilizing keyboards. This was an ominous omen for many of the fans, for a band which had written much of their material during their classic era on acoustic guitars. One of these tracks was "Crazy Crazy Nights," a song that was intended to be the album's leadoff single long before the band had entered the studios to record the album. As was often the case, Paul original demo changed very little when recorded by the band, though the "crap that they all say" line was changed to "rap" for some odd reason. Written with Adam Mitchell, Paul is fond of the song though in hindsight would prefer more guitars and less keyboards. He's commented, "It's a really good song, but I'm not terribly fond of its sound on the album. There are some songs that I think are absolute crap, but Crazy...' isn't one of them" (Classic Rock, 11/2001).

Adam, who participated in the recording of the demo, at a studio on Sunset Boulevard, also felt that the song had lost some of its essence during translation from demo to album cut. He commented, "I remember the lyric in that song is awfully good. I remember we really worked hard on the lyric on that particularly. Paul absolutely had the idea. "Crazy

Crazy Nights" was a big hit worldwide, but Paul and I were both disappointed to some degree with the record because the demo we did we felt was so much better. We demoed that in a studio on Sunset. But the difference between the demo and the record was in the chorus when the crowd comes in and sings along with Paul, "Crazy crazy crazy crazy nights." [Chants] The crowd on the demo we did was much louder and it really sounded much more like an arena. It just sounded bigger to me compared to when I heard the record — and Ron is a great engineer who has done some terrific records." Only reaching #65 in the U.S., the August 1987 single can be deemed a failure. A live performance video was filmed at Olympic Auditorium, Los Angeles, CA, on August 8, 1987 and directed by Jean Pellerin and Doug Freel. With the song's return to the KISS live set in the band's latter years though, it is firmly entrenched as a KISS classic.

I'll Fight Hell to Hold You

Written in New York and based on a title by Paul. Bruce Kulick was responsible for the main riff, while Adam Mitchell assisted in the over-all writing of the piece. Paul wanted a strongly passionate song. In 1999, Die Ärtze bassist Rod González, contributed a disco treatment to the German KISS tribute album, "KISS Deutschland: A Tribute to KISS," which was followed by the release of a CD-single version featuring a radio edit and 9-minute "Super Sound Maxi Mix" (Universal/Motor Music, 587 216-2).

Bang Bang You

Where Gene may have been guilty of being Spinal Tap-ish on his writing of "Spit" in 1992, the same can be said for Paul (and co-defendant Desmond Child), who resurrected "Love Gun" in this ode to sexuality in 1987. According to Paul the song was "the classic story of boys and their toys" (HP 1/88). As the album's "Uh! All Night" the song was performed with enthusiasm throughout the "Crazy Nights" touring cycle.

No, No, No

Originally titled "Assume the Position" — and later "Down on All Fours" — this song was written by Gene, Bruce and Eric Carr... The song started out with a Bruce riff which he and Eric developed into a song idea at Eric's apartment in New York. Gene later completed the song. According to Eric, "I just set up a double bass drum beat on my drum machine. I just got this feel in my head and I started coming up with this real staccato stuff for the verse" (KISS Neon Glow #1, 1992). This would be one of Bruce's favorite tracks on the album because "It's the fastest, ferocious thing, and it features me a lot" (KISS Fire, 1.3). It would also be a song he performed all of the guitars for during the recording and also become a showpiece during live performances during the tour.

Hell or High Water

Written by Gene and Bruce Kulick the initial idea for the song came from Bruce during the "Asylum" tour with Gene adding the lyric and song-title when refined for use on the album.

Very little changed between Gene's demo and the album version, other than the rough edges being polished off. This tune was occasionally performed live during the 1987–88 "Crazy Nights" tour.

My Way

Written by Paul Stanley, Desmond Child, and Bruce Turgon, this song would not change much from Paul's original demo of the song (which has circulated in collector's circles for many years). Bruce was the bassist in the band Black Sheep, with Lou Gramm (later of Foreigner), who had toured with KISS during the "Alive!" tour in late-1975. Unfortunately, the band lost the support act slot due to an equipment accident...

When Your Walls Come Down

This was another song created from a riff Bruce Kulick had come up with during the "Asylum" tour. Added to a chorus which Paul already had, the final piece was polished off with the assistance of Adam Mitchell. The song would get a rare live appearance on the "Crazy Nights" tour, but did not work out well.

Reason to Live

Not only the second single released off "Crazy Nights," "Reason to Live" was the album's mandatory power-ballad. Written by Paul and Desmond Child, Paul recalled, "I remember calling up Gene and playing it to him down the phone... I played the song to Gene and obviously the bomb had gone off at the other end. He was speechless" (Kerrang #155). Paul was defensive about the inclusion of such power ballads on KISS albums, a situation which had first started with "I Still Love You" in 1982. He commented: "If a band was to be honest they would tell you that at that time the only hope for airplay was a ballad. Somehow to make it more palatable they got labeled power ballads. A ballad is a ballad" (Box Set Liners). There are some minor similarities with

Foreigner's "I Wanna Know What Love Is" from their "Agent Provocateur" album (1984).

Assisted by a Marty Callner directed video, this single reached #33 in the UK, solidifying the overall success of the album in that market. In the US it only reached #66 on the Billboard charts, but did reach #34 on Billboard's "Mainstream Rock Tracks" charts which tracked the "most-played songs on mainstream rock radio stations." The premise of the video is simple according to Paul: "The video's about me and a gorgeous woman!" (Scripps Howard News Wire, 1987).

Good Girl Gone Bad
Written by Gene Simmons and two, then newcomers to the KISS song-writing camp, Davitt Sigerson and Peter Diggins. Davit was a friend of Gene's while Peter was Davitt's song-writing partner whom Gene never met. Prior to writing with Gene, Davitt had recorded solo material and written songs which were recorded by the Jim Vallance related band Prism. He had also written material for Jeff Paris, Eddie Money, and Loverboy, and had co-written with Desmond Child.

Lyrically, the song was based on something obvious out of Gene's community college period: "A young lady who Gene went to college with, a girl who started out the demure virgin, all coy and unclaimed... then met up with 'The Tongue!' The only sad thing about the tale is that when she finally did give way it was in the back seat of a car and with someone else, a friend of Gene's in fact" (Kerrang #155).

Turn on the Night
Written by Diane Warren and Paul Stanley in March/April 1987, this would be Paul's first collaboration with the rising Los Angeles song-writer who had then just had her first #1 hit with Starship's "Nothing Gonna Stop Us Now." This was the final single off the album, but only charted in the UK reaching #41. Live performance segments for the video were filmed in

Worcester, MA, on January 27, 1988. The video was directed by Marty Callner.

Thief in the Night

Essentially, this song would see KISS covering their own song. During 1984, while Gene had been producing Wendy O. Williams, he had given this song, written with Mitch Weissman, to Wendy to record. By the time "Crazy Nights" was being recorded this was one of two songs from that earlier era that were considered for use, with the other being "It's My Life." According to Gene, the band recorded this song simply because he had always liked it and nothing more.

Are You Always This Hot

According to Gene, "There were 50 songs written and 12 recorded. 11 were used. There's one other song called 'Are You Always This Hot' that was recorded but not used... We never finished it. Maybe it wasn't right for the album" ("15 Years On" CD Interview). The song was written by Gene Simmons and Adam Mitchell. The song has not yet made it into collector's circles, unlike some of the demos from the album, but is intended to be included on Gene Simmons' "Vault" box set.

Adam had originally written another song, using the same title, in 1981, which he demoed. Gene simply liked the title enough to write a song with Adam around. Adam recalled, "I had written another song entirely on my own, and demoed it on my own, and called it 'Are You Always This Hot.' And my demo actually ended up in a movie, 'The World According to Garp...' It's the scene where [Robin Williams] is driving the babysitter home, and she's young. And she gets in his car and she flips on the radio right away, as a teenager would do, and the song that comes on when she flips on the radio is my original demo of 'Are You Always This Hot...' If I remember, Gene liked the title — it's exactly the type of title Gene would like — and we wanted to try and do something for KISS. But

for whatever reason it didn't work." By the time the movie made it to video it had been replaced with "Long Way Home" by Alice Cooper.

Sword and Stone (Demo)

"Sword And Stone," another of the KISS power anthem cast offs, was written by Bruce Kulick, Desmond Child, and Paul Stanley. The song was demoed for the "Crazy Nights" recording sessions and the style of keyboards and guitars mix well with a powerful bass riff. Recorded at Electric Lady Studios the track is nearly a complete KISS track, though it was not fully recorded for the album because producer Ron Nevison was not particularly keen on the song. The song was offered to Loverboy to record, and Paul Dean covered it on his 1988 "Hardcore" album.

Within two years the German band Bonfire, who had in 1987, been recording in the studio next to KISS, covered the song for the KISS involved "Shocker" soundtrack. One of the better KISS songs of the late-1980s this song circulates in excellent quality on the demo trading circuit in a couple of forms. The catchy chorus, "I feel the power runnin' through my bones / I am the sword, you are the stone / I swear forever we can stand alone / I am the sword, you are the stone / I am the sword... you are the stone," is often considered a better example of Desmond's work with the band.

A second variation of the song, almost an earlier demo, starts off with a more pronounced drum roll and has less emphasis on the keyboards. One minor lyrical difference occurs in the final line of the chorus with "I am the sword, you are the stone" being changed to "I am the sword and you are the stone." This "rougher" version is 15 seconds shorter than the more polished primary recording. Oddly, Eric Carr, Bruce, and Adam Mitchell also published a song called, "You Are the Wish, I Am the Well" which bears some structural similarity to the chorus of this song.

No Mercy
Written by Gene Simmons and Bruce Kulick around the time of the "Crazy Nights" album sessions this song never got past the song-writing stage... A later demo of the song appears on the Gene Simmons Vault, dated to the "Hot in the Shade" era.

Dial L for Love
This song was written by Eric Carr, Gene Simmons, and Adam Mitchell. It had previously been thought that this song had never been fully recorded during the "Crazy Nights" era, so the inclusion of a pristine studio vocal was a surprise on the Vault. Eric had commented that the song was not good enough (at that point) to make it onto the album, and that it was felt that it was a work in progress. As the primary writer, Eric had taken the song to Gene and Adam for polishing, something which he had done several times. Gene has commented: "Eric and I co-wrote a song called 'Dial L for Love,' a real fine tune. If it won't be on a KISS record it'll be on somebody's record" (Rock Scene Spotlights #2). A rough demo, which did not include any completed vocals, was finally released in 2011 on Eric's "Unfinished Business" album and was wrongfully assumed to be the best there was to get an idea about the song. A full-fledged studio quality demo, including vocals, was included on Gene's 2018 "Vault" collection.

The Troubles Inside You
Written by Eric Carr and Mitch Weissman, Eric would demo the song with Weissman on bass and lead vocals. Nothing would ever come of the demo, though a rough version would be included on the release of "Unfinished Business."

It's My Life
After being discarded in 1982, the song which could have been KISS' anthem for the 1980s was considered for use on

"Crazy Nights," according to Gene Simmons. It is not clear whether the Kulick-era lineup ever demoed it or whether it was just a thought to use it. One may well shudder at the thought of what the "Crazy Nights" production qualities would have done to the song.

When Two Hearts Collide (Demo)
During the 1987–89 period Paul was gearing up for the possibility of working with Cher, and he was mentioned as a possible producer for her. At the same time he was writing material specifically geared outside the scope of KISS. Some of this material was included on the "Paul Stanley Compilation" publishing tape which was circulated in 1989 to prospective targets. With material which dated back to 1986, this tape included "When Two Hearts Collide," "Best Man for You" and "Jump the Gun." "When Two Hearts Collide" was written by Paul and Adam Mitchell and was originally intended for Cher's use.

In 1989 Paul commented that he had also written a song with Desmond Child for her with the possibility of doing a duet with her. Unfortunately, those plans were trashed due to the scheduling of the "Hot in the Shade" recording sessions. Running 4:36, with strong keyboards, this light ballad seems the least completed of the demos included on the tape. The song is pure syrup: "Not everybody survives / To get out alive / When two hearts collide / The night seems so long / The pain should be gone / But I'm feeling it inside / But I thought that I'd made up my mind / But your lips moving closer to mine / This is not what I planned / Can anyone stand goodbyes / When two hearts collide."

Best Man for You (Demo)
Another of the keyboard-laden Paul demos from his home studio recording era of 1987–89, though this 4:28 demo has some similar characteristics with "Reason to Live." It is not clear where this demo was directed, though there are vocal

elements which would be used on the recording of the "Crazy Nights" album, notably transitions. The amount of keyboards on this demo tends to indicate that Phil Ashley was part of the recording process, since Bruce doesn't play on the track. The song was written by Paul Stanley and Jean Beauvoir with a catchy chorus: "If you follow your heart / It's the best you can do / If you reach for my hand / I'll be there for you / Baby, don't hesitate / 'Cause you know I'll be waiting / 'Cause I'm the best man for ya."

Don't Let Go (Demo)
This song was another of the demos put out by Paul for publishing, and was written with former KISS producer Vini Poncia with whom the band were working around the time of the "Hot in the Shade" album. Running 3:35 the song is a ballad which has a catchy chorus. The verses, such as "Girl, I keep coming back / To the words that spoken / And the promise we made / If we let it slip away / And the vows are all broken / We'll regret it too late / Are you cryin,' I see tears in your eyes / That you claimed didn't go there / But I can't help but wonder / Is there rain in your heart?," mainly have keyboard backing.

Jump the Gun (Demo)
Another of the songs from the "Paul Stanley Compilation" publishing tape, "Jump the Gun" was a 4:28 song that Paul Stanley co-wrote with Geoffrey Lieb. Geoff is better known by his stage name Jeff Paris. He was a synthesizer player in the early 1980s and has co-written a vast amount of material with other song-writers and artists, including Vixen and Mr. Big. While Paul did not perform the lead vocals on the demo, it is likely that those vocals were by Jeff. Jeff recorded the song, perhaps building on the original demo, with Paul being on backing vocals and perhaps rhythm guitar, for his 1993 album "Lucky This Time."

My Way (Demo)
Running to 4:00 the lack of any lead guitar work indicates that this demo was recorded by Paul with a drum machine.

My Way (Vocal Lead)
Simply 2:32 recording of Paul singing the vocals to the song without any backing music.

Reason to Live (Demo)
Running to 3:55 this demo also lacks lead guitar work but is an identical arrangement to the album recording.

Bang Bang You (Demo)
Running to 3:22 this demo also lacks lead guitar work but is an identical arrangement to the album recording.

Crazy Crazy Nights (Demo)
While Paul's songs rarely differed much in the translation from demo to album recording the original demo had a much deeper layer of voices on the chorus (recorded by Paul, Eric, and Adam Mitchell at Electric Lady Studios) which were later lost in the mix on the album version. According to Adam, "It was almost like a whole arena singing along" (KISS Online).

Hide Your Heart (Demo)
Like other Paul demos little changed when the song was recorded for the album. In the case of "Hide Your Heart," the song would not be used on the "Crazy Nights" album, though the demo version of the song does have a longer instrumental introduction to the song and some minor arrangement differences which result in the song running 4:27. The most noticeable difference between the demo and later album version is the guitar solo which is completely different.

Good Girl Gone Bad (Demo)

Hell or High Water (Demo)

Demos of both of these songs were included on Gene Simmons 2018 "Vault." Unusually, these demos are fully formed and differ only slightly from the versions recorded by the band for the album.

INTERVIEWS

Christopher K. Lendt

Former vice president of Glickman/Marks Management recalls the state of KISS in 1987 and an ambitious bid to reignite their career

KissFAQ: Chris, before talking about "Crazy Nights," specifically, let's set the stage. "Lick it Up" had been break-even at best on the road and by 1987 had only gone Gold. "Animalize" continued the trend, with mediocre gates becoming the norm. You mention that by the end of the "Asylum" tour the album-tour cycle had become drudgery. The band comes off tour in April 1986 — from your perspective, on the business side, how had that tour done in comparison with "Animalize," before and "Lick it Up," which I believe had only a breakeven proposition?
Christopher K. Lendt: My recollection is that "Asylum" did reasonably well. I don't remember the specific statistics as compared to "Animalize." It did reasonably well. With Bruce Kulick playing, the band was settled in terms of the lineup for "Asylum," it was the people that were with KISS until the 1990s, until Eric Carr passed away. At the end of the "Asylum" tour we expected KISS to go back in to the studio and do a new album that would come out at the end of that year. But KISS were keen on not just doing another album with another producer, they needed to do a new album with a really big producer. And that producer was Ron Nevison. Unfortunately, Ron was very much in demand at the time, he'd been working with Ozzy Osbourne, and it would be nearly a year until he was available to work with the band.

The business managers, myself, Howard Marks, and Carl Glickman, went along with the idea because it was important artistically and creatively to KISS that they wanted to have an album with the imprimatur of Ron Nevison. He'd done the

Heart albums that were very successful. He had a very deft hand in the studio at producing radio friendly pop-edged records with a diverse group of artists. So that set the stage for waiting a year until Ron Nevison was available. Basically KISS had a year off to rehearse and get songs ready to be screened by Ron, and then go into the studio as soon as he was free. Our belief at the time was it was debatable whether it was worth the wait, in terms of what made sense to KISS economically. It's not a reflection on Nevison, he was a real talent, but how much difference it would make to KISS was debatable.

How tough does it make for you from the business perspective, when the band isn't on the road, the band isn't in the studio, or selling a new record; to deal with the loss of all of that prospective income stream for a whole year?
In KISS' case it was a problem, but it wasn't unsolvable. They had only recently gotten their finances back together, and it would plug a big hole in their finances because we would have to wait another year to collect the album advance. There would be no income coming from touring or merchandise, so yes it would be a problem and it made things a bit tight.

So Gene had a lot of external projects lined up to tide him over. How involved were Glickman/Marks in helping him with say getting roles in movies such as "Trick and Treat" or "Wanted: Dead or Alive," which came out around that time, or production with Black 'N Blue, and probably others.
All of those activities, I can tell you Glickman/Marks management, including me, had practically nothing to do with, at all. Whatever I knew about "Trick or Treat" or his work with Black 'N Blue, I knew from speaking directly to Gene. He might mention a few anecdotes about what he was doing and when he was going to be out of town and when he'd be back. I haven't the slightest idea how much he was paid for any of those projects because I believe the money

flowed directly to him and don't recall that it was commissionable by us. So, whatever he did on his own were his own projects. He scheduled them, he participated in them, he made his own deals (or someone on his behalf), but I don't recall it was us.

By this time KISS has no specific manager. Aucoin is long gone. I believe Howard may have been helping out as that role developed depending on what the band needed?
Yes.

So, what's going on with Paul at this point because he seems to have had nothing lined up that actually took place? I know in Billboard, in the middle of the year, it's rumored that he's going to do a solo album; then a couple of months later that print a retraction saying that he's decided against doing one at that time. There also the possibility of the Guns N' Roses album production that we've heard about in both Slash's and Paul's autobiographies. Is anything being done to help Paul, Gene's got all these things going that he's obviously set up on his own. Is anyone helping Paul to try and do something externally during that year gap, or is he just off on his own thing?
Well, the Guns N' Roses production, my recollection is that Howard Marks may have had a meeting with Paul Stanley and someone from Guns N' Roses, but it simply didn't come to fruition. Paul probably tried to find what he would consider to be higher profile projects for him to do, but for whatever reason they didn't happen and then, you know, time marches on.

Indeed, KISS is also rumored, in early 1987, to be playing that year's Donington "Monsters of Rock" festival, which they don't. Do you remember anything about offers for one-off shows like that coming in?

I recall that they played Donington the year after I was involved. There was a Donington show in 1987; I believe that one was with Bon Jovi.

That's right, they were in England at the time and Paul ended up on stage with them that day while Gene declined.
I was physically there. We were backstage at the show, but we flew with Bon Jovi in a helicopter to the site. And Gene and Paul appeared on stage at the end of Bon Jovi's performance, but we were never scheduled to be in the show. And if one of the promoters made an offer for KISS, it's possible, but they didn't accept it because they certainly wouldn't have been the headliner. I don't even know what position on the bill they would have offered KISS at the time.

It probably would have been similar to the following year where they opened for Iron Maiden...
Right, I know about that, but that I wasn't involved in.

I guess, ultimately, that "Crazy Nights" was an attempt to copy the Bon Jovi playbook that had resulted in the insanely popular and commercially successful "Slippery When Wet" album. Would there have been business meetings where musical direction for the new album was discussed, or at this point is the band just figuring all of it out for themselves, and not communicating it with the business office?
My recollection is that the recording was done in Los Angeles. I never met Ron Nevison until he came to New York to do a listening session, which I wrote about in the book. It's possible that Howard Marks may have gone to Los Angeles in that period and met with him, I don't remember. But basically, Ron Nevison was calling all of the shots with the band. I didn't hear any negative feedback, except after all was said and done. They were happy with the album and the way it had turned out, but I sensed that they didn't feel that Nevison did anything really remarkable. In other words, the

album was completely professionally done, and they were satisfied with the results; but it gets back to whether it was worth waiting for a year because there was nothing groundbreaking or spectacular or extraordinary about the album.

You detail the listening party in "KISS and Sell," which is at least a nice contrast to the one held for "The Elder," where the jaws were left agape...
Yeah, more favorably received!

How did Glickman/Marks get involved in the business process once the album is completed? What is the role, one the band is ready to move forward?
What our job was, was to make sure that all of the marketing opportunities were capitalized on. That the record company knew that the band had a management company trying to not only bolster what the record company was doing, but to spearhead KISS' touring and merchandising, and to market the album. It's important for fans to understand that the artist doesn't get involved in day to day discussions and the ordinary business machinations of the everyday dealing with the promotion department at the record company, the marketing department, the business affairs department. There has to be a manager, or a management team, to handle all of those functions. The record company has to know that the band has people behind them who are looking over their shoulders, frankly, to make sure that things happen as they're supposed to happen.

The management company, at that time, was responsible for seeing that a tour was booked, for making sure that there was an outside publicist to augment the publicity efforts at the record company, which KISS paid for. The management company was responsible for ensuring that there was a line of merchandise available to be sold at the concerts. And for the album cover, artwork, and graphics that were to be used for the album. There's a lot of leg work to be done, and

someone has to constantly check on the record company that if KISS are playing in Louisville, KY, or Dallas, TX, or Pullman, WA, that there's a record company person who's going into the stores and knows the album is in stock, and doing a local promotion with a radio station in conjunction with the promoter. There's a lot of wheels that have to turn properly in order for sales to be maximized, and in large part that's what our company was responsible for.

So, at the listening party, the album is seen as being a good album, albeit a not spectacular one, that didn't blow anyone out of the water. Were there any challenges in getting the album promoted at PolyGram — particularly when bands such as Def Leppard, Cinderella, and Bon Jovi were in ascendency at the label and KISS are not?
Yeah, that's always a problem and that's why you need somebody to represent the band's interests because otherwise you get lost in the shuffle. What you're talking about is the competition from within your own record company, not to mention all of the other record companies that are going to have albums out at the same time as KISS'. And some of the market that is going to buy KISS is also going to buy other hard rock records from those other acts and labels. So you're right, those groups were in ascendency and KISS was their competitor. At that time Def Leppard were at the top, selling millions of copies of albums, so it was pretty hard to get the attention of the record company and keep their attention when we had that kind of competition.

One of the things that stands out in hindsight, and of course hindsight is always 20/20, is that KISS releases "Crazy Nights" at the same time Aerosmith releases "Permanent Vacation," Def Leppard has "Hysteria," and Guns N' Roses are hitting with "Appetite For Destruction." Not to mention Mötley Crüe and Whitesnake... So, that one year delay seems to work into a perfect storm of competition that kind

of dooms the band without a spectacular album and a large dose of luck.

Exactly. At that time, the radio stations that played Aerosmith, Def Leppard, and Guns N' Roses were for the most part the same stations that we wanted to play KISS. They're only going to add so many records every week. Chances they're not going to add all of those bands, and they'll go by their instincts and maybe some listener feedback, and go with the one that instantly gets the best reaction, which is probably the one that has been doing the best in the recent past.

So Bruce Bird was brought back in to help on the promotion side and try to get them more radio play. Was it a lost cause for KISS trying to get radio airplay in 1987?

I wouldn't say that it was a lost cause. There were always some stations that had been loyal to KISS based on their success with the band in the past, but it wasn't getting any easier. They were not the KISS of yester-year; they were the modern KISS without makeup and costumes. In some ways that gave them more credibility, they weren't seen as a throw-back or a nostalgia act. But on the other hand, the mania of the original KISS wasn't there. KISS was now another hard rock band, a very good hard rock band, but look at who they were competing with, giants.

Absolutely, coming back to the vision for "Crazy Nights," would it be fair to say that the album and Ron Nevison's involvement was 100% Paul Stanley?

I would say largely that was true.

Was there any attempt to persuade him to go with a different producer so that there wasn't a year's gap because of the financial strain it would put on the organization?

I'm sure it was discussed, but I don't remember any other names coming up. There certainly would have been people

who were available. Here again, they didn't want to go back to the people who had done albums in the recent past like Michael James Jackson, or before that Eddie Kramer. Obviously, they weren't going to go back to Bob Ezrin, at least not then. So they would have had to take a chance on someone new, and I'm not sure that that was something that they were inclined to do.

Paul wanted this to be a big album, I think you described it as "big and important," in your book. Even though it's not a direct analogue around the thinking that surrounded "The Elder," didn't it set off any alarm bells that they were trying to reach for a next level again, and the last time they had attempted that sort of thing, it hadn't worked out too well?
Well, in fairness, most of us who were longtime allies of the band felt that they really did need to do something that was, maybe if not spectacular, but they really needed to do something that was a step forward. Something, perhaps, that would have been seen as more important and would get them a lot of publicity, in a favorable way, because of the caliber of their producer. I think it was a legitimate objective. I don't think that anyone at that time was delusional, in the sense that they were going to do a concept album, or do a completely different genre, or cross over into a different kind of musical experience. It wasn't so much overly ambitious, to the point where it may have been a bit unhinged, I think it was simply ambitious to the point where they wanted to prove themselves. That they could do something musically and production wise in the same caliber as many of the same artists we've mentioned, who also received accolades in the press for doing breakthrough forward-thinking albums that were really state of the art. Albums that were very progressive within their genres. In a long-winded way, what I'm saying is that there wasn't the kind of thinking going on that what they wanted to do, or that we were heading for "The Elder" again. No, there was no reaction of that kind. It just created a business dilemma because taking a year off, for

KISS at that time, potentially put them behind the eight-ball financially, which obviously we had to say we couldn't recommend.

What about Gene at this time, at business meetings, because Paul's really driving the car. That's the impression we get from Gene and Paul's books, is that because of his outside projects he's very much distracted from the business of KISS. Is that a fair appraisal?
He had all these side projects going with the acting and producing groups, and that's what kept him happy. He's a very ambitious person and always likes to be involved in things. At that point he was happy to cede the KISS responsibilities, creative wise at least, to Paul who wanted to take control in any case.

You've mentioned that you didn't meet Ron Nevison until the album listening party. Had you heard any of the demos or musical ideas they were thinking of, before they went into the studio, to get an idea of the music direction in which they were heading?
I probably did, but my only recollection is that they wanted to continue in the direction of a heavy metal/hard rock sound that was not so intense or aggressive that it would not be suitable for pop stations. So, they wanted a kind of sophisticated production of hard rock music. Not head-banging music or intense heavy metal music, because KISS had moved past that. Music that was more song oriented that had a very professional studio produced patina that was very much in the style of what was working at the time on the stations that played competitors such as Def Leppard and Bon Jovi. It's hard rock, but not head-banging. It's an aggressive guitar sound, but not so aggressive that it splits your ears. It's melodic and structured in the way that pop records produced for rock artists are, but they weren't trying to be Melissa Manchester.

In comparison with "Asylum," in terms of the economics of the recording of the album, was it about the same cost as the previous few albums?
I think with all the costs, and the advance paid to Ron Nevison, it was more expensive.

In terms of Ron, was he perhaps given too good a deal on the points to save on up-front costs and load it on the backend if the album performed?
I remember that he had a very good deal. At that time he was in a position to negotiate an excellent deal for himself. I remember Howard saying that there was really no negotiation with him. He got the big advance and whatever his points arrangement was. He had come off very successful albums, so he was in a position to command a really good deal. It was basically take it or leave it. And if we didn't want to take it we would have had to find another producer, but somebody in the music business who's reached his level of success, they take what they can because that time may never come again.

So, at the listening party — this is the first time you hear the music — what's the mood?
I don't remember who was or wasn't there. It was generally upbeat. The band was proud of what they had done. People liked the sound, it was very hard-rock pop sound. I don't remember anything standing out in my mind as to their reaction. The listening session was well received.

At this time you switch from ICM to CAA for booking the tour, was that a positive or a negative in the long run?
CAA came into the picture because they had started to get a real foothold in the music industry. They had already become a dominant force in television and then motion pictures, so CAA was seen as a way for KISS to bolster the market place. The agency was looking for bands to take on. KISS had a name and a track record of years of arena performances, so

I'm sure they were very interested. Here again, it was a way to shake things up for KISS' benefit and go with an agency that was on the rise.

One the tour starts, response is pretty dire. White Lion seemed a good pick as an opening act, though they only really hit big after their opening slot had ended. It seems KISS just couldn't get any luck. Was there anything else that could have helped the band on the road?
The opening act was always seen by KISS as being critically important. For a period of time it was difficult to get really promising bands to appear with KISS, because KISS weren't really seen as a really big deal. White Lion, I remember them, but I can say where anyone would have done anything differently. They had the album that they wanted, they had the producer that they wanted; they had a new agency behind them that was motivated in marketing the band and selling them to promoters very aggressively. I'm sure they would have been thrilled if some band came down the pipe who were about to break out with a top-10 album.

How serious was the possibility of the tour being cancelled? Some of the early attendances were pretty dire.
Yes, there was. In fact, I was in Los Angeles at the time and I got a phone message from Howard Marks that the tour was now confirmed to go, which leads me to believe that there had been some doubts whether it would have happened. Otherwise I wouldn't have received a message like that.

The IRS issue, you go into quite a lot of detail about that in your book, and obviously it's not settled until after your time with the band. When does this really become an issue for the band in 1987? Is it during the recording of the album that they're cognizant of the issue facing them?
It was brought up in business meetings at the time, and to my recollection it came to a head toward the end of 1987 and finally culminated in early 1988 when we had a business

meeting with them in Cleveland, OH. And that was the final straw that led to us being dismissed.

And Peter Criss also comes back into the picture, as far as you're aware did he sell his image back to the band?
The settlement with Peter Criss, during the time that I was involved, my recollection is that there was something carved out in the agreement that he owned the rights to "Beth," since he considered that his song. I don't remember if he owned the rights to the "Cat" makeup. I'd have to go back to the book, but whatever I said there is probably 99.9% accurate since nobody ever contacted me or challenged me on anything that I wrote in the first place. The problem with these agreements is they were so complicated and in some cases so poorly drafted that they created more questions than they answered, or caused problems. When reality set in, what was in agreement made no sense, and had to be renegotiated. I know that happened with Ace Frehley. Not one person that had sophisticated business knowledge could understand that agreement because it was so unclear. So I don't exactly remember whether he did or didn't. Maybe he did, because he did a solo album on Tony Nicole Tony records with the makeup on the cover. It's really an abstract issue.

Howard Marks, it sounds like in your book he remained totally devoted to KISS. Have you read Paul Stanley's autobiography that came out a few years ago?
Yes I did read it, I can't say I read all of it, but I did read parts of it.

Is it difficult to marry up what you know how things worked, and what you're aware of, with how presented his view in his book questioning Howard's judgment?
I can simply say that Howard Marks and Paul Stanley were extremely close personally and professionally for many many years. Paul Stanley had a father-son relationship with Howard Marks. He'd talk to him multiple times a day on the

telephone, or come into the office. Howard Marks knew many aspects of his life beyond simply Paul Stanley as his business client. Paul Stanley trusted his judgment and benefitted for many years from the negotiating abilities and business acumen that Howard Marks had, and used on behalf of the band. Now the whole thing blew up when largely because his psychiatrist instigated in him the belief that we were doing bad things and the tax shelters proved it. So Paul Stanley's faith in Howard Marks was undermined and eventually the psychiatrist took over a business role.

But that says more about the state of mind of Paul Stanley and his psychiatrist, that a medical professional becomes your business manager, than it does about Howard Marks and Carl Glickman who probably made an error in judgment in putting the band into those tax shelters. However, those tax shelters were perfectly legal. They were fully disclosed. There were other very wealthy people, during the late 1970s, who had done similar things. Unfortunately, those tax shelters blew up because the government claimed back taxes, not that they did anything illegal, but they didn't allow the write-offs that they had originally promised. So it was a bad business judgment that happened as a result of unforeseen circumstances.

A lot of memos circulate from business meetings, and while obviously not all of them and they don't paint the full picture, it's clear that the KISS partners are present when financial investment decisions are being discussed, even if they don't understand them. So the band was aware of the investments and what was being done on their behalf?
Yes. And they also had an outside lawyer who had partners who came to the meetings. So it's not like we handled their legal affairs too, they had completely independent lawyer and an accountant. The accountant reported to them too. It wasn't that they were unaware, it was a matter of whether

they accepted that these problems existed and eventually we'd have to something about them.

So, in you view is there anything that could have helped "Crazy Nights" be a more successful album? Was there anything that you felt that the record label, band, or you didn't do, or was it simply the vagaries of the market?
I think the album got off to a reasonably decent start and they were able to tour on it. You have to realize that less than six months later I am no longer involved. What happened — from March 1988 forward, with respect to that album — I really have no idea. All of a sudden you drop your management in the middle of an album campaign that may jeopardize your relationship for a period of time that you might not be able to recover from. So, I don't know. I can't imagine anything. They got the producer they wanted, they got the producer they wanted, they were reasonably happy with the album. There were no tracks on the album that became hit singles [Ed. In the United States]. The tour, from what I understand, did fair to middling business at best, and some of the shows had to be cancelled. So, if you ask me, "what could have been done differently," during that period of time with that set of facts, I can't think of anything.

In your book you've been very clear about the demise of your relationship with KISS, but had you been involved in the booking of the Japan tour before you were fired?
Yes, I was involved, and was dealing with Bobby Brooks, who was an agent at the time. He passed away in a helicopter crash [Ed. Along with Stevie Ray Vaughn in 1990]. I remember discussing it with him, and we had some back and forth during negotiations.

What about the Monsters of Rock run through Europe during the summer?
No, nothing at all.

How about the compilation, "Smashes, Thrashes, and Hits," had any advance discussions for the occurred by the time you left?
No.

Ozzy's "The Ultimate Sin," produced by Nevison, had been released in February 1986. It struggled to Platinum certification in May, and ultimately stagnated. Didn't the reception of an album from an artist similar to KISS, working with Ron set off any discussions or concerns? Was anyone looking at this while the band was waiting for him, and it not turning out as well as the Heart album?
I seem to recall that Paul Stanley had a very good relationship with Ron Nevison and seemed to be very knowledgeable about his track record. This was largely his decision, to go with Ron Nevison — it wasn't like we were selling him on the idea. Paul had already been sold on the idea, and we were simply trying to put the pieces together to make it workable. Sometimes a producer has a great track record, but to extrapolate from that, that he's going to do the same job for you, perhaps that's overreaching. This is what he felt would work for KISS and he was very confident about it.

Do you think that anything could have saved Glickman/Marks' relationship with KISS, with everything that happened in the background, or was it just done by that point after 12-years?
I'm sure if Hilsen wasn't around, we would have soldiered on. I also have to concede that for us to have been involved for 12-years, it is almost an eternity in the life of a rock group. It's true that after a while people do get tired of the relationship they have with other people. And usually you get tired of a relationship, especially a long standing one, when your fortunes decline and you start to have problems, even about things that you may have known about. So we ended up being the fall guy.

You interacted with the band members at one time or another, can you just give us a quick appraisal of what you thought about them individually. Paul Stanley?
I would say *very* focused, very intelligent, very mercurial, and very artistic. Paul Stanley had the most artistic temperament of all the KISS people that I knew.

Did you work with him the most?
Initially, I was closer to Peter Criss, and then he left the group so my involvement with him started to wane, particularly after he did his first solo album. He moved from Connecticut to California, so from that point on I had very little contact with him. Ace, I had a good rapport with, but I wasn't really close to him. Paul and Gene I knew much better, but Paul I probably spent more time with, talking to and being with in the later years of my involvement because Gene had moved himself to Los Angeles. So, Paul was around more and was the main person from KISS who was still living in New York.

What about Gene Simmons, how would you describe him?
Also *very* focused, and somewhat bombastic. Somebody whose personality was actually quite different in private than his persona was in public. And I mean that in a favorable way. Behind the scenes, when the cameras were off, he was a very thoughtful, often generous, person who you could have a really good conversation with. But then when the cameras were on, or he was onstage, or there was an audience, he became overly aggressive and bombastic. That's just how he works, he just switched himself on and off, in terms of his personality, depending upon the environment — like an actor.

The man of 1,000 faces, so to speak. Eric Carr?
Very decent and kindly, but a little bit timid. Someone who ended up in a situation, a stroke of good fortune or good luck, that happens maybe one in a million times. He was someone who went from total obscurity, to being a part of

one of the most famous groups in the world, in a very short period of time. And that created problems for him. He wasn't used to it, and there was no transition for him. One day he was a drummer in Brooklyn, playing in local bands and working a day job, and the next day he was making hundreds of thousands of dollars a year as an employee of this famous rock group. So he had a lot of adjustment problems. I sympathize with him; it's really more than I understood at the time.

So he goes from basically cleaning stoves to KISSteria in Australia!
There was in-between for him.

What about Bruce Kulick?
Bruce was a real journeyman musician. He had a very unassuming personality and was very solid worker, an excellent musician and easy to get along with. Again, somebody who had worked for years as a professional musician, but suddenly got a stroke of good fortune and became associated with this famous group for years. He seemed to know how to handle it, so he didn't have the adjustment problems that Eric Carr. Bruce Kulick was a more mature personality.

He'd been on tours with bands such as Meat Loaf, so had more experience that sort of drama.
He had a much wider range of experience and a level of maturity that worked in his favor.

You worked with the band for 12-years, what is your fondest memory of your time working with the band?
Let me answer it this way, the earliest days, say 1976, 1977, 1978, they were by far the most fun, because everything was happening at that time. Every day was an adventure. Everybody from the original band was there and those were the most original and unique experiences. So it was the most

fun, we were all a part of this big organization and KISS was a household word and one of the most successful acts of the time. After that I had many good moments, many wonderful travel experiences, such as Brazil or Australia that I enjoyed tremendously. By the time the 1979 tour was finished you could see the wheels starting to come off.

Phil Ashley

KissFAQ: Phil, let's start with a little basic background. What led to your interest in music and when did you start playing?
Phil Ashley: I studied classical music as a child and when I was about 12-years-old, I started playing in rock bands. So, I started pretty young! I always wanted to be a musician and I didn't have a particular style of music that interested me, I would just jump into different styles. I loved classical, I loved rock, I loved pop; and then, by the time I was 16 or 17, I was playing jazz. So, that gives you kind of an idea, I was all over the place but I always just loved music.

That's a very broad spectrum from an early age, especially to not be pigeonholed into any one genre. What would you call your first professional gig?
I left college to go on tour with Rupert Holmes. He was the "Piña Colada" guy.

I remember that song!
I played keyboards for him, so that was like my first work with "national" recording acts. I always look at that gig as the beginning of my whole kind of approach. Right before that I had been a college student and I had a 20-piece big band in New York that was put together for me by New York studio musicians. We would play all around town, and I was basically just would write everything. Even though it was with professionals and everything, I always look at that as just more of an experience. I went from that straight into Rupert's band.

Did you decide early on that you had a preference for session work, and the variety it engenders of working with

different acts and styles, rather than being in a single band type situation?
It took me a while. I was with a band called the Uptown Horn Band, who were a horn section and they played a lot of acts so they had a deal on EMI. I joined the band right before we went to England to record the album. I recorded the album, but as a result of some corporate stuff, a bunch of acts got dropped, and they were one of them. I looked at it and just said, "This isn't really my kind of thing." Doing sessions, I love the variety. I like walking in every day and not knowing what I'm going to be doing. It became more of it really fitting for me to be more of a studio musician, rather than let's say in one band and I'm playing the same sort of stuff, over and over again. It's like when I started studying and at 10 or 11 my teacher said I had to make a decision between performance and composition. I chose composition. I like difference.

Right, so there wasn't anything that really forced you out of an interest in band situations?
No, it's a personality thing. It's not really about which I think is best; it's just the nature of my personality.

It certainly seems to have served you well! By the mid-1980s, you're doing a lot of session work with a diverse group of artists: Mick Jagger, Debbie Harry, Aerosmith, Prince, and Billy Idol... You recorded with Lou Gramm, who's doing his first solo album, "Ready or Not." How did your interaction with Lou come about?
It's funny because I was playing with my big band at the Ritz and the drummer in the band was Lou Gramm's brother, Benny. So, during a sound check he said, "Let's go visit my brother, he's doing an album over at Electric Lady Studios." The album they were recording was 'Foreigner 4' [Ed. Released in 1981]. So we went over there, and I had not been in a recording studio like that before, ever. I was kind of stunned, but Lou was very friendly and was showing us

around the studio. So, when it came time for him to do his solo record, I was highly recommended.

That's amazing, that your first look in a studio was such a legendary one! Projects were coming at you fast and furious at this time?
Actually, timing-wise it was very interesting, because I finished Lou's solo record and I was doing video for "Ready or Not," and that's when I was flying out to Los Angeles to work with KISS. It was like the same time.

Oh right, that's much closer together than I'd thought.
Yeah, Lou's album was a little before "Crazy Nights." Lou's a great singer and I really was happy to be on that record.

That's a really fun album as well. You got to play some of his early solo dates that he did in the U.S. in support of it as well didn't you?
Yes that's correct, but I had to leave Lou's band because by then I was also recording with Mick Jagger. I was doing his second album, while I was doing "Crazy Nights." So, when Mick asked me to go on tour with him and Jeff Beck, Lou was very gracious and let me. I got someone else to fill in for me with Lou, Gary Corbett. He was the person I also recommended to KISS for their tour. He's a good guy, but I was just too busy and so all over the place. It was amazing that I had any time to sleep.

Do you recall where you were recording with Mick for the "Primitive Cool" album? Were your sessions for that in Barbados or at Wisseloord in Holland?
I started in Barbados because they had someone else start the record, but then Mick remembered me so I went down to Barbados and recorded with him. And then, actually, right after I finished the keyboards for "Crazy Nights" in Los Angeles, I ran back New York to finish up the album with Mick.

And you also did the "Throw Away" video with Jeff Beck which looks like it was fun to be a part of?
Yeah. Then I ended up doing two tours with him. Actually, that day I went out there to do the video I visited KISS, because they had just started doing their rehearsals for the "Crazy Nights" tour, and Gary had just started working with them. So, yeah, all of this stuff was happening at the same time!

That's what I find so amazing. You're having to juggle and pick and choose between you know, Lou Gramm, Mick Jagger, KISS, which it must have been absolutely amazing to have all of those on your plate at one time. And around the same time you're also working on remixes for Aerosmith with John Luongo?
When I was in town I would work with John, he kept me pretty employed. But I was also working with Debby Harry as well, so I was just flying from one studio to another. It was great and it actually was really enjoyable. I had an office in Electric Lady Studios, so a lot of the acts started coming down to the studio to work with me there. It was easier, so yeah, it was great and a lot of fun. Couldn't ask for more, right?

Absolutely not! One question I've got is about the remixes that had become popular again in the second half of the 1980s, stuff like Aerosmith's "Dude (Looks Like a Lady)" and "Rag Doll." You were doing those with John. Was there any talk about doing any for any of the singles off "Crazy Nights"?
I don't think so; I introduced Paul and John later on. He did the remixes for "Let's Put the X in Sex." That was the first time I believe that John and Paul actually did something. But, for "Crazy Nights," no I don't remember that.

Okay, some fans may be relieved that there's no 12-minute "Extended Crazier" version of "Crazy Crazy Nights" sitting in the vaults waiting to be unleashed on them?!

There could be but I wouldn't know anything about it!

How did you meet Paul Stanley for the first time? I guess by 1986 you're working with him doing demos at Electric Lady, some of which eventually get recorded for the "Crazy Nights" album.
It's a funny story. I was sort of the staff synthesizer player or consultant over at Electric Lady Studios. They were doing the "Asylum" album, the album before "Crazy Nights." Paul wanted to try keyboards on "Tears are Falling," so the studio manger, Mary, recommended me to him. I went into the studio and we started working on the tune, and he recognized me. But Paul and I definitely could not figure out where we knew each other from, but there was definitely something, we knew each other! But we couldn't figure it out. After about 20 minutes or 25 minutes he figured it out: We actually grew up a few blocks away from each other and knew each other as teenagers and had played together. Also, we had both changed our names. I didn't really know anything about KISS, so I didn't realize that, you know. I knew him as Stan, so he had gone on to do those things with KISS.

He didn't realize that I had also changed my name and had gone on to do all of these other musical things. So that's where I reacquainted myself with Paul. It was a real mindblower for both of us, two guys from Queens. So when he wanted to work on songs for "Crazy Nights," he spoke to me about it and asked if I would get involved on the demo side. So I did all the demos with him and Electric Lady. We would program the drummer machine, I played the keyboards, Paul played the guitar, and then we'd go in the studio, we'd do vocals and so forth. Those demos were what were used as the templates for the songs on the album, when it was recorded out in Los Angeles.

One of the unused songs, or maybe it wasn't even considered for "Crazy Nights," was "Time Traveler," which

was released on their box set in 2001. There was some other material, such as "Best Man for You," "Don't Let Go," and "When Two Hearts Collide" which often gets groups in the '87–89 period. I think those are the big demos that circulate, some of which certainly date to this time? What do you recall of those?
We did a lot of songs that didn't go on the record. Two of those titles I remember, but again titles may have changed too. I do remember we did stuff that did not come out and that's always part of every record, but the first and last ones you mention I believe I remember those.

"When Two Hearts Collide" and "Time Traveler"?
Yeah.

Do you recall working on "Hide Your Heart" at this stage? I think Paul first did that in 1987 and it got left off the album, possibly due to being offered out to other artists, and was then used the following year on "Hot In The Shade."
Absolutely. That was recorded in Los Angeles for the album after "Crazy Nights." I remember singing some of the chorus with them besides the keyboards. That was my one vocal debut with those guys!

Were any of the other KISS guys around, when Paul's doing these demos? What about Bruce Kulick, for instance?
Bruce came in to do some solos. Eric also came in to do some vocals and that was about it because it was New York where we were doing the demos. Since they were just going to be rough sketches, they were never supposed to be full band recordings. They were really to help Paul figure out the songs since he was going the slightly more pop direction. He really wanted a very close handle on the arrangements and that's what we were concentrating on, basing drums and voicings and so forth. They were well-done demos, but the idea was always that they would be rerecorded with the band. I think

Bruce did some guitar solos, but I don't think that we finished them all.

They wouldn't have needed them at that stage since the arrangements and backbones of the songs were the most important thing.
No. Paul's a really hard worker and the idea was to maximize these tunes, make them the best they could be.

Was he talking about any of these songs being offered to other artists at this time? At the time it was invariably reported in the trade magazines that he was writing for Cher and looking for other artists to place material with. I think he did a song, "Jump the Gun," that went with Jeff Paris. Paul Dean picked up one of his songs from the period, "Sword and Stone." Was he talking with you about what this material's for? Is he saying hey, I think this is a good song for Cher or so and so, or is this all, as far as you're concerned, for the next KISS album?
No, everything was pretty much for KISS, except "When Two Hearts Collide." I believe he did that one for Cher because I remember recording that and he kind of wrote it for her. But everything else was really just write, write, write, write and what does it sound like, and trying different things. So, it was always, as far as I knew, just for KISS.

Were you helping Paul with any of the arrangements, making suggestions, or, "Hey, Paul, try this," because you come from a different perspective? He's very much from a guitar oriented band, but in 1987 is looking for crossover with a slightly different sort of sound. There was a suggestion that gets blown out of proportion that he was writing on keyboards — he even called himself a "kamikaze keyboardist" who kind of just jumps in and hopes to be in the right place at the end of the song. That's why you're there I expect.

Well again, Paul wasn't really a keyboard player, so he would hear things and understand the top note of voicings and things like that. For me that's a really easy translation. I also play guitar so this is what I do with people — I try to pull sounds out from that and what they're trying attain. I maximize what they're doing. He had very definite ideas and the idea was to flesh them out. So my background being, playing on so many different kinds of pop records and things like that, obviously I would help him with those kinds of things. It was a lot of fun and we had a gas. We used to work in my office and then run to his car and listen.

How easy or difficult of a process was it with Paul, because he's very particular. He has a very definite vision in his head of how a song is going to sound, even if he can't fully express it himself musically. If he's describing what he's hearing in his head to you, and you're translating on the keyboard into sound, how did that process go? Was it tough or did you kind of click and easily present what he wanted?
Total click, we had similar musical references. Paul and I as teenagers had similar sources, in the sense that we both loved Led Zeppelin and Cream and that kind of music. He may have gone much more into the performance side, and I had gone much more to the other side, but we had a basic understanding of where we were going with this stuff. For me it was a breeze working with Paul. I mean I worked with Paul for a number of years on things that weren't KISS — we even did one of the tours in the... I forget when. He wanted to do a classical piece for the opening of the KISS show and he came to me. I did all the instruments using synth and samplers, and we had a gas. That was a real stretch I'm sure! It was an interesting experience for him and it was a great experience for me so he and I gelled when it came to working together. He did his homework, he did his work. That's what I'm used to dealing with, people like that.

When you're recording at Electric Lady, are you in the proper studio, or was the side room just a place to lay down quick and dirty multi-tracks? He was known in the '70s for sometimes doing the full 2" 16-track treatment in a full studio for his demos. Was he still doing that when he worked with you?
Oh no, well we started in my office because we do a lot of the programming in there. The drums are programmed, the bass is programmed, and then once we needed to get to get it on tape, we would go in the full studio. Dave Wittman, who engineered a lot of records for KISS, was the engineer for most of this.

Did you have any equipment did you have in your office for tracking and recording?
No, it really wasn't for tracking or recording. I had banks of synthesizers, so the idea was that I could program stuff in my office but we would always hit tape. This was the 1980s and digital recording was still in its infancy in terms of computer recording.

What sort of tape's being used in the studio to capture these demos?
Probably 24-track if I remember correctly. Yeah, we're using the full studio, and Electric Lady was a state of the art studio at that time. We were using the facility as if we were recording final records, whatever you want to call it.

When it comes time for KISS to record the full album, was it always planned that you would be participating in those sessions? Or did you get a call later on saying, "Hey Phil, can you come out to California and do the sessions with Ron Nevison?"
Paul was very adamant from the beginning that he wanted me on the record. Ron even came to New York while we were doing the demos and he was thrilled that we were doing so much preproduction work. He said, "You know, you guys are

doing my job for me!" I went out there, and I ended up working with Ron on another album after that. It was always going to be, I think, at least from my perspective. It was just a matter of having to figure out the schedule. That was always the hard part.

It sounds that in 1987–88 you had a very crowded schedule?
It was so crowded that I remember that when I was doing the video with Lou, and the director wanted another take, I was like, "Shit, I'm going to miss my flight to Los Angeles to start with KISS in the morning!" I remember that. So, yeah, it was just crazy. While I was doing the "Crazy Nights" sessions, Mick was calling me and we were discussing what we were going to do once I got back to New York! That was my life and it was great! I loved it and KISS were part of it.

Do you remember which studio you did the keyboards at in California? Was it at Can Am Studios or were you out at Rumbo?
Rumbo.

Were other band members around when you were doing it or did, were you just coming in and doing the sweetening with Paul and Ron, or were there listening back sessions with Gene and the other guys?
Yeah. Gene was there the whole time. Bruce was there a lot and I think Eric was there. I just don't remember off hand, but I remember Gene for certain because we went bowling. In fact, I'm pretty sure Eric was there when we went bowling too! Anyhow, once I started working with KISS, I actually started working with Gene on a couple of the records he was producing for his label. I don't remember what are those were bands called.

When I spoke with Gary Corbett he made a comment about Gene that he simply did not like keyboards. Was there any of that undertone that you got from him, that he wasn't

totally thrilled to be doing an album that was a little bit more pop oriented with a strong keyboard essence underlying the music?
Absolutely, that was his opinion and a totally valid opinion. And yes, he expressed it very clearly. You know, I looked at it as well, and it was simple: "You guys make the decision." That's really not my. My role is to maximize what I bring to the table, whether you like it or not. So that was for them to iron out. Gene was always good about it. He used to do the ice skating thing too. It's fun, but everyone has their opinion.

Gary also said that when he did his sound check with the keyboards Gene would start fake ice skating around the stage to let him know exactly how he felt.
Yeah, he did that in the studio. Gene is a character and you know that's part of who he is. He's not the first one and he's not the last one and we all have opinions and he expresses it particularly that way. I've done so much work with Gene over the years that, you know, what can I say, it's just part of him. When they were producing Crown of Thorns, Paul and Gene, I did the keyboards on that; and they needed keyboards on that band. The focus of that band was guitar-based but definitely had to also have keyboards. So, Gene knew it.

In hindsight, how happy were you with your work? Obviously, you probably didn't have any time to sit back and listen to it and critically analyze it after you finished, with going out on tour with Mick and everything else that you were doing in the studio. But, were you happy with the production when you did finally hear the finished product, how Ron had done, and how your contributions sounded?
Very much so. I was actually surprised how loud the keyboards were in the mix. It's a hard rock band! When I worked with Ron we had really done all of the parts in preproduction, and he was happy. He said to me, "Look, what do you think? Do you have any ideas that have we have not looked yet?" And I said, "Sure!" He just basically said, "Okay,

go for it," and that was a very good experience for me because I love working with producers that give you that kind of openness. So, for the keyboard recordings, he really gave me a free rein. There are parts on there that were not part of the preproduction work, but I had a gas doing that stuff with Ron. So, for me it was a very positive experience and I'm looking for different things than let's say other people may look for. I'm just looking that the whole product is good. If I do great keyboards and the drums sound like shit, it's not going to work. So, I was just happy with everything. I liked Ron's production so I was a fan of his, his stuff with Heart.

And then of course, two of the three singles released in support of the album, "Reason to Live" and "Turn On the Night," were very keyboard-oriented. When it comes to KISS touring, to support the album, were you pretty much lined up to be the touring keyboardist?
We never discussed it.

So, you knew Gary Corbett from around Electric Lady or the New York City scene and recommended him to Paul?
Yeah, because when I made the move from Lou to Mick's band, I had Gary take over with Lou. Gary was great because he came to the rehearsals, he understood the program, and he slid right into the Lou Gramm gig, no sweat. And that really showed me that he could do this, so when it came time for the KISS one, to me it was a no brainer, and I knew Gary would love the gig. So it worked out well for everybody. Gary was very professional and that's what I know they needed. They needed somebody that they didn't have to think about, that would just do the gig, learn the parts, and so forth. So, Gary was the perfect guy.

Was he the only person you recommended? Or did you give them a list?

No, I said try Gary first. We'll get back to it, but I just said I think he's the right guy. He had already proved it to me, you understand?

Absolutely. I was listening to some of the Lou Gramm stuff on that European tour with Gary, some live shows from Germany, and they sounded good. Let's move to, "Smashes, Thrashes and Hits," the 15th anniversary KISS compilation released the following year. They're back in New York, well I guess at least Paul is, and you work with him on the two new songs. Is that correct, or did you just do the remixed versions with John later?
Now are we talking, "Let's Put the 'X' In Sex?"

Yes, and "(You Make Me) Rock Hard."
I don't really remember "Rock Hard," but then again I could have worked on it. I remember "Let's Put the X in Sex," because I went to Paul's apartment and that's where we started programming it and he was working with Desmond Child.

That's right.
I met Desmond back during "Asylum." So we started in his apartment and then we moved over to Right Track to record it with KISS. So I did the horns, yeah, I did quite a bit on that particular single. I guess that was it. I get a little confused, because then there was another record, the one with the pyramid I think.

Yeah, "Hot in Shade" with "Hide Your Heart" and "Forever."
Right. For that one, I flew out to California to do in a studio out there. Yeah, so that was a different time. So as far as "Let's Put the 'X' In Sex," yes, I did a lot of work on that.

I think they're out at the Fortress Studio in Hollywood, when they were working on "Hot in the Shade" and Cherokee Studios too.

That's the studio, I remember that well.

Oh good, I always like to know where these things happen. So, you've worked with a tremendous amount of acts, where does KISS kind of fall in your wheelhouse of musical experiences? It's always tough to ask someone to rate, you know, an iconic band that's been around for 45 years!
You know what; the only reason why KISS is slightly different for me is that the relationship I had with Paul. He's the only person that I knew as a teenager that I ended up working with so much later on, and that was always a different bond. There was a certain friendship there, like when he first got married, I was one of his groomsmen. I did a string arrangement for the wedding that they walked out of the thing for. I think it was "Forever," so for me KISS was really this relationship with Paul. Paul would also come to my shows. When I was with Joe Satriani in the 1990s, he would come to see me play with Joe. So, it's a little different. I always look at the different artists I work with only as that I'm there to maximize what they do.

With KISS and Paul, I really felt I was able to accomplish that. So, that's the sign of success for me as far as where I stack all these things. I don't really say, "Oh, this is going to be a hit, or this not going to be a hit." I just do the best I can and when you work with lots of artists you don't really like to compare them. They're all unique, so I learn different things from different people. Lou was so different than Mick. Mick was so different than Tina Turner. Cher was totally different, Michael Bolton totally different, Satriani totally different. So everyone's different. The exciting thing is bringing something to those different things. The work I did with Joe Satriani is very different from the work I did with Cher.

Absolutely.
So, that's how I look at Paul. It wasn't that I didn't know anything about KISS, and when they did "Asylum" I had

played a little bit of the keyboards on that song, but he asked me to come out to help him with the show. I had programmed Eric's syndrums for his solo, and then I eventually did some opening music, but they flew me out and were doing rehearsal, Paul came up to me and said, "You've never seen us, right?" I said, "No!" So he kind of introduced me to KISS, so it's a little different. There was a little more of a friendship.

One of the things it's interesting to ask people who knew Paul pre-KISS — especially people who grew up with him, before he was basically anyone of note — is, was there anything about him, in his youth, that you would have said, "I'm not surprised he actually made it as a musician." There's many kids who artistic and talented and play around with music when they're young and then either don't pursue or make it. Were you surprised or not surprised that Paul became the success that he has been for so many decades?
That's a hard question and I'm not good at that. The only thing I do remember of Paul is he had a vision. We used to talk, I remember at the bus stop, and he was much more image conscious than I was. I thought it was really interesting, it was very like a vision he had and this was way before KISS, so I saw that he had a vision in terms of an understanding the sort of symbolism of music and so forth. He and I were both very into the London fashion at that time, all that kind of stuff, but as far as knowing that he would make it, I could make a huge box of all the people you think are going to make it and they don't.

Right.
I mean growing up in the era, in Queens, it's like everybody was in a band. And very few got past 30. So there's a couple of my friends that are studio musicians, but Paul was the only one that really became let's say an icon or a star. But did I see it? No, because I'm not good at that kind of vision.

Were you actually in the same band as him or just playing in bands around the same scene?
No, what happened was we had a mutual friend and this guy said, "You've got to meet my friend Stan!" So I said, "Okay," and walked over to his house with this friend and went to his bedroom to hang out. He had his guitar under his bed I remember, he pulled it out and we started jamming and it was fun. I was playing guitar in those days and while we didn't continue, in terms of playing together, we always talked music. We were always running into each other, whether it was parties or at the bus stop — because he went to school in the city — and I was always going into the city. So we'd always see each other and stop and talk about music. This was our thing, but we weren't in the same bands because I was doing more of the Allman Brothers type stuff and he was doing a bit more of the hard rock stuff. We were kind of like in different worlds but at the same token, always discussing music. We were definitely two music addicts. There was no two ways about it!

That is just one of those absolutely fascinating pieces of minutia that you don't necessarily expect to find out when you speak with someone. We're talking about "Crazy Nights" in 1987, to find out something about 1970, or whenever it was, is just absolutely fascinating. Thank you for sharing that.
It was one of the jokes with us because he lived only two blocks away. When I moved to Long Island, I moved to the same town as his parents. At one point I actually lived across the street from them. So it was just like so crazy all these connections.

Diane Warren

KissFAQ: Diane, thanks so much for giving me some time to talk with you about your writing career with KISS.
Diane Warren: I love KISS and Paul Stanley's a really good friend of mine.

So the purpose of this call particularly is to celebrate the 30th anniversary of the band's "Crazy Nights" album, on which of course appeared your first co-write with Paul.
Fuck, 30 years ago!?

Yeah, I'm sorry.
Fuck me, oh my god. That's crazy, how can that be? I was like 5 when I did that song!

(Laughs) You were? And now you're 15!
Yeah, I was a real prodigy. Isn't that funny how that happens? Wow, I can't believe that's 30 years. Jesus, that's crazy.

So, at what point in your life did music become something special, something that you wanted to participate in?
When I was little, you know? I always knew I was going to do this. I kind of always knew I was going to write songs.

Is there a particular song or artist that was your "Ed Sullivan" moment, so to speak?
The Beatles on Ed Sullivan. That was definitely a moment.

There's a whole generation that was affected by that moment.
I know, isn't that crazy? I mean, it's not really like that anymore. It's so fragmented but, yeah.

Did you play any instruments? I think your bio says that your father bought you a guitar...
I taught myself guitar and then later on I taught myself piano.

Which do you prefer to write with? Do you have a preference?
I write on both. Probably keyboards more, but I love writing on my guitar too. I write different kinds of songs. You know, I'm still like trying to get over the 30 years thing.

So, how does Diane Warren enter the orbit of the KISS world? Were you working with Desmond first, or were you working with Paul Stanley, because Paul was working with Desmond a lot during that period?
I'm trying to think how I met Paul Stanley? Maybe it was through Desmond Child. I'm pretty sure I met Desmond first, I think it was 1986. So I want to say I must have met Paul though Desmond. I don't know how else I would have met him. I can't remember shit. One other really cool thing is from this, aside from a really good friendship, Paul and Gene are great. I've become good, good friends with Paul through the years. I remember him, a long time ago, saying, "You need to make sure you have a trainer. That you always work out," and stuff. You know what, if it wasn't for him, I wouldn't have had the same trainer for almost 30 years now.

He's been religious about staying fit and taking care of himself as much as he can for the rigors of what he does. He's a great role model for people to follow.
Yeah. He's a great guy.

What do you remember about writing "Turn on the Night" with Paul at this time? How was the session set up? Did you guys meet in person, was it over the phone?
We worked together, I remember that. You know, it was just a fun song. I thought it was a really good song. We wrote some other things together and then later on I wrote a song

called "Nothing Can Keep Me from You." I think that was the first outside song that KISS ever did that they didn't write, and that was really cool. It started from doing that song with Paul. It was a cool song.

How does a song like that start for you? I mean, are you working on a keyboard with a melody?
I think I was probably at the piano and he was on guitar. I honestly can't remember, it's a long time ago.

He was a new collaborator writing with you. How do you, do you prepare to write with someone if that, that situation does arise?
Yeah, I don't write with a lot of people. I write by myself usually, so I didn't prepare. I don't prepare, I just come in the room and see what happens.

As much as you can recall, did it happen quickly or was it over a period of days that the song came together?
It was pretty quick. I take a long time on my own songs, but if I'm in a room with somebody it's usually pretty quick. It's 30 years ago, so the hard part is going to be remembering all the stuff! I think it was probably a couple of sessions, but I do remember loving the song when we were writing it.

It became the third single from the album, so Paul obviously loved it as well.
Cool, yeah, he loved that song.

If I was to ask you if there was a Diane Warren fingerprint on the song, would you be able to say that's me without a doubt?
I'm sure I'm in there, all over the place and I'm sure Paul is. I was going to say, like a big chorus is usually me, but a big chorus is KISS too.

Which would probably be why it was a good combination as well with how the song turns out.
Yeah, exactly.

You were obviously coming off the No. 1 hit with the Starship's "Nothing's Gonna Stop Us Now." Did working with KISS open any new doors for you, or was it just something on the resume that just expanded you cachet within the industry?
I think it got me writing songs for more rock artists, definitely because of that.

Because Aerosmith came along and after that and Bon Jovi.
Aerosmith, yeah. There was Cheap Trick, Bon Jovi... I wrote with a lot of rock artists, you know. All those hair bands too, like RATT, and people like that. I've always done all kinds of songs for all kinds of people, but the KISS thing definitely opened the door for more bands to work with me.

It might seem a rather inane question, but when you heard KISS' fully-recorded version was your vision for the song fully realized in how they captured it in the studio?
I remember loving what I heard, but I'm going to be honest, it is a long time ago!

It is, there's been a lot of songs for you since!
Yeah, like a million songs ago! But I remember loving the record when I heard it.

Do you recall Paul talking about it as a single possibility or was that something that the just completely handled on his own without talking to you?
I remember he thought it was a hit. We both did.

Success is wonderful, but when a single fails to chart, like this one did, do you ever go back and analyze it, or do you just walk away?

No, I move on.

You walk away?
I move on. The charts don't always matter. The songs can live on. Some of my most memorable songs, the songs people love the most, weren't my highest-charting songs.

You're so prolific, and you've done so many different genres. Do you have any emotional attachments to these songs once they are written or recorded?
Thanks. It depends on the songs. Certain ones will be more emotional, and I'll be more emotionally attached to.

You wrote "(You Make Me) Rock Hard" with Paul for their "Smashes, Thrashes, and Hits" compilation. Was that the following year or was that an idea that started around the same time as when you were doing "Turn on the Night?"
I don't remember, it was like probably around the same time. I think that was my title, and it was kind of a joke.

I have to ask you about "Nothing Can Keep Me From You." KISS fans have a mixed opinion on that, especially with the Aerosmith song the previous year, for the "Armageddon" movie. Paul was originally reported as going to co-write with you for their movie project. Do you recall anything about the situation that happened that resulted in that not happening?
No, I just remember that I played him the song and he loved it.

It was good enough for him then to not need his involvement?
Gene really loved it too. That was great, you know.

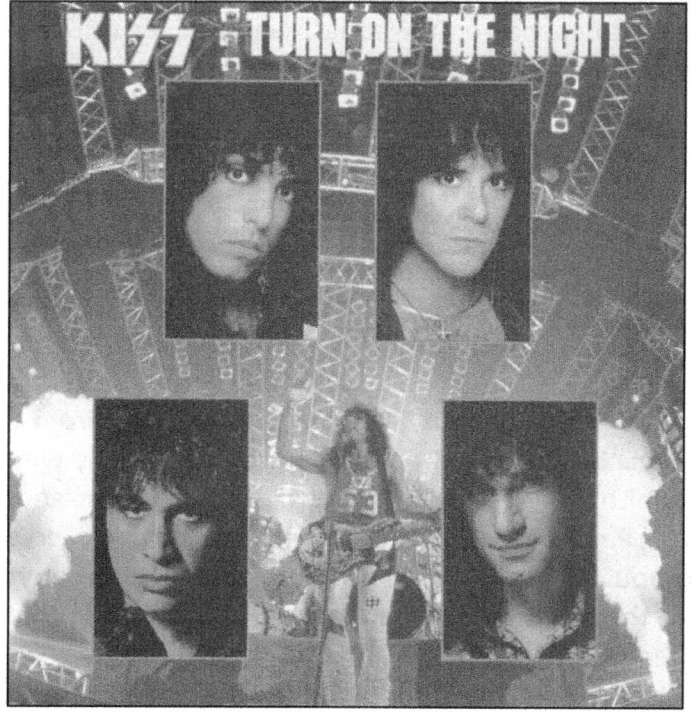

Adam Mitchell

KissFAQ: Adam, you originally came into the fold in 1982 for the Killers/Creatures albums; and then don't really have anything on KISS albums, such as "Lick It Up," "Animalize," and "Asylum." You're brought back into the fold for "Crazy Nights," though by that time you'd been writing for Gene projects such as E-Z-O and Black 'N Blue. What was your contact like with the members of the band in the intervening years?
Adam Mitchell: In the intervening years, I still was doing a lot of stuff with Gene, but I was also busy doing other things. I was screen writing, and it wasn't like I didn't want to anything with the guys after "Creatures of the Night," or anything like that. Paul and I had always remained friends and we used to go out almost every night. At one point we even double-dated roommates. So, we wrote all the time and we'd go bowling, the whole band or whoever else Gene or Paul would invite. So socially they were still very much in my life. Gene and I were still writing for bands he was working with like Black 'N Blue and E-Z-O, what a great record that was we did with that Japanese band!

That one was with Val Garay as well, right? I always found them to be a Japanese version of Living Colour, some great music on the album.
Yeah, that's right. It was a great record, and a number of people have come up to me over the years, even other musicians, and said how much they liked that record. So Gene and I had been doing that, and we wrote something for Silent Rage [Ed. Adam wrote "All Night Long" with Bruce Kulick for the "Don't Touch Me There" album], so we still were doing a lot of things — so KISS was still very much part of my life. I was more involved in doing other stuff, and I wasn't even writing songs that much. I was really focusing

more on screen writing at the time. So, at some point, I guess they were going to do a new record and Bruce was in the band by then. Bruce and I hit it off right away.

"Crazy Nights," where does the base idea for the song come from, you, Paul, or Bruce? What's the seed, a riff, or are you coming in at a more developed stage to refine?
By this point it was the mid to late '80s and they were taking a different approach — a slightly more pop '80s' approach. In any case, Paul and I always wrote, but he came over one day and he said, "I want to write something about ... like that feeling that you get in the arena when you're on stage and how it's like really magic. And the whole thing really starts to take on a life of its own." He says something like, "Crazy, Crazy Nights." That's what he was describing and I thought, "Well that's a good title," so we just took it from there.

How does a writing session with Paul go?
Well, it depends ... I mean first of all, I mean I'm a huge believer — and this is one of the things when I'm teaching songwriting I really try to emphasize — that all great songs, not great records, but all great songs are *ideas* which are set to appropriate music. "Detroit Rock City" is not about the guitar riff, it's an *idea* which is set to music. "Crazy Crazy Nights" and every other song that I ever wrote with Paul or with Gene is first an idea set to music. Sometimes, occasionally, you'll get a record where the music or the great riff somehow makes it works as a record. For example, when Paul and I finished "Crazy Crazy Nights" we had to go and play it for Gene. Gene naturally has to agree it should be on the record ... So, Paul and I went and played it for him. We'd done a demo at my house we, as we'd usually done, but if it didn't work as a song first it wasn't going to work as a full-blown record.

Do you both have guitars? Are you sitting down across from one another and saying, "Okay, what about this chord

progression," or, "Hey, I've got this idea." Where does it come from, a root melody or lyrics?

You know, I can't remember exactly who started playing what, but we always worked at my place and with two guitars. There was one other song we wrote, which just never made it a record, called "Nightmare" we wrote at a place Paul had when he was first moving to L.A. But yeah, otherwise we always wrote in my studio at my house, and we just sat down with two guitars and a plugged-in and just start throwing ideas around. Paul was very good with lyrics. Paul's a big Bob Dylan fan, as we all are — I mean all Bob Dylan did was change the entire world — so, Paul has a very, very keen sense of lyrics as do I. We would just start throwing ideas around. One of the interesting things about "Crazy Crazy Nights," is that it's an unusual song in one sense. Absolutely all of it is written in the present tense, and most present-tense songs are really hard to write because they tend to just lie there. There's no dynamic tension that you get in most songs from the change between the past and the present — or the present and the future — as there is in most songs. But this song, in particular, had to be a present-tense song because it was really all about that feeling of being in the arena and the vibe in the arena. So, it is all in present tense except the very last line where Paul says, right at the end, "Nobody's *gonna* change me because that's who I am."

That's right. I've never noted that before.
Yeah, seems like a small thing but that line is very important because it brings a lot of dynamic tension, just that one line. I know that's a hard concept to grasp, but that one line being in the future. [The] "Nobody's gonna change" [lyric] me has a huge contextual frame around the rest of that song. But anyway, because the rest of the song's in the present tense, we had to come up with huge images. "This is my people / This is my crowd / This is our music / We love it loud." You know, "a million strong." You know, all the images in that song are really big, and I've talked about this before but one

of the really interesting things has happened, even over the last, however many years it's been since I talked to Tim McPhate, is the number of other versions of this song that there are. Paul and I wrote it as this big up-tempo "arena" vibe song. But the number of other slow versions, beautiful versions, of "Crazy Crazy Nights" that I've heard, that have come along are fantastic. It's a testimony to the strength of this song.

Oh, without a doubt. A good song that can be translated between genres and styles is a great song. It's not one-dimensional.
For sure. There's even a version done by Gregorian monks! I think Bruce Kulick told me about it and I thought he was kidding! But he wasn't. Also Kurt Nilsen did a version. And there was a version used in a vodka [Ed. Smirnoff, 2011] commercial that played throughout Europe which was beautiful. Even though Paul and I wrote it to be one thing, I never dreamed it would be something else. So we actually wrote a really good song.

It stood the test of time, obviously to be reinterpreted in different ways and be used in ways that were probably never originally envisaged.

It's one of KISS' biggest hits and in Europe you hear it all the time. It's still one of the most popular songs in Europe. They always play it when they go over there. I was in London about a year ago and you just hear it all the time. So, we wrote a really good song. We wrote a really good song because it accurately reflects the feeling that Paul walked in the door with.

You totally nailed it because it's a massive song. I remember in Britain in '87/'88, you couldn't escape it. I never got to experience that sort of reaction to KISS when living in

America, so that makes the song one of my big KISS anthems.

Yeah. I remember they put it on the Christmas hits collection that they put out at the end of the year, "Now That's What I Call Music" [Ed. Released on Nov. 23, 1987], and that sold another 2 or 3 million records.

You went into HMV or any record store and it was all over the place. Picture discs, CD-singles, poster sleeves. It was absolutely mental.

Oh, yeah, yeah. I don't know if it'd be, you know, the top 100 British songs of all time, but in Britain it's still huge. But the thing that really impressed and surprised me, and still does, is just how many other beautiful, slow version of it there are. That I never dreamed would happen and it works. It's a really good song.

I went to a KISS show in April this year and they brought that back into the set list. They had started doing that song again, in 2010, when Tim spoke with you. It was actually an experience to see 2017 KISS still doing the song. 30 years later, the song it's now a "classic" in their catalog.

It's a classic, yeah.

Who would have thought that in 1987, '88, when the album doesn't quite meet expectations, in the U.S., at least?

That's for other reasons. The album actually sold several million in the U.S. as well and the album actually did really well. I think it was that period and KISS, when they were between kind of getting away from the heavy rock of "Creatures in the Night" and "Lick It Up," and getting into consciously being more commercial for whatever was going on in the '80s.

Oh, without a doubt. You had very polished acts. Bon Jovi is obviously the keystone with which to measure what was going on.

That's right.

Their 1986 album, "Slippery When Wet," was highly polished. Same had been the case with Def Leppard's "Pyromania." And, of course, Ron Nevison had done "Ultimate Sin" which took a somewhat similar approach.
Yeah.

The chorus is massive on the demo, very much the sort of anthemic nature you expect from KISS with the bigger drums and I love it without the overt keyboards. A different beast completely that made me reappraise my opinion of Nevison's version. Were you involved in demoing material for the album?
Yeah, and Paul and I were both disappointed in that. I'd love to hear the original demo. We didn't do the demo in my studio; we did it at some studio on Sunset Boulevard. But, the chorus in the demo was fantastic because we wanted to sound like an arena.

And it does.
It does, and when I heard the record I was somewhat disappointed, but I thought, "Ron's made a lot of hit records, so wait and see." You know, when Paul came in it's not like he said, "We have to write a classic." We were just trying to write a good song and follow the feeling that he had when he came in the door with his idea.

He's got a very clear vision with his songwriting. I've always found, that whatever songs make the records and become classics, Paul's gone into their writing with a very definitive idea about what he wants to accomplish.
Oh, absolutely. I mean, Paul's a songwriter's songwriter. He's a real songwriter, you know. That's not to say Gene isn't, but what Gene cares about is what works.

Yeah, they're coming from different angles. There's something impeccable about Paul's lyrics most of the time. They don't often come across as throwaways. But those differences are what make them such a dynamic partnership. The contrasts...
Yeah, really. Well, I mean, Gene's the God of Thunder! (Laughs)

You can't argue with that, can you?
(Laughs) How subtle can you be?

Let's talk a little about "I'll Fight Hell to Hold You." I think Bruce had a little bit in that one as well. I was surfing YouTube today, and found a disco version of the song from 2001. I don't know if you've ever heard it?
Oh, my God, no. You've got to be kidding me.

Rod Gonzales. It's even got a Barry Gibbs-esque falsetto going on with the vocal and electronica throughout. "Saturday Night Fever" dance moves in the video. It's insane. The problem is, everything in the song that you just said about "Crazy Crazy Nights" being covered, in a sick and twisted kind of way it works. I had a big problem with Paul going so high in his vocal range on the song, that it becomes a little bit too high for my personal taste. I mean, obviously he knows what he's doing, but how do you recall that one coming together?
Well, again, it was probably the same with all of the songs that Paul and I wrote. We wrote nine or ten songs for different KISS albums. If I'm sitting down with Paul to write a song or for a KISS record, it's got to be a KISS song, not an Adam Mitchell song. I'm there to help Paul or Gene, in that case particularly Paul. I'm there to help Paul write a KISS song and bring whatever skill I can to help him write a KISS song. So in virtually every occasion, Paul would come in with an idea, often just a title.

In the case of "I'll Fight Hell to Hold You," he'd have a title, and then he would usually start singing, trying to turn that title into music that made emotional sense. Again, this goes back to the idea that songs are ideas set to music. Good songs, are not just music looking for some words. Occasionally records are written that way, but most, 99.9 percent of great songs, no matter whether it's country, pop, young modern pop, or whatever; it's an idea first. He had the idea that "I'll Fight Hell to Hold You" was expressing: "The strength of my love," you know, a common them in a million other songs.

So, a seed of an idea and two guitars and you're bouncing ideas off one another?
You know, it's in that whole genre, so once again we just sit down and start plunking away on the guitar and then try to craft a lyric that expressed and supported that idea. Offhand, I couldn't tell you the lyric for "I'll Fight Hell to Hold You" because it's been a long time since I wrote it. Once it started I could probably sing along, but (laughs) I've written an awful lot of songs in the years since! Anyway, that was my writing process with Paul. He, almost always, had some title or an idea that he would want to express, and we would work it out together a way to express it.

This was one of the songs from the album that always stood out for me. It's the heaviest of the keyboard songs of the three that you wrote with him. Was Paul ever using a keyboard during any of these sessions, or was it strictly guitars? Did you ever just tinker around?
We'd always write on guitar. I think there were a couple of things when we first started — and I know I did with Gene — where I would play keyboard. But basically, no. KISS is a rock band and rock means guitars. Whatever keyboard in the song came in was probably more Ron Nevison's influence. The third song we did on that record is "When Your Walls Come Down."

Right, there's a dynamic difference with that song, to the other two. It was one of the rarely performed tracks during the tour. It's much more of a traditional kind of rock song and doesn't really stretch into the anthemic "Crazy Crazy Nights" declaration.
Well, at least just "sound" wise, that's my favorite song on that record. I mean the engineering. I just like the sound of it. That one, to me, doesn't sound thin. It sounds really full. And again it was an idea that Paul had, and I can't remember precisely *who* he was singing about. And if I could remember, I wouldn't tell you! (Laughs). But, there is undoubtedly a person behind that song. That's the one, when I listen to the record that I really like. I think the sound on it is great.

One of the things I notice with the whole of the album, and I don't want to get into a critique of Ron Nevison's production, because it's so subjective and really doesn't serve any purpose in hindsight, is the sound of the drums. On the demos of "Crazy Crazy Nights" and "I'll Fight Hell to Hold You," I don't know if they're programmed or if Eric was around, but they sound richer. They sound more like a traditional drum kit than the album versions which are very thin to my ears. They're lacking the sorts of dynamics and bombast we'd become used to on the previous three albums.
Yeah, that's my problem honestly and I've spoken frankly about this before. The album, you know, I think, was recorded on a SSL digital board. I'm not a fan of the digital boards, particularly at that time when they hadn't been around very long yet. I never liked SSL boards in particular and the album to me sounds thin. That was my initial misgiving right from "Crazy Crazy Nights" onwards. The drums...well, normally what we would do in all the other demos, like for "Creatures," and certainly for the ones on "KISS Killers," and then some of the later songs was... I had a drum machine and would program them. Like, for example, on "Creatures of the Night," for "Danger" and all those other

songs, I would just program the drums and then poor Eric would have to try and copy what I had programmed — (Laughs) which, in the case of "Danger" was not easy to do because the tempo was just so, you know, super up-tempo da, da, da, da, da!!!

Yeah, that sounds like a drummer's nightmare, to try and replicate naturally something that might have sounded good, but not necessarily have been realistic in reality.
But I think in the case of "Crazy Crazy Nights" we demoed it live at the studio. I don't remember what the drums were, but I'm pretty sure they were Eric's old drum kit.

I think Gene at times sampled Eric's drums anyway, from reels he had of takes on various songs, to put together some his demos. Just take a little bit at the right tempo, and loop it, and then chuck his stuff on top.
Yeah, that's right, he did. But, you can over-polish records some times. We had some friends over here the other night and I was just looking through some music channels on cable, to put some music on. And inadvertently a '60s music channel came up and they were playing stuff like Dylan's, "Like a Rolling Stone," what an incredible record. A lot of those '60s records were made under the most primitive conditions, but the energy is there and the drums are great but yeah, if you're not careful, you really can over-polish songs, and a lot of records in the '80s were simply over-polished.

Right, in many cases, they used electronic kits, or the sound became synthetic and over-processed in the mid '80s. And for the right sort of material it worked, but for other styles it could get dodgy.
Yes, it became synthetic. I mean, Bon Jovi's records were polished, but they were really well done, felt natural, and again Bon Jovi had great *songs*. Really great, and that's part of why they're still huge to this day. They have fantastic songs and their records "sound" pretty good. I think they might

have been all done at the Power Station in New York - or most of them - which is a great big drum sound studio anyway. But, it's easy to over-polish records and that was my problem with "Crazy Crazy Nights." To me, it was just was too thin sounding in the end.

Another big difference is that Bon Jovi always had a keyboard player integrated in the band from day one. It was a part of what defined their sound, even if it took a couple of albums to really put all of the pieces together.
And that was really a different sound for a hard rock band. You know, they were more a pop rock band.

Bruce Fairbairn, who did "Slippery When Wet," did a fantastic job with the scope of sound he captured. Okay, perhaps that's more down to the engineering, the separation there between the instruments and the overall balances. It's near perfection. But, for KISS, the balance is a bit off. It's too much of a dynamic change from what "Asylum" had sounded like, or "Animalize or ... It's like a sonic speed bump in the middle of the road.
Here I think, they're in a difficult position because Bon Jovi had just come along. They were new then. They were all young. This is their sound and Bon Jovi is not faced with the problem of the way their music is changing like KISS is. "How do we transition here?" All things considered, I think KISS managed that transition incredibly well and the truth is they came out of it bigger than ever.

Yeah, KISS was fighting and grinding all through the '80s from one album to the next they kept working and trying and Paul was steering the ship alone. I think that's without any doubt at this time with Gene working on side projects. That's not to denigrate his contributions in any way. But Paul was really fighting to keep Kiss relevant. And "Crazy Nights" is a massive statement of, "Here we are. We're still

relevant. We're not dead yet, and we can do the same thing everything Bon Jovi's done as young whippersnappers!"

Yeah, exactly, and if you think about how it's really not easy. KISS came along and it would be easy to say, "Oh well, it was just the makeup that made them a big band." And then that's all over — and as soon as they took off the makeup it was over — but they did take off the makeup, and they still survived, and they still sold records. As I said, "Crazy Nights" sold a lot of records and they did make that transition. So that's pretty amazing. And you think how long they've been around now, since 1973, or whatever it is.

Yes, 45 years strong at this point and still going.
And they are bigger than ever.

"Are You Always This Hot" was the twelfth song recorded for the album, but was apparently deemed superfluous. This song always comes up when you're asked about the album, so go ahead and roll your eyes now! Let's talk about it in "The World According to Garp," which I watched that yesterday.
(Laughs!). I got a check for that just the other day!

Wow, you did?
Yeah, I actually did get a very small check, yes.

What's the context of your original demo for that song being in the movie? Because, when I was watching the babysitter scene yesterday, it was an Alice Cooper song that comes on when she turns on the radio in that scene.
Well, the thing is, when it went to video, I don't know why they changed it. Maybe they had to pay too much. In the original movie in the theater release it was in there. But in the later video release all of a sudden it's not in there. I hadn't seen the movie in the theater, or maybe I had, I can't remember. But I didn't even know my song was in the movie until I was watching the video one night. And that scene

came on where the babysitter turns up the radio as Garp gets in the car to take her home. That was definitely my original demo of my original song - to be clear, not the later one of the same title I wrote with Gene. The one in the movie is my original demo that I wrote all myself with me singing and me playing. That's what's in "The World According to Garp." A couple of years later, Gene heard it said, "I'd like to write another song with this title, I just love this title so much." So, he and I wrote another song called "Are You Always This Hot." Same title, different song.

Was there any resemblance between the two apart from the title?
None whatsoever.

So KISS fans probably shouldn't go searching for really old copies of the "Garp" video, to find yours?
Mine was more like a Chuck Berry, sort of rock and roll thing. And like I said, it's me singing, me playing bass, me playing drums, guitar, everything. But it's a totally different song ...

Right, it's certainly not on the current iTunes version. That features "A Long Way Home" by Alice Cooper in the scene.
I can't remember what the original was if it was Alice Cooper or not. I can't remember what the theatrical release was because they may have changed it again, you know, depending on how much they have to pay to license the song. I did get a huge check the other day for, like, (laughs) $80.00.

You're still getting at least some money out of it at least. So, that's a good thing.
Yeah.

A demo of "Dial L for Love" was released on Eric Carr's "Unfinished Business" several years ago. You co-wrote that with Gene and Eric. What do you recall of that one, and

working with Eric on song ideas? How did the process work with him? Did it ever get lyrics?
You're asking the wrong guy, it's so long ago! We did finish it and we did do another demo of it. I think it might've been Eric's original title which Gene loved. It fit right in with "They Call Me Doctor Love," "God of Thunder," and stuff [like that]. Gene likes that kind of title, you know, big. I remember being over at Gene's house at the time; before he built the mega mansion he had a smaller house on the same property. I remember being over there with the two of them working on it. But what we actually did I have no idea.

Well, that's fair enough. The last few questions I have are just some quick comments on a few other songs that you did with band members. One is "Street Legal," that surfaced a few years ago. That's a song you wrote with Gene, apparently (according to publishing documentation). I could play you a little bit of it if it'll jog your memory.
Yes, please ...

(Plays sample)
No idea! You could tell me somebody else wrote it, and I'd believe you.

I won't torture you with any more of that: "I don't care how old you are, you're old enough for me!" It's like an attempt at a 1988 version of "Christine Sixteen."
Yeah. Honestly, you could've told me somebody else wrote that and I'd believe you. It vaguely rings a bell. I'll have to ask Gene if he actually remembers that one. Where did you get the demo?

That came from a studio reel sold on eBay that had that had a couple of takes of that song and "Something Wicked This Way Comes," which Gene gave to Doro a couple years later, and had nothing to do with you.
I completely forgot about that one.

You can see why they didn't use it. But, musically it's decent.
Yeah. That wouldn't have been one of my ideas. It sounds like one of Gene's titles, you know. His titles are usually big and, and edgy like that.

That's one that's going to grab your attention when you hear it! Maybe it's going be on his box set. Phil Ashley recalled a demo for "When Two Hearts Collide." That was a song that Paul was writing for Cher, I believe —
Paul and I wrote that. "When Two Hearts Collide" it was my idea. Yeah, I remember Phil. I hadn't thought about Phil in a long time. Nice guy, but no, that was my idea. That was an exception in that we wrote it at Paul's apartment in New York when he was still living there. No, I remember that very well. He was, he was trying to do something with Cher at the time, which I don't think ever came to fruition, but yeah, we did write it with Cher in mind.

There's so much stuff in this period. He was writing with Vini Poncia as well. Do you remember Paul coming to you and saying, "I'm writing for other people, I want you to work with me on this idea for someone else?"
Not specifically him saying those words. But Paul and I had always stayed in touch and I did go to New York specifically to work with him on that song. I was still living in LA at the time. There were a couple of other ideas too but those weren't songs I particularly enjoyed writing. I never liked writing songs for artists unless you're actually in the room with the artist. Because whenever you come up with an idea that you think might work, or your publisher say, "Oh, I hear they're looking for this or they're looking for that," trust me, they almost always end up looking for something else and the whole thing will have been a waste of time. It's like writing for movies — my least favorite thing in the world to do. There are too many people involved with too many different opinions, so it's better when you just sit down and try to

write a good song. And then, if somebody else wants to do it, fine. Let it find its own home.

I guess if the artist's in the room with you they could put their fingerprints on it and become a part of the process or the song in some ethereal way?
Exactly. I'm trying to think if I've written with any other artists other than KISS. I never expected KISS was going to be more than two days' work anyway. It just so happens that we clicked and it turned out to be all those years. But no, with some exceptions — Tommy Conners and Willie Mack in Nashville are great guys I always liked writing with - but normally, no I don't I enjoy co-writing. It's like having somebody else inside your head. Again, with exceptions. Paul and I wrote some great songs. And Gene and I wrote a lot of good songs. But generally I prefer to write myself. With KISS, it was easy because they knew what they wanted. So for me, "Okay, I totally get this and then get on with it." You're right there with the artist and they can say yes or no right there. But when you're sitting in the room trying to write and the artist *isn't* there, who knows what they want?

You might as well be herding cats to a certain extent.
Oh yeah. Totally.

Indecisive in that sense. I have one more question; before I ask you about what you're up to currently, and that's obviously Gene is working on his box set. Has he been in touch with you about any material that may appear on it?
Yeah, absolutely.

Are we finally going to get to hear "Chrome Goes Into Motion?"
I don't think that one's on there, but there are several others that he and I had written. Including the very first song I ever played for him when he came over to my house. It's called "Something Seems to Happen at Night." He really liked it and

so we took my original track and put his vocal on it. There's at least five other songs on there that I was a cowriter on.

Very cool. Like what?
"Are You Always This Hot," our version of that I think is one of them...

Okay, don't give me anywhere! I don't want to ruin any surprise or suspense for the fans! We're so far away from the '70s and '80s when things in music were a surprise. We'll keep that all secret. So what are you working on these days? You have a new album out?
Yeah, a new album came out a couple of months ago and it's doing really well. It's an Americana album called "Back When We Were Cool." On iTunes, search for Adam Mitchell, "Back When We Were Cool," and *please* download the whole album from iTunes. Don't use Spotify because the truth is all songwriters get ripped off unmercifully by Spotify. We get paid something like a thousandths of a cent per play. It's criminal. So please, download from iTunes. It's a really good album. (Laughs) Ask Gene. He loves it. On the sales chart that it's on, the Americana chart, it took a jump from number 98 to number 45 in the first week. Life is good and I'm excited to see what lies ahead!

Bruce Turgon

KissFAQ: Bruce, let's set the stage a little bit. What was your inspiration to learn to play an instrument, and ultimately perform professionally?
Bruce Turgon: I started playing woodwinds in grade school and then like so many, I saw the Beatles and the Stones on the Ed Sullivan Show and from that point on, playing in a rock band was all I wanted to do.

You were a member of Black Sheep, a Rochester, NY band that included future Foreigner vocalist Lou Gramm. You released a single and two albums. Could you tell us a bit about how that band came together?
Lou and I were in the two big club bands of that time and I would see him periodically at different shows. We both wanted to be in a band with a heavier approach and write our own material and we got together to pursue that.

Black Sheep opened for KISS on several occasions during their "Alive!" tour. What do you recall about how the band got the opening gigs at these shows?
Black Sheep was the main hard rock/alternative band in the area, and was opening shows for many national acts that were coming through. I don't remember the exact timing, but I believe we had just released our second album and our management got us on the bill

From an opening band perspective, what was it like opening for a band that was just starting to break; and one with the live performance they put on?
I was struck by how relentless their approach was and the power in the delivery of the material. It was different than what I had seen up to that point

What did you think of the band, and did you interact with any of the members at any of the shows?
The first show that we did with them was in Rochester, and I don't remember meeting any of them personally. However, I did meet Paul at sound check when we played the Orpheum in Boston — I didn't recognize him at first as I'd only seen him with makeup.

A feature in Goldmine suggests you only performed a single show opening for KISS. Ads for several other shows suggest that other slots were at least scheduled (Rochester, NY, 10/5; Columbus, OH 10/11; Boston, MA, 12/14; Waterbury, CT 12/18; Louisville 12/27/75). Do you remember how many shows you actually opened for KISS for?
Rochester and Boston for sure. We played Columbus a few times and I don't recall if we opened for them there.

Lou has recalled that Black Sheep ultimately broke up following the crew truck hitting a patch of ice and much of your equipment being destroyed. What do you recall about that event and the ultimate demise of the band?
Yes, we were returning from the Boston show and that's exactly what happened. As much of the gear was damaged or destroyed, we were unable to continue with the other dates we had booked and the band never recovered from it.

Lou landed on his feet with Foreigner. Where did your career path take you?
I was offered a gig in LA with a metal band on United Artists. Although that never transpired, I started working in the LA scene, both with my own bands, as a songwriter and as a hired gun for Billy Thorpe, Nick Gilder and others. I joined Warrior, a metal band on Virgin, and eventually began work with Lou on his solo career, Shadow King and Foreigner as well as my own projects on Frontiers Records.

How did you ultimately end up writing "My Way" with Paul Stanley and Desmond Child?
Phil Ashley was playing keyboards on Lou's solo album, and was working with KISS as well, and he mentioned me to Paul. I was in NYC and Paul and I got together and worked for an afternoon on the music bed for what would eventually become "My Way."

Was it a situation where you actually sat with either, or bounced ideas off each other remotely?
Paul had a small demo studio and we worked together there.

How would you ultimately define your contribution to the song?
It was in its very formative stages at the beginning of my involvement. Paul had played some chorus keyboard chords and I embellished on that idea as well as a verse riff/groove and basic melody.

Paul has commented, "It really became more of a challenge to me to see how high I could sing. There's times where if I sang any higher dogs would run into the street." With 30 years hindsight, how do you rate the song?
I like it and that album certainly shows the range Paul was capable of. At a time when I was working heavily on Lou's albums, it was a departure for me musically and I enjoyed working with Paul on it.

Were there any other of your suggestions/contributions to the songs that didn't survive to the song's final studio form?
Not really. I would have liked to have spent more time exploring other musical ideas with Paul, but as I said, I was in NY to work with Lou and there really wasn't time.

Obviously, you've worked with numerous people during your career. In terms of your life experience, what is the

first thought that comes to mind when thinking of this song?
I've been fortunate to be involved with a lot of great players and projects and this is certainly one of them.

Ultimately, you recorded with Lou on his "Ready or Not" solo release, the criminally underrated "Shadow King" (one of my guilty pleasures), and with Foreigner for the "Mr. Moonlight" album. What are you up to these days?
I'm glad you enjoy the Shadow King album — there seems to be a real love/hate dynamic with that record and I appreciate when someone says they get it. Besides all the work with Lou on "Ready or Not", "Long Hard Look", "Shadow King" and with Foreigner, I've also done a solo album on Frontiers, "Outside Looking In" as well as "Places of Power". I currently own a recording studio in northern CA, and will likely do another solo album at some point as I continue write.

Tom Kelly

The sole credited additional background vocalist on "Crazy Nights" describes a #1 studded song-writing career and session work that included Mötley Crüe, Alice Cooper, and KISS

KissFAQ: Tom, as way of introduction, let's start with a bit of background since you started out on the performances side of the business before moving into session work and song writing. What was your entry point into performing?
Tom Kelly: I started out playing in bands, playing guitar actually. When I was 14 I was a singer in a band; and I didn't even play an instrument in that band. Then I eventually started playing guitar and as I moved up the ranks I ended up playing bass guitar for many years for a lot of groups.

You worked with several notable bands, including Dan Fogelberg, Fools Gold, and Toto before transitioning into writing and session work.
I worked with Dan Fogelberg when I moved to California in 1974–1975 and toured as his bass player and background singer for a couple of years. I was always writing songs and before the song writing became my paycheck I worked however I could. One thing I broke into was background singing so I sang vocals for many groups and artists and that kind of sustained me until I figured out how to write a hit song.

Let's touch on the band Fools Gold, which included you, Denny Henson (guitar/vocals), Doug Livingston (guitar/piano), Ron Grinel (drums) — essentially Fogelberg's backing band — you released a couple of albums with them?
I had a partner from the Midwest that I played in a group with and we were Fools Gold. I put together Dan Fogelberg's

back-up group which became Fools Gold eventually and with songs that I wrote. My partner, Denny Henson (who now lives in Nashville), we were the singer/songwriters in the group and we did a couple of tours. You know the record business had a lot of money back then. I mean unlike now, a record company would pay for all kinds of expenses, forward money, and then try to recoup it, but you'd be sent on the road. We had subsidies for tours. We opened for Loggins and Messina. We even opened for Fogelberg, and then later accompanied him [for his set]. But, as 1975, 1976, 1977 kind of were ticking by there were plenty of months of the year that I wasn't on the road. There was usually just a summer tour on and off for six weeks, so I think the first person that hired me as a background singer was John Boylan who was a well-known producer back then.

He produced a lot of hit songs and for Epic Records and it was just a word of mouth thing. Keith Olsen was very instrumental in giving me background work. He produced one of the Fools Gold albums and he knew I sang high. I sang high and I could hit at full voice and do that whole high tenor rock and roll thing so he started hiring me and he hooked me up with other sessions. Then he hired me and Bill Chaplain who was in the group Chicago for a long time. We were kind of a duo for a while. It was just word of mouth. You know, somebody would hear those vocals, and decide, "I want those guys." Over the years I did session work regularly with Bill Chaplin and Bobby Kimball from Toto. I ended up touring with Toto for their first tour for about a year, because they needed a high voice. Richard Paige from Mister Mister and his partner, there were a handful of us that just rotated and we worked a lot.

How did the transition from the performing side to focusing on song writing occur?
I worked, I would say 3 or 4 days a week and I was still writing songs and hoping to break through. I was realizing that I was

pushing 30 and making it as an artist was looking more and more difficult. I had two kids at home and a wife, so I kept singing the background vocals, because it paid very well. I kept writing songs and eventually the songs took over and I was too busy writing songs and working with artists to do background vocals. I was making money writing songs, so I kind of phased out of performing.

"Fire and Ice" was the lead single off Pat Benatar's third album, "Precious Time," in 1981, co-written with Pat and Scott Sheets (a member of the New York 70s punk band, the Brats). That was your first song to become a hit reaching #17. More importantly, Pat won the Best Female Rock Performance Grammy award in 1982 for it.
That's correct; it was my first hit record. I had written a song and then she got her hands on it and rewrote the bridge and some lyrics; so we ended up being co-writers on it.

You're particularly well known for your extensive songwriting partnership with Billy Steinberg. You met at Billy at a party hosted by Pat Benatar's producer Keith Olson, right?
Correct; yes. You've done your homework.

Billy has described you as a "far superior musician." Was there any underlying delineation of roles within the partnership?
Yes. Billy Steinberg is primarily the lyricist. He actually was an artist and had kind of come up through the punk ranks. He wasn't a trained musician or perhaps as sophisticated as I am, but when I met him and we worked together, I was just blown away with how cutting edge his lyrics were. So, we got together and it was pretty clear, off the bat, that he was going to write the lyrics and I was going to write the music, although we both dabbled in each. He likes to write a lyric first, almost like a poem, and then I would write the music to it. Not everybody does it that way. I think Elton John and

Bernie Taupin start with the lyric. It just really clicked, you know?

How did partnering with Billy change your writing?
It was just, all of a sudden writing a song was easy. I used to be able to write a melody and a chord progression really quickly and then it would take me ten times as long to try to write a lyric to it. And then my lyrics weren't that good! Mine is more musical than it is lyrical, so we were a good complement together. I sang the demos and did harmonies and produced the productions of demos when we wrote a song. I always had a recording studio at my house.

One of those songs was the original demo of "Like a Virgin," which became Madonna's first Billboard Hot 100 #1 — could you describe that song's creation and the transformation it underwent for her?
Good question. Billy wrote the lyric and we literally worked Monday through Friday and we'd get together. If we had phone calls in the morning we'd take care of that, but he'd usually drive to my house at noon and we worked until dinnertime and call it off. But he would come over —and this was before word processing and computers — and he would type out his lyrics on a typewriter. He was really structured about it. So, he'd come in and present me with his latest lyrics and "Like a Virgin" really stood out. I mean actually, you know the first, the opening lines of "Like a Virgin" say, " I made it through the wilderness / Somehow I made it through / Didn't know how lost I was until I found you." It was about kind of getting through a relationship and starting a new love and he was going through that. That's why he wrote it, and I had certainly related to it. I had just gone through a divorce when I met Billy and had met somebody new around that time. I was so moved by it that I tried writing a ballad to it and, you know, it just didn't work.

I just couldn't get it and then I tried writing something that was almost a ballad, like a medium tempo thing, but beautiful? Unlike other lyrics of his, which we usually wrote fairly quickly, we kept putting that one down and coming back to it and coming back to it. We knew that in 1983–1984, when that was written, the word "virgin" was like saying "fuck." It was really nasty and so we knew it was going to raise eyebrows. After trying to write it at least three times and then giving up [until] I was just clowning around out of frustration. I had just purchased a Jupiter 8 synthesizer and was getting into that world of synth. We'd always been pretty organic with guitars, acoustic guitars and acoustic piano, but there was a patch on the Jupiter 8 where the left hand was a bass and the right was kind of an orchestra. It's the same sound that's on Madonna's record, and if you heard my demo, I just started playing in all the Motown R&B bass line and just started singing it in falsetto and just being really playful with it. I probably sang the first three or four lines, and we looked at each other and started laughing and just said, "This is it!" It was fun and playful and sexy. Billy immediately altered some lyrics to make it more playful and finished it that same day and started demoing it the next. I'm sure I did the demo in one afternoon. It was on a 4-track tape recorder.

You and Billy were working on the "i-Ten" album at the same time, right?
There was a gentleman in A&R at Warner Bros. Records, Michael Ostin the son of Mo Ostin, who was the President of Warner Bros. Michael was a young guy looking for new songs and artists. Up to that point, Billy and I had not written a big hit. Sure, I had written "Fire and Ice" and he wrote a song for Linda Ronstadt called "How Do I Make You" [Ed. #10, Billboard Hot 100, 1980] and they were hits. But they weren't Top 5 hits or No. 1's, so we'd been working together for maybe a good 2 years or so, and started getting the idea of making a record. I mean I was the primary singer and

musician again, but just as a team and as songwriters, we thought, "You know, why not make a record?" Everybody else was making records. So, we had a meeting with Michael Ostin. In fact, he came to my home studio, which at that time I believe was in North Hollywood, and we actually played them a bunch of songs that were of the style, kind of like Foreigner and Journey — you know, kind of high singer rock and roll, which I could sing. We even debated whether to play him "Like a Virgin," because we knew if we made a record of our songs as artists that "Like a Virgin" wasn't going to fit in there. Nothing else was in falsetto, nothing else was R&B, so we were looking to get a record deal with Warner Bros. through Michael, and we didn't want to confuse him by throwing this other thing in. We played him all of our songs and he was impressed and he started talking about Madonna. I hadn't even heard of her.

So out of shopping for your own deal Madonna unexpectedly ended up with one of your songs?
Her first album had just come out and had her first hits was. Billy knew who she was. He pays attention to that stuff more than I do and we just kind of looked at each other and said, "Oh, let's play him 'Like a Virgin.' Maybe it would be good for Madonna." So, we played him the demo and he just flipped. He said, "This is perfect for her. You know, she's got this, she wants to do this sexy image." So he took it and within days we heard that she'd loved it and was recording it. And a little time went by and the MTV Video Music Awards had just been on for a few years back then, and I remember coming home from dinner and I'd recorded it on the VCR because I knew Madonna was going to be on the show. Nobody goes on those shows and sings a song no one's heard before. They all go on and they sing their hit song, right? So, everyone knows it and loves it...

The funny thing is, while we were with Michael Ostin and he heard the song over at my house, Billy had this image that he

said, you know, "I could see Madonna on top of a wedding cake," he said, "coming down singing this song." That was Billy's image of this song for her, and obviously Michael mentioned that to her because, now here I am waiting for Madonna to come on and I assume she's going to sing "Lucky Star" or whatever her first or second hit records were, and then they introduced Madonna and there's this fricking wedding cake that she's standing on top of in a wedding dress with all this cleavage and she starts coming down the steps singing. It was awful. I mean you've probably heard this story, but she comes down and when she gets halfway through the song she drops to her knees and starts rolling around on the floor. The microphone is slamming into the stage floor making all this noise, and she's not singing in the microphone. When she is, she's singing out of tune and her voice is trembling. She's rolling around on the stage and the camera angles are terrible because they didn't know she was going to do this. When it ended, it was kind of like about four people clapped and it was just like, "What happened there?" My first reaction was, "Oh my, God, I'll never work in this town again." I'm humiliated, you know? But, of course, you know, as she went on to discover any publicity is good publicity for her, and it turned into a story. When they released the song, it jumped to No. 1. I think it was there for 7 weeks so it was like a dream come true for us.

So, you released the "i-Ten" album, which included your original version of "Alone," later covered by Heart.
That was the album we were trying to do with Warner Bros. with Michael Ostin. Billy and I were trying to do was take a bunch of the songs that we recorded and make an album out of it, and that ultimately became I-Ten and Epic Records signed us.

You've worked with seemingly everyone, from Dionne Warwick to Streisand, to Arlo Guthrie. By 1986, you're doing work with Alice Cooper co-writing "He's Back (The Man

Behind the Mask)" for the "Constrictor" album and singing backing vocals on the song. How did that collaboration come about?
I worked with Arlo Guthrie? I did so many sessions over the course of several years; I don't even remember them all! That's funny! I can't remember how I met Alice. It might have been on the golf course because we're both avid golfers. At that stage I'd written a bunch of hit songs. What year was that?

It was on his "Constrictor" album released in October 1986.
Yeah, 1986. We had probably written three No. 1 songs by that time, and when you've done that people come to you and people start noticing who's writing the hit songs. I don't know if that's why Alice's people maybe said, "Why don't you write with Tom Kelly?" Maybe he was comfortable with me, because we'd played golf before at Calabasas. Anyway, we spent several days wood-shedding at my house. I think we probably played golf too. We'd play golf and then go back into the house and work on the song with his guitar player, Kane Roberts. He was a big, strong, muscular guy and that's how it comes about. Once you've written a few hit songs, you know, people will come to you. There was a time when we couldn't get anybody to listen to our demos, but eventually it comes around the other way if you've been successful.

In 1987 you have two songs, the #1 hit "Alone" and "I Want You So Bad" on the Heart album "Bad Animals" produced by Ron Nevison. "Alone" had originally dated from the i-Ten project. How did those songs placement come around?
I did know Ron. Did he work with Survivor?

Yes, he produced their debut album released in 1979, "Vital Signs" and "When Seconds Count" in 1986 on which you contributed vocals.
Okay, so I met Ron as a session singer. One of the great blessings I had, and advantages I have as a songwriter, I'd

been doing session work for so long that I knew everybody. I mean, it's a very intimate process, the creative process and performing in the studio with the producer and the artist. Everybody gets really close, because you're essentially making a baby together. You're making and creating a song and arranging it, so I was pretty close with an enormous amount of successful record producers and artists. Even by the time I started seriously writing songs with Steinberg, I'd been doing session work for 4 or 5 years. If I wrote a song, and I thought I want to get this to Tina Turner, I could go to the producer and call him on the phone. In the case of Ron Nevison, I was working on a project with him — I can't exactly remember who it was, Patty Smyth or Survivor, but I'm not sure — but Ron mentioned to me that he was looking for a song for Heart.

The original version of "Alone" provides a striking contrast to the power-pop of Heart's version. How do you feel when a song of yours is transformed away from your original vision? Is there an emotional detachment?
I said that I think "Alone" is perfect for Heart, but i-Ten version is different. The opening line and the chorus have different phrasing and different lyrics. I knew it wasn't right, that it didn't kick in properly for a hit chorus. I mean I always loved the verse in "Alone," and I thought it was perfect for Ann Wilson. It's a very rangy song, which is exactly what she kicks ass on, so the bottom line is Steinberg didn't think it was a hit song. He didn't think it was good for Heart, but I insisted on it and got him to write a new lyric for the first line of the chorus and I rewrote the melody of the first line of the chorus so that it just came in a little bit more in your face. We demoed it, I think even without guitars. It was just orchestral; there was acoustic piano in it and a synthesizer. It was a very simple demo, just a handful of tracks and I sang the vocal and did the high harmony and we threw that together in several days and with the new opening line for the chorus. I took it in to Ron and he and Heart loved it and they recorded. It was

the first single from their "Bad Animals" album, and just boom, went to No. 1. So, we were just on a roll.

Nancy has commented that Heart loved performing "Alone," but without what she called "wedding cake" production that she felt in hindsight represented the album version. What do you make of that in relation to the production Ron Nevison did on the album?
He pretty much took the same structure that our demo had and did the same dropouts. The verses were very tender and sparse. He improved some of the sounds with keyboards — maybe made it a bit little more sparkly — and maybe that's what Nancy's talking about. But it was also still bombastic, had the big power chords and the thrashing drums so it was timely. It seemed to be the right sound for the right time, and it was a very melodic and an acrobatic vocal for Ann. You know, she copied almost everything I did on the demo, even adlibbed some stuff, so that's always flattering.

You also sang backing vocals on the album? Is it this connection with Ron that leads to you working with KISS on the "Crazy Nights" album?
I did backgrounds without vocals on "Alone" and on a number of songs on "Bad Animals" with Ron and Ann and Nancy. I was on mic with both those girls. They liked the way my voice blended in with theirs, to make sure it just didn't sound like all girls. So I did a bunch of strong background vocals for that album. Nevison had hired me before that, so he brought me into the Heart thing because he was happy with what I had done with him before. They were singing my songs, so I was just pretty cozy with everybody. My guess is, my ticket to KISS was probably Ron. He was their producer too.

Particularly with Heart, what was Ron's guidance for backing vocals, or as the song-writer were you pretty much given free rein?

I was hired by so many people to do the same thing, to hit the high notes and hit them full voice and kind of kick ass. It was just kind of a razor blade kind of a voice that just cut through. It really cut through. I sang the high part on "Jessie's Girl" for Rick Springfield. When I first started with Keith Olsen he never stopped hiring me because apparently my voice could blend with just about anybody. It just has a texture to it that kind of cuts through. It doesn't sound weak up there. It sounds really pushed and intense. So, I pretty much knew what my job was going in there. It was to sing the high harmonies and to kick them hard and make them really cut through with energy and intensity. That was my job. I did many sessions where I sang soft falsetto things and even lower parts, but if I was hired by a rock and roll band, that's what they wanted.

In general, how would you prepare for a session? Would you listen to the band's material or their demos, or go in with a clean palette?

Just go in. It's better that way. It's fresh. Everybody woodsheds around the console and listens by the speakers and tries parts and suggests things. It's just the creative process in the studio. You just go through it, and a lot of times it was obvious what needed to be done. If it was, for example, on "Jessie's Girl," Rick had already sung a melody and put a harmony on it, so I just put all the high parts on top of that. They wanted to just stack it up, because he couldn't quite hit the really high notes. Maybe a few times somebody sent me some material ahead of time and said, "Here, listen to this and come up with something," but that was very rare. You usually just walk in cold, you know? Show up at 1:00 at Cherokee Studios and shake hands and start listening to the song and start arranging something and putting it together.

After Heart's "Bad Animals," Ron works with KISS on their "Crazy Nights" album. You're the sole non-band member backing vocalist credited on the album. Why?

I had already written three No. 1 songs by then, so I wasn't doing that many background sessions, but you know if KISS asks you to do something you do it.

(Laughs). What about the members of KISS? Had you known any prior, and how was the experience working with that band compared with say Alice, Heart, or REO Speedwagon?
That was the first time I'd met them, I'm pretty sure. It's possible I had done something before for them. You know, a lot of the power glam bands, like Mötley Crüe and Poison, were produced by a friend of mine, Tom Werman. Tom often hired me to come in and belt out the high parts for those records. KISS was more unique, but still working in a similar genre, so it's logical that I sang with them. I'm pretty sure I just met them [for the first time] when I came in to sing with them.

Going into the studio, how did you find the KISS band members on a personal level? What direction were you given?
I was impressed that they were really warm guys. You know, Gene does his shtick about making money. He was always joking about making money. Paul was very warm and they were just regular guys. I was impressed that they were relaxed. I guess they knew who I was; that I was a songwriter and had had some success. There was mutual respect and it was just guys making music and having fun. It was a lot of laughs. I remember being on mic with Paul. His lead vocal would be down, and then he and I would harmonize together on some of the songs. I couldn't sit here and rattle off all the song titles for you, but I just remember having a good time. You know, we were young and in a creative part of our lives. There was a lot of energy. They were hard workers. It wasn't like working with Mötley Crüe, the KISS guys knew what they wanted. They had the image that they created and they seemed to really have their vision and be really disciplined about how to do it. It was a genius to hide yourself behind a

mask that's allowed them to continue working well into their senior years! It was enjoyable, and I just thought they were great guys.

"Crazy Nights" was very much Paul's baby, and he was driving the artistic direction of the band. When listening back during a woodshedding session, did you mind the sort of feedback that might require take after take after take, to reach the point where the artist's vision was realized?
No. If it was my own song, like singing with the Wilson Sisters on "Alone" or "I Want You So Bad," then of course, that's more my baby. But, otherwise, I'm just going in there to make them happy and do a job. Like you said, it was Paul's baby. Ron Nevison is a perfectionist, and if it took five or six times to get it in tune — or to get the right timber in my voice or something else — it was going to be done until it was right. So, I wouldn't listen to a KISS or any album and say, "Oh, I wish I had done this," or "I wish I had done that." It was simple, I was there to do my job, and I feel confident that I did it well. They wouldn't have let me leave if it wasn't right and everybody was happy!

With working with so many different artists across several genres, were there ever any acts that you simply didn't want to work with — and I'm not looking for names, just whether the situation ever arose for you professionally?
Yeah, there were artists that that I declined, I just said, "No thanks" to and some that I worked with that I regretted working with. It's part of the creative process. You've just got to wade through that stuff sometimes and keep going.

You bowed out of active work in the 1990s. What led to that?
I've had three families with three different wives. I've still got kids, 12 and 9-year-old boys I spend a lot of time with. I play a lot of golf. You know, maybe I'm a burnout. I worked so many years doing this, and truthfully it's hard work and it takes a

lot of energy. As the 1990s went forward, I was still working with Billy Steinberg, but you could just feel that things were changing. Where we came from and what inspired us — I think was probably 1960s music from the Beatles to Motown, the British invasion, a lot of Roy Orbison — were our big influences and I can hear it in the songs we wrote. "Like a Virgin" was my Smoky Robinson song. It was like a Motown Smoky Robinson song to me, I sang it in falsetto. I could feel things were changing and rap music was really becoming popular. The best of it, I like, but I don't like terribly dark, ugly, violent, negative, angry lyrics.

It was becoming harder for us to write a hit song, so I just slowly started phasing out of it because it just didn't feel comfortable and I was tired of it. When you do something for a long time you sometimes just get tired of doing it. I had proven to myself. I was a No. 1 songwriter, had five No. 1 hit songs, and I had really achieved all my goals. I was getting older and so I started picking and choosing more what I wanted to do, unlike Steinberg. He was really a workaholic and I say that with admiration, because a lot of his drive pushed me to go for more and more. It was good for me, being kind of laid back and not particularly ambitious. So we balanced each other out really well and it was a good chemistry. I'm not saying I couldn't write a song right now if somebody had a gun to my head. I think will write songs again at some point in my life, probably not a lot but I've just been on a long break enjoying life, enjoying the outdoors, and enjoying my family.

When you look back at your career and accomplishments, where does the KISS work figure in?
It's right up there with my achievements as a singer. They're legendary and it was fun knowing them and seeing that they're really just nice guys doing their job too and following their dreams. Singing with KISS is something I'll never forget and it's up there with some of my greatest accomplishments.

I admire those guys. I knew their manager, Doc McGhee, really well and played a lot of golf with him. Doc had his 50th birthday party at Pebble Beach, and Gene and Paul came to that, and as soon as they saw me we all reconnected and reminisced. People reach "legendary" status, but when you get down to it we're just people and had mutual respect for each other. It's a good bond and something I won't forget.

Gary Corbett

KissFAQ: Gary, before we get into talking about you working with KISS during the "Crazy Nights" tour, let's set the stage with where your career was "at" in 1987. First, why the keyboards as your instrument?
Gary Corbett: It's something that happened at a really early age. I think it primarily happened because my aunt had a piano in her house and before I was of age to go to school my mom was spending a lot of afternoons with her and I would have to keep occupied. So I used to sit at the piano and just play. I was a 3 or 4-year-old kid so I wasn't really *playing the piano*; I was probably more banging on the piano. But I was picking out melodies or doing things enough that my parents said, "Let's get him some lessons and see where it goes." So it started there and I started taking lessons when I was 4. I basically I learned how to read music before I learned how to read English. So, it's been my whole life and I don't remember a time when I didn't play.

Was there anything in your upbringing that made music inevitable?
Nothing in particular, but, there was never a doubt about it. From the time that the Beatles came out, the Rolling Stones and then, ultimately the Dave Clark Five — because they were the first ones of the British Invasion that had a keyboard player — once those guys came on Ed Sullivan, I was hooked and I knew that that was what I was going to be. I used to wear Beatle boots with my Cub Scout uniform! I was always into it as a little kid and there didn't really seem to ever be a doubt in the house that that's what I was gonna do, because it's what I said I wanted to do. I started earning money at it at 10 years old. One thing my dad always instilled was if you want to be a musician, you can't just be a *rock* musician. You have to be able to earn a living as a musician, and that

involved learning more than just [the style of music that] I wanted to play. So, I always had that approach and learned all styles of music. I learned pop music, but I also learned older big band music and played with older musicians — I was always the youngest person in the bands I played in. I never had another job my entire life.

That's a fantastic story to have. That you've had a passion for music since age 3 or 4 and made it your life. What was your path into professional music? You said that you're always the youngest member of the bands that you were in. When did you start playing in bands and when did they get serious enough to really start saying that you're going to make a living doing it?
My first band was at 7. We were called the Mosquito's. I started working and getting paid doing gigs at age 10. At that point I wasn't old enough to get myself to gigs, so my dad was my chauffer, roadie, equipment carrier and setter-upper. I took piano lessons at a place that taught all instruments and they also had these classes that they called the "combo" classes where they would invite the more promising students for each of the instruments, and on Saturday afternoons one of the teachers would actually put together bands and basically teach you how to play with a band. Playing with a band is a little different than sitting and playing the piano by yourself, so you have to learn to play differently to accommodate the fact that there's also other people playing. It was just another afternoon activity I guess to keep me off the street, but we used to do these things every Saturday. The woman who owned the school was enterprising enough to capitalize on it and hire us out for sweet 16s, bat mitzvahs, bar mitzvahs, and younger kids' parties. Nonetheless, we would be working on Saturday nights and we'd play for a couple hours at a party and I'd get paid 10 or $15.

I started doing that at about 10 and then I started working with the kind of bands that played at weddings and bar

mitzvahs and all that stuff where I had to put on a black suit and go play with a sax player! At that point it was always older guys. I also used to spend my summers in the Catskill Mountains at a bungalow colony — which was popular back in the 50s and 60s — and people would rent these cottages basically for the summer. They would have a recreation hall, and every Saturday night there would be entertainment. So they'd have a trio: a drummer, keyboard player and a sax player. They played dance music for a few hours and then around 11 or 12 at night they'd have a singer or a comedian come in and do a sit-down show, and then they'd have dance music again afterwards. So, being up in the country for the summer, at around age 13 or 14, I started doing that where I had a set gig at the same place every Saturday night. I did that for three or four summers and then once I got my driver's license I was able to do a lot more.

So where were you growing up? When you say the Catskills, it screams upstate New York to me.
Yes, I was born and raised in Brooklyn and lived there my entire life until 1997. It was a regular thing for people from the city. My parents always wanted to get us out of the city for the summers because that was when all my friends would get in trouble. You know, too much free time on the streets in Brooklyn... Plus the summers in New York City were so much hotter and more humid than upstate, so it was a nice way to have a vacation for the summer. My mom would be up there with us for the whole summer. My dad would commute back and forth. He would come up to the country on Friday afternoons and he would leave Tuesday morning, drive straight into work. His job allowed him to take Fridays and Mondays off during the summer so that he could be up there with us, so that was the way I grew up. Until I was 17-years-old and got my driver's license, every summer was up at the bungalow. Of course, as a kid you can't wait until you could stay home with your friends, but my parents would never allow it! Once I graduated high school that's when I

really started trying to get into a touring band and into the real music business.

So what is your entry point into what we might call the real music business?
I graduated high school June of '76 and that summer started with me having a gig up in the Catskills. I guess very much like the resort in *Dirty Dancing*. It was kind of schlocky and it wasn't a really good gig; it was a trio with me, a drummer and, believe it or not, the instrument that played the melody was a trombonist. Two weeks into the summer I had had enough and quit. Then I got a call, to come back to the city. There was an act, a woman named Cherry Vanilla, who started out as a public relations person for David Bowie's company, MainMan, Ltd., as punk rock was starting, she decided she wanted to be a singer and I got a call to be in her band.

Max's Kansas City was a happening club, and she was a regular, and we would travel on up to Boston and played the Rathskeller Club. Max's Kansas City did a record of all the top acts that played there, and on Max's '76 album we did a track [Ed. "Shake Your Ashes"]. We'd been up to a studio in Massachusetts to record it so I guess you could say that was the first chance to actually "make it."

So, once you've got your first break, you've got your foot in the door, so to speak. How do you start moving up the musical food chain?
In 1977, I got a call to play with Ian Hunter. He had just released the album "You're Never Alone with a Schizophrenic," and a buddy of mine, Tommy Mandel, was actually the keyboard player, but his father had passed away the night before they were leaving for the tour, so I got that last minute call asking, "can you be on a plane tomorrow and fill in for him for a couple of weeks?" I did, so I guess that's really where it all kind of got started. I started meeting

people... As a matter of fact, a lot of the band on that gig had just finished the first Meat Loaf tour which included the Kulick Brothers. Ellen Foley was the opening act for Ian on the shows that we did, and they kind of shared the band. It was a really kind of cool band. The drummer was a guy named Hilly Michaels, who was in Sparks. The bass player was Martin Briley who had a song, "You Ain't Worth the Salt in My Tears," which was a big hit back in the '80s. The guitar player was a guy named Billy Cross who played with Bob Dylan at the time. And Ellen was singing backgrounds for Ian. The band just backed up both acts, so it was a really fun musical thing. David Johansen was also there. Cleveland International was the company that was managing all these artists so it was kind of their "A list" guys backing everybody up. So, I had the pleasure of being able to be a part of that for a couple weeks. It was a lot of fun, but that's where I started meeting people and going into the city more and trying to find the next gig.

That sounds like a lot of fun, what about trying to find a regular band to be a part of?
At that point I had auditioned for lots of bands, including one with Michael Bolton, called Blackjack. As a matter of fact when I first started working with KISS, Bruce Kulick said, "I know you from somewhere!" We started talking about it and figured out that he remembered me from the Blackjack auditions. He said, "That's right, you were that really young kid who had come in." I think it was down to me and the guy who actually got the gig, Alan St. Jon that went on to play with Billy Squier. I was banging around a bunch of studios, and started to play around New York City a lot more. I found a band through the Village Voice that played at a club called Great Gildersleeves in Manhattan [Ed. 331 Bowery between 2nd and 3rd Streets] that was a really cool live music club. The band was called Falcon Eddy, and they were really hot at that club. We'd play every weekend at either Great Gildersleeves or Tracks, Privates, and Hurrah's. There were so

many clubs that had live music that we worked two shows a weekend, every weekend just about. We opened for the Kinks and lots of different people. We opened for the Scorpions — I think it was probably their first tour in the states. So I played with those guys for a couple years and, you know, one thing leads to another...

The importance of networking old school, face to face, and getting your name around and then you get a phone call. Let's jump forward to 1984 and talk about "She Bop". Cyndi Lauper shares a history with KISS for also playing at NYC clubs such as the Coventry and opening for the all-female band ISIS. How did that collaboration come about?
We're back at the Great Gildersleeves playing with Falcon Eddy. We were supposed to get signed to Tommy Mottola's company, but it never happened, so I left the band and joined Tom Dickie and the Desires who were managed by Tommy. Tom Dickie came from a "Gildersleeves" band called "Susan" and when he left that band, he formed Tom Dickie and the Desires. We did two albums on Mercury Records. During the preproduction for the second record one of the guys they were looking at to produce was Steve Lunt. He'd been in a band called City Boy. Steve and I, even though he didn't end up producing the record, ended up hitting it off and decided we were going to do some writing together. He was managed by Dave Wolf, who ended up being Cyndi's manager. Blue Angel had just lost their deal on Polygram, but being on the New York club scene I was already a huge fan of Cyndi and her band. She was so awesome live with that band! So what happened was, Steve told me that Cyndi was willing to sing the demos for us when we finish writing the songs. We were recording simple four-track demos and had already written the music for "She Bop." The track was complete — including the whistle solo in the middle. Everything was done. We had the song titled. Steve had a notebook full of titles that we would go through and we would look at them and just pick an appropriate title for whatever we thought the music sounded

like, just so it would be easier to remember and reference in the future. Instead of saying, "You remember that idea that sounded like ..." He's British, and explained to me that "Bop" was a slang term for masturbation, so we just laughed about it, and I said, "Yeah, okay, that's a good title for the music."

When Cyndi came over to sing one or two of the other songs that we actually had finished, she accidentally heard the music to "She Bop" and said, "Wow! I really like that. Can I write the lyrics with you and I'll do it on my record?" She had just gotten her solo deal. Blue Angel had sold something like 20,000 records, so in my mind I thought it'd be great if she sold the same number for her solo record; and to have a song on it! So, we just said, "Yeah, take it." We never expected what happened to happen. There was just that social type of thing, the networking, and the social aspect that used to be such an amazing part of the business back then, which no longer exists. That was how everything got done back then before the internet and social media. There really was no other way.

What a great part of your career, to be part of something so special — which that album is regardless of anyone's preference for a particular style of music. It was impossible as a teenager in the early 1980s to not be aware of Cyndi's explosion on the popular scene with that album and her quirky style.
Yeah, and I still get checks a couple times a year. It's unbelievable what it turned into...

Getting paid for your art, that's an important part of it!
Yes, absolutely! It's funny because at the time, while I was trying to peruse the dream of being in a band and getting signed to a record deal, I always did the wedding band stuff on weekends because, like I said, my dad instilled that in me that you can't call yourself a professional musician if you can't earn a living being a musician. You're not going to just sit

around all week and wait for your "rock" band to do something. You're going to work. If you're going to be a musician and you're not going to go to school for something else, this is how you're going to do it. So, that was just part of what I did. There was a gap between the time the album for Cyndi was finished, and became a hit, so I was still going out and doing these gigs on weekends and putting on my tuxedo and going and playing cover stuff and Top-40 stuff.

When the album came out and the song took off, I was still playing in the wedding band because the money hadn't started coming in yet. It takes 9 months to a year before you start seeing royalties after a song becomes a hit. So, during that time period I still had to put on my tuxedo and go play weddings. People would come up to the bandstand and say, "do you guys know "She Bop?" And the singer would say, "Yeah, that guy over there wrote *it*. And they'd say, "Yeah, sure. If he wrote it, what the hell's he doing here!" That used to kill me, absolutely kill me, but eventually the checks started to come in, and I was able to burn my tuxedo and stop doing the wedding gigs.

I think Gene Simmons would approve of your work ethic! So let's get into 1987 and KISS's "Crazy Nights." Phil Ashley, of course, recorded the keyboard parts in the studio and had worked with Paul Stanley during the writing sessions. So, how did Gary Corbett enter KISS's radar range? How were you approached to tour with the band?
After I started getting my royalties, I went out and bought a bunch of gear. I bought my first computer which was an Apple IIe computer — because computers were just starting to be used to make music. Since "She Bop" had been a result of us experimenting with drum machines and synthesizers, I also bought my own four-track, drum machine and DX7 synth. I started doing a lot of work in studios around Manhattan as a programmer for people, because at that point it was a new thing, and when something like that is new

everybody wants to use it. It became the way in the 80s that many records were done. It seemed there were no more drummers playing on pop records at the time, as it was all drum machines! It took a while before there were a lot of people who could actually do it themselves, so I worked a lot, as a result. I used to work at Electric Lady Studios all the time.

One time I happened to walk out to the coffee machine, and there's a guy standing there, so we started talking. That guy was Phil Ashley. I told him how I was getting a little tired of the programming thing, because when you're programming you're not playing with a band and you're not bouncing ideas off of other musicians you're being creative in a different way. It's fun, and it's great to be the source of all the parts, until you have a creative block; and then there's nobody else to pick up the slack. So, it was getting a little bit old to me to not have a band to play with. That's really what I loved doing, so I told him that I was at a point where I was ready to hit the road and take a break from the studio.

That's been something I've always had to do. If you look at the names on my resume, even style-wise it, it goes from one style to another because I'm always needing change like that. We exchanged numbers and went back into the studios that we were working in. About a week later, he called me up and said, "Listen, I got myself in a bit of a jam and I could use your help, if you're still interested in going on the road." I said, "Sure!" He said, "I got myself kind of double booked on two different tours, and I would love for you to cover one of them for me." I said, "Sure, who are you playing with?" And he said, "Lou Gramm from Foreigner." And I went, "Oh, that's great, man! Who I am gonna play with?" He says, "No, you're playing with Lou Gramm, and I'm going out on the road with Mick Jagger." Mick had just done his solo album [Ed. "Primitive Cool"]. So, I ended up getting the gig with Lou. About a week later he called me up again, and he told me he had just done the record with KISS, and that they had thought

about actually wanting to take a keyboard player out live. Because of his relationship with Paul they weren't really going to be doing cattle call auditions. They were basically trusting Phil's recommendation and all I basically had to do was go to a meeting at the office with Paul Stanley and Chris Lendt. We sat and talked for a few minutes, and they pretty much said, "Okay, you're hired!" That was it, but it was Phil Ashley who recommended me.

What did the interview entail? The sort of, "Do you have a passport? Are you ready to go?" vanilla questions, or was there anything technical or anything else asked to judge you personality-wise for what they wanted?
It was more personality-wise, because from a musical standpoint, Paul trusted Phil. Phil was really involved in the demoing process of many of Paul's songs for the album. At that point everybody else in the band had moved out to Los Angeles, so for Paul, when it was time to write songs for the next KISS record, he didn't have the guys from the band to lean on. He had his friends in New York and he ended up doing a lot of it with Phil. Phil had a room that he kept at Electric Lady Studios where he had his own personal little 12-track setup and his computer, and all that stuff. So, they ended up demoing all the songs there and when it came time for the record, they recorded it with Ron Nevison and Phil played keyboards. It was just that he was very connected to it and Paul trusted his musical judgment — especially, I guess, when it came to keyboard players! Paul really didn't know much about that end of it, and Phil did, so from the musical point they really trusted his judgment. It was more about the personality and just to see that I wasn't some nut job. That I fit in too or I could possibly be a good hang or whatever. It was more about that than anything else.

What was your initial impression of Paul from that first meeting?

It was a little overwhelming walking into that office, you know. Of course, I had been aware of them for a few years, and they were huge. I wasn't really a die-hard KISS fan, but when you meet somebody of that magnitude it's intimidating. I guess it made it easier because it was just him and wasn't the whole band. It would've been a lot harder if I walked into the room and it was all four of them and management and everybody else there. It probably would've been a lot more uncomfortable. Paul can be a very charming personable person, so it wasn't an uncomfortable situation at all. Chris Lendt was there and he was very nice. The only uncomfortable moment was when they finally said, "Okay, you're hired." We started talking about the set list. They said that they weren't sure what the set list was going to be, so they would really like me to be familiar with everything, which was like, 20 albums. I guess that was more of a test than anything else, so when they asked me what albums I needed — because at that point it was still vinyl — I said, "All of them!" They kind of looked at me funny, but they handed me a few envelopes stuffed with albums.

I was actually leaving for a tour with Lou. We were going on tour in Europe, so I wasn't even going to be back in the country until the second week of KISS's rehearsals. They were actually going to start the rehearsals without me so I flew from the last gig with Lou in Munich straight out to LA and then started with them. I never even went home between tours! My entire time on tour with Lou in Germany I was listening to KISS albums. I transferred all the albums they gave me to cassettes and I had my auto reverse Walkman with my headphones and speakers that I traveled with. I slept with it on continuous loop so that I could subliminally absorb it! I listened to it with headphones as we traveled from one city to the next. It was basically my background music for the entire European trip, but that's what I needed to do to really learn it all properly.

So had you done the tour's musical rehearsals with Lou before the meeting with KISS?
Oh yeah. We had already done some shows with Lou in the states although that tour didn't make it all the way through in the states. What happened was Lou's tour had started and Phil was going to do the first 2 weeks and then I was going to step in. During the first 2 weeks of the tour, there was some stuff going on at the record company and they said they're going to postpone the tour. So, I never got to go out and do any of the shows in the States, but I did all the rehearsals and everything as an understudy with Phil. I'd go to rehearsal every day and just watch, but I also had a recording of the band running through the set — minus the keyboards — and once the band left at the end of the day, I would stay behind and crank it through the PA system and run through the show.

So, I was already up to speed with Lou, and then they added this European tour. I was finally going to get to do some shows, so I was really excited about it because he was always somebody I had idolized. That part of it was a thrill. I was a huge Foreigner fan at that point. When I was still doing the work up in the Catskills in the 80s when I was engaged to my wife, we had a conversation, while driving up for the summer, and she asked "If you could play with anybody in the world that you want, who would it be?" I pointed to the cassette deck, with "Foreigner 4" playing, and said, "It would be that guy!" At the time, the Lou gig was actually the gig of a lifetime and I was really thrilled to have it. I really loved playing with him and it was a great band. He was still in great physical shape and his voice was still amazing. I used to get goose-bumps every night with him.

He played a really good set for that tour, didn't he? He's got some Buddy Holly, the Beatles, Humble Pie, the Small Faces, and all the stuff from the "Ready or Not" album. It, it looks like a really fun tour to have been a part of.

Like I said, it was a great band. Bruce Turgon, who was his right-hand guy in that situation, had co-written all the stuff for the "Ready or Not" album with Lou. Lou's brother, Ben, was playing drums. He is a great drummer. It was an awesome gig to have. It was just sad that there wasn't more of it! I did get to play with him again in 2003, but he had already gone through his health issues and it was hard for me to actually go and do it because it really hurt me to see him in that condition. I actually ended up doing the second solo record, called "Long Hard Look" [Ed. Released in 1989]. We even did the one of the Small Faces songs that we did in the 1987 show on the second record and I played on that.

That was "Tin Soldier," right?
Yep, that's the one. Yeah, I'm on that. Was it Eric Thorngren that produced that record?

Yes, Peter Wolf and Eric Thorngren.
We recorded at Lou's house up in Katonah, New York. He had a studio above his "garage." It wasn't your typical garage, it was a 10-car garage! He was a muscle car collector so it was this huge square building on the property of his really nice estate. He had a whole studio upstairs with a Neve console and a 2-inch 24-track machine. So I would drive up there and we would go play racquetball and then work on the record and have dinner with the family. And that was how that the second record was done. It was great to work with him. You know, it's nice to get to work with someone you idolized like that.

That's a great story! So, you were spending your tour of Germany doing your prep work for the next tour; listening to the KISS tapes. Were you in touch with them, while you were on tour with Lou? From their perspective, wouldn't it have been difficult for them to be waiting for you while they're starting to get things going and did they ever

consider just going with someone else because of your availability?
What they had told me was that it usually takes them a week or so to knock the rust off — because of not playing together since the last tour [Ed. Which had ended in April 1986] — or the recording of the record. There was so much other stuff that needed to be addressed for the tour during the first week. It's kind of a matter of get up and get everything running properly anyway. So, they really wouldn't really have missed me much; and as long as I came in prepared I could get up to speed pretty quick. They were confident that I would actually do my homework and be ready to go so they didn't really worry about it. I think they actually welcomed the fact that they got to get into their routine before I was there.

So, you flew directly from Germany to Los Angeles and you're rehearsing with KISS. Were these the musical rehearsals or are they the full stage production rehearsals by that point?
It was a little bit of both. We were rehearsing in a rehearsal studio. Do you remember the set for the "Crazy Nights" tour? It had that kind of semi-circular ramp that went around the drums toward the back of the stage. They had that part of the stage in the rehearsal room that we were in, so that they could get used to being on it and running around and doing their thing. That really was the most impressive thing to me at the first day of rehearsal. I get off the plane after flying from Germany, and before I even go to check into a hotel they took me straight to a TV studio where the band was taping a an episode of "Top of the Pops," which was that British TV show. They tried to do an American version of the show, but that didn't last long. But, in the '80s, when MTV was so successful, every network tried to do their own video show. And that's when I first met Gene, Eric, and Bruce. I walked in the dressing room as they were getting ready to go on. That was a fun night, and the first rehearsal was the next

day. I got to the rehearsal room and everybody was off in their own little corners.

Eric was over in one end doing drum stuff with his drum tech, Paul was dealing with his stuff, and Gene was off on the phone doing his business stuff and everything. It was very quiet, a very business-like environment. But when they said, "Okay, you guys ready to play?" everybody just walks up to the stage, puts on their instruments and from the downbeat of the first song; it's a full-on KISS show! They were running and jumping and it really floored me that they could just flip a switch like that and all of a sudden there's a full-on KISS show going on in the room right in front of me. It was very impressive and that really showed me something about their talent for putting on a show. They might not have been the best musicians in the world, but as performers and entertainers they had a keen sense about that, that I've never seen anywhere else. Obviously they managed to sustain themselves as one of the top rock shows of all time, so it wasn't by accident and they worked real hard at it. It really gave me a new respect for what they did.

So when you properly meet them for the first time — I don't think we can call the "Top of the Pops" introduction a proper meeting of them since they were about to go into basically work — what are your initial impression of the band members? We've already talked a little about Paul, so let's start with Gene.
Gene can be a little intimidating. The first thing he said, as I walked into the dressing room at "Top of the Pops," was, "I want your jacket!" I had bought this leather jacket while I was in Germany, and it was really cool — it had buckles and all this stuff on it — so that was the icebreaker. It made me relax a little bit because he gave me a compliment. I don't remember talking much to him at that point. But Bruce, that's when he and I started talking and realizing that we kind of had met before, and we had the whole conversation about

Blackjack. Eric and I hit it off immediately, because he also grew up in Brooklyn with a very similar background to me. We played at some of the same clubs growing up and there were a lot of similarities between us. I didn't have a rental car — I was staying at the Hyatt on Sunset and he was still living in New York — so for the time that we rehearsed he would rent a suite at an extended stay type hotel and he did have a rental car. The arrangement was that he would swing by and pick me up on the way to rehearsal every day and drop me off, so we had a lot of time at that point to kind of get to know each other. We just hit it off, we just had so much in common that it clicked, instantly.

So you're working at these rehearsals, was it always planned for you to be an offstage player for the tour?
For that tour? Yes, absolutely, that was always the plan. Of course, Gene, to be honest with you, never really wanted keyboards in the first place. Gene didn't like the keyboards. Gene didn't want the keyboards, and he let it be very well known. He used to tell me that keyboards were not a rock and roll instrument. And he meant it. Forget about Jerry Lee Lewis, or Jon Lord, etc. Keyboards were not a rock and roll instrument and at sound check every day whenever the soundman would get through with everybody else and say, "Okay, Gary, could you give me a little bit of keys?" As soon as I would start to play by myself he would start fake ice skating around the stage. Because that's what keyboards were to him — it was music for ice skaters. Gene is Gene and the one thing about being on tour with those guys is that they were hilarious, but you had to have a "thick skin". They all had really sharp wits and there was heavy sarcasm going on. We were all New Yorkers, so I got it, and I could dish it out just as well. It was constant. There was always somebody busting somebody's balls! I think that was more important, when we had our initial meeting, just to make sure that I was a person that could deal with it.

There were a lot of times when it came time for a tour, you got these crew guys that grew up being KISS fans. And they couldn't do their jobs if Gene or Paul were nearby because they were so enamored that "they're," over there. We had a pyro guy that Gene fired in the middle of a show while he was onstage playing. He looked over at the guy and said, "You're fired", and through a series of hand gestures, and "demon" looks, had the pyro guy get away from the pyro rig and give the button to his bass tech," and Dave Rule (Gene' bass tech) had to trigger the explosions for the rest of that night until they could replace the guy. Fortunately, I wasn't like that, so I was fine. I used to laugh, you know, it was kind of funny, and they would throw picks at me and I'd pick 'em up and throw 'em back. It got to the point where I had my own bags of guitar picks just as ammo to throw back at them. It was fun, but Gene's got really good aim with a pick. He could hit the sound guy at the board from the stage. It was amazing.

They turned it into an art form what they could do with picks.
Yeah, they really did!

Did you have any input on the sweetening and where and how the keyboards were going to be used in the show or did they, Paul in particular, have a very clear vision of exactly where you were going to feature and how you were going to feature?
No, they had no idea at all and I don't think they really gave it much thought up to that point. I think that all that was important to them was the stuff that was on the "Crazy Nights" album —that I covered the keyboard parts where there were actually keyboard parts on the record. I had the choice that I could either just play those six songs, and then having nothing else to do, or I could figure out something to do. So I played on every song during the show, and as time went on I was basically doubling pretty much everything that

Gene and Paul were playing. When they're running around doing the show their playing could suffer a little bit, so I would play the stuff that the rhythm guitar part was playing and also pumping the bass stuff so that if they didn't hit every note it wasn't as apparent. As samplers became a thing, I also started doing some background vocal samples in the choruses of probably half of the songs in the set and some sound effects.

There were nights when the fire marshal would show up in the afternoon to watch a pyro run-through and then say, "Well, you can't use the explosions but you could use the colorful stuff." Gene would have that spot in his bass solo where he fired rockets from his guitar up at the PA cabinet and it would explode and confetti would fall out, and there would be explosions that would go with it that came from the pyro guy. But in the buildings where they couldn't use the concussion stuff, I would have these samples of explosions that really rumbled through the PA, and it became part of my job to trigger them at the appropriate places. He would do his bass solo and go up to the side of the stage and point his bass up, hit the button, the rocket would fly up and then I'd hit the key that triggered the explosion. The siren in "Firehouse" was another thing that I did, and the talking in the middle of "God of Thunder" was something that came from the keyboards. It grew as time went on what I did, but I always played every song from day one.

So you're really you're really thickening the sound for the band, aren't you? You're, you're helping them mask faults and making the show richer. What's the core equipment that Gary Corbett's using in October/November 1987? What was the equipment that you took out on tour?
On that record they used the Roland JX-10 keyboards. There was the Jupiter line which was a very popular analog synthesizer with very typical '80s sound. It was the sound in "Reason to Live." Bruce would play the keyboards on stage

for that song during the show because they were so predominant. I guess they felt if the keyboards were there and nobody onstage was playing them, it would be apparent that there was somebody else. So for the first half of the song they actually had a keyboard up onstage that Bruce played. It was also a Roland JX-10, and he would start the song and we both played together, but then — like halfway through — he'd swing the guitar around and walk away from the keyboard and, of course, the keyboards continued. Because of that they bought the two JX-10s, so they had the one that I used and the one that he used. For the rest of my rig, I had a Korg EX-8000 which was basically Korg's version of that type of synth. I would MIDI them together, which means that I would play the Roland JX but also hear the sound of the Korg layered with the Roland when I played — so it doubled it to be even thicker. So, basically what ended up becoming my signature sound, if you will, was a combination of those two synths and on one song I might dial in a little bit more of a gritty sound on one so it wasn't as smooth; so it wasn't that typical keyboard sound and it blended better with the guitars. What I was going for, especially on the songs that didn't have keyboards, were sounds that were guitar-ish and just basically filled the sonic spectrum; that you couldn't really distinguish from the guitars.

When you listen to one of the pro-recordings from the tour you can hear the thickness of the overall sound, which I guess is you doubling the guitar chords throughout the songs. It sounds lush, and different from earlier tours.
Basically I became like an expensive effects unit and it was the kind of thing where you only noticed it when it stopped. It wouldn't stick out so much as much as just filling everything in, but it was more apparent if I stopped playing that something had just fallen out of the sound, but you couldn't put your finger on what it was. That was always how I approached it, which was different than many keyboard players because most keyboard players are very technically

oriented and schooled and when it comes time to play with a band they always want to stand out and show what they learned at their lessons. I never cared about being noticed. I just wanted to make the band sound better and do what I was hired to do.

Eric's drum solo involved a lot of synth. Did you work with Eric to help him on that aspect of the show?
Yes. He wasn't a very technical guy. When I got there, he had already had the Simmons pads that were all around the top of his drum kit and he had a synth module in a rack that those pads were connected to. Each one of those pads would be a different note. So if the song was in the key of E, at the last note of the song when the last note was ringing out and everybody's just bashing out, he would also embellish it by hitting the appropriate pad and adding a low rumble to the end of the song. So he was already doing that when I got there, but when I started doing the sampler stuff with the vocals and sound effects and everything, he got interested in it and bought a sampler. We would do that for his drum solos. I remember going and sampling all these different Metallica guitar riffs, that he would trigger from the Simmons pads. He would start a guitar riff that would loop around once it played through, and then he would play the drums to it. But we always sampled guitar riffs. If it was a song that started with just a guitar on a Metallica record, we would sample the four bars or the two bars of the riff — just the guitar, never a full band thing — and we had all these different little snippets across each one of those pads. He would incorporate it into his solo. I helped him do all that stuff.

What are you doing on stage while he's doing a solo? Are you still at your keyboards triggering stuff while he's doing the drum solo or is it "break" time for you?
No, break time. Definitely break time!

During "break" time, what's going on backstage? Are you, or any of the band members, talking about what's going on in the show, or is it simply a matter of catch your breath and just relax for a few moments?

It depends on which tour. By the "Hot in the Shade" tour, they had thought enough about my placement to actually build something as part of the stage to actually hide me properly. On the "Crazy Nights" tour, when I first started working with them, although they didn't want me on stage and they really didn't want people to know I was there, there really was no place to put me where they could be guaranteed that nobody would see me. Typically, I would be on the floor behind the stage left PA stack, which meant that people on the sides could see me and knew I was there, but I wasn't visible to the main audience. On the "Hot in the Shade" tour, they actually built something we used to refer to as the "condo," which was off on Gene's side of the stage and it housed my keyboard rig and also Gene's bass rig. His bass tech would be in there, and there was a little ramp that came down from the right side of the stage. It was only like a 3-foot ramp that came into the "condo" from the stage.

So, I had the view right across the stage from the side of the stage, but there were opaque curtains. It was a pipe and drape type thing, so I was kind of covered at that point which then meant that it became a little bit of a party room during the show as well. The fun thing about touring with those guys was that it seemed that every band that came out in the '80s opened for KISS, at one time or another, they were all huge KISS fans. Guys like Slaughter, Faster Pussycat, and Danger, Danger. They would be with us for months at a time, so you become friendly with them and it was a very common thing for Mark Slaughter or Ted Poley to be standing next to me while I played. And they'd be singing backgrounds with me, and having fun, just because they were fans, like little kids at that point. So my "condo" became kind of a meeting spot. It

actually was good once I had that little hiding spot because it allowed us to do a lot more fun things.

Mark Slaughter, he's an awesome guy. Let's get back to November of 1987 here. Six songs from the "Crazy Nights" album debut at the first show in Jackson, Mississippi: "When Your Walls Come Down," "Bang Bang You," "Hell or High Water," "No, No, No," "Reason to Live," and "Crazy Crazy Nights." Were those the only songs from the album that you rehearsed or were there other new songs tried out during the rehearsals?
There might've been one or two others that were rehearsed, but they either never really sounded great or there was something about them that they didn't like. Maybe they didn't feel the other songs were necessary, especially if they weren't going to be singles. I think that album was more of a Paul album than a Gene album. Gene was so busy at that time, pursuing his acting, and he had the record company, so I don't think his attention in the off season was on the band, as much as it had been on previous albums. When it came time to write the new record, I think it kind of fell more on Paul's shoulders. Gene did have a couple of songs, I think "No, No, No" was one of his.

Yes, so was "Hell or High Water," which wasn't performed much.
There's a couple that were Gene's songs, but the main vibe of that record is definitely a Paul record.

Absolutely, and none of them will deny that Ron Nevison was Paul's choice. He had no choice but to try and carry the load on his own. Were there any of those "Crazy Night" songs that you could choose as a favorite that you really enjoyed performing every night, that immediately struck you as your sort of song?
No, because even though I'm a keyboard player, I like the heavier stuff and that's probably why I was able to do what I

did for them. Even though I'm a keyboard player, I understand Gene's feelings about keyboards, although I might not agree with them. I know what he's feeling, so I was very careful in my approach to never step outside of that zone. I understood that and I did appreciate the heavier stuff and the earlier songs more. For me, songs like "Rock and Roll All Nite," and stuff like that were the songs that I was really familiar with from KISS before I ever worked with them, so those were the songs that I kind of looked forward to.

Well, that answers the next question as well... Which was, of the classic stuff, what was kind of more in your wheelhouse?
"Strutter" was fun. Or "Heaven's on Fire" was fun. I also liked "Tears are Falling". I used to sing a lot of backgrounds too, so that was fun for me to be a part of the background vocals. I really enjoyed the challenge of making it sound as huge, and KISS-like as possible. Overall, it didn't bother me to be off stage, but it's a little hard to not be on stage when you're playing and there's a huge audience. However, there were times, like during the "Monsters of Rock" tour [Ed. Summer 1988] when people were throwing bottles full of piss from the audience at Donington where I was kind of happy to be offstage because I knew I'd never be hit!

There are certainly times when being offstage had its benefits! So, on the early part of the U.S. tour, the audiences were pretty unspectacular. It's well documented, mid-60 percent at best, and even lower in some cases. Shows, such as one in Lake Charles, Louisiana are cancelled. What was the mood of the band as they set out on this tour, and then started seeing those sorts of results?
It was dark. The sarcasm kind of turned to that stuff. We would be in the dressing room and Paul would say something like, "We should order a pizza for the audience," or something like that. They'd make a joke about it, but you know, at the same time, they were also figuring out ways to

hang curtains in strategic places in the arena to block the empty seats, because they didn't want it to look like a half empty arena. That's a really ugly thing to see from the stage. I guess for the sake of making it still look like a full room, they added curtains to the venues to close it down a little bit. Then the expense of the tour became an issue, and I was actually let go for a time because they decided that the tour wasn't doing well enough that they couldn't afford me anymore. So they actually sent me home.

What did you do in the interim?
Well, I didn't get any warning about it, to be honest. We had a break at Christmastime and I was home in New York and doing my Christmas shopping. I was in Greenwich Village, so I stopped by Electric Lady Studios to say hello to all the people there. I was doing my thing, Christmas the next day, great, and then we were supposed to be leaving again the day after Christmas. So, I get to Electric Lady and a call came in to the studio for me and it was Paul. I was sitting in the lounge with a couple of my friends and I answer the phone, "Hey, Paul, how's it going?" And he says, "I'm really sorry, man." I said, "What do you mean you're sorry?" "Oh, you didn't speak to Gene yet?" "No, I didn't speak to Gene." "Oh, um, well, we really can't afford to, you know..." So basically, I was now out of work and it was so last minute that there wasn't even time to get my gear off the truck. So my gear went back out on the road without me. It wasn't a very happy time. I'll tell you I wasn't very happy with them, as you could imagine. Then they went back out on the road and after like one or two shows, they called me up and said, "Listen, man, we really need you to come back out on the road... What we'd like to do is figure out the shows that are important and bring you back out and have you come out for some shows, and go home for the ones that don't matter as much," and all that stuff. So I ended up going back out and I ended up doing probably another 3 or 4 weeks of that tour and then it ended for me because they couldn't afford it anymore.

Were you still around when they shot the "Turn on the Night" video in Worcester, Massachusetts [Jan. 27, 1988]?
No, I don't think so.

So you hadn't rejoined at that point? When you are out on the road with them, was there any fun shenanigans on the road in the States, or did the overall mood just somewhat kill the fun?
Not so much on that tour. At that point, although I went back out, I was not really as jovial and happy to be around them as I had been; because of circumstances. As a matter of fact, there was even a point when I did go back out where they decided that as part of this thing to save money, I no longer traveled with them but was going to ride the crew bus as a crew member. So, needless to say, I was not really in a joking mood when it came to those guys. Now, don't get me wrong, I spent more time on the crew bus at the venues during the day than I did anywhere else, because those guys were the guys that were having all the fun. I could hang out on the crew bus and smoke cigarettes and not worry about it. I would just be myself more with those guys, and a lot of them were friends of mine from New York City that I knew from other things. So, I spent a lot of time with the crew, but the difference between being hired under the arrangements that I traveled and was treated as a band member to all of a sudden I'm with the crew, was a bit of a kick in the nuts. Instead of being in a room at the Four Seasons, my day would start on a crew bus at a venue with everybody else inside working and putting the show up. I would just sit there until the band showed up for sound check at around 4 in the afternoon with nothing to do. I think I did that one night and they could see that that was not going to work.

So, I ended up going back and traveling with the band again. But I only ended up staying for another couple of weeks before things completely fell apart. It really wasn't a lot of fun at that point. The last show I played with them was at the

Nassau Coliseum [Ed. Jan. 29, 1988] and I left there that night without saying goodbye to anybody. I just basically left, took my gear, and went home because I was still living in New York. My wife came to the show and at the end we loaded up my gear, and split. The Roland keyboard that I was using belonged to them, so it stayed behind. I didn't hear from them again until the "Monsters of Rock" tour was a possibility. They called me up and asked me if I wanted to do it, and at first, I said, I wasn't interested because of everything that had happened.

Ultimately, we came to an agreement that I would go back out with them, but I would travel as a band member like we had originally agreed. If the band was on the road, then I was going to be on the road. I wasn't going to be flying back, doing the back and forth thing. Everybody agreed, and then from there, for the next few years, everything was always great. So, I guess with, like a lot of things, you have to stand up a little for yourself. You get a little bit more respect and then you can get back to being who you are with each other.

So in the interim between leaving the tour in January and the "Monsters of Rock" tour, I guess that means you didn't go to Japan with them?
No, I didn't.

Let's fast forward to June and the rehearsals at SIR in New York getting ready to do a couple of gigs in July. Did you do the North Swanzey, New Hampshire show at the Cheshire Fairgrounds on July 4 with them, and the club gigs in August?
Yes.

So you were back by then and the set list had changed with songs like "Strutter" and "Deuce" returning, starting to skew the set's content back in favor of the classic stuff. A lot of the "Crazy Nights" stuff is now out of the set. All you're

left with is, "Crazy Crazy Nights," "Bang Bang You," and "No, No, No." Even "Reason to Live" is gone. What was the mood of the band at this point and their reaction to you? You had stood up for yourself and now you've agreed to do the "Monsters of Rock" dates. Did it strengthen your relationship in the sense that you had confronted them about not being happy about arrangements?
Absolutely! I never had another problem with them and there was never any of that sort of uncomfortable background stuff. All the way, until the time I stopped working with them after the European leg of the "Revenge" tour, I never had another issue like that with them. And it was awesome!

How were those club gigs then from your perspective, the Ritz in New York and the Marquee in London a couple of days later? What were those like to play with a band like KISS in a small venue?
It was fun! At the July 4 gig, my keyboard tech Tony Byrd had bought one of those handheld 8-millimeter video cameras, which were brand new at the time. So at that Fourth of July gig, I ended up borrowing his camera and we walked around the venue filming. Basically, we made a really funny video of back stage and all this stuff. When it came time to go to Europe, the day before we left, I went and bought my own 8-millimeter video camera. So, I have all of that on video. I have the Marquee Club on video and I have all the Donington, and "Monsters" stuff. It was a new toy, I would take it everywhere with me, including on stage or on the side of the stage. I would hold it with one hand while I played or set it down on the rack next to my keyboard and leave it on while I played. I'd walk around and film Eric doing his drum solo. The Marquee Club was mayhem. They were packed in like sardines in that place, but it was so cool because it's such a legendary club that to be there and have it be so packed was really cool.

Of course, a couple of days later, you're playing in front of 100,000 people at the "Monsters of Rock Festival" at Donington. Would that have been the biggest audience you'd ever been in front of, at that time?
Yeah, it was. It was huge. It was unbelievable.

You mentioned the throwing of the bottles of piss and everything — which bands such as Twisted Sister have discovered is a very Donington thing — if you've ever seen Dee Snider talk about the audience throwing actual crap up on the stage... What was that like? Just give us a quick overview of your "Monsters of Rock" experience in England.
I spent a lot of time at the site. The day before, Eric and I had gone down, because he had to do some last minute tweaks with the drums. That's who I hung out with all the time when we were on the road because Gene and Paul didn't come out much. Bruce was newly engaged and his fiancée was with him at that time on the road. So, I have lots of footage I shot on that trip. Most was me behind the camera, with Eric as the focus. We went to Hyde Park, the original Hard Rock Café, and then the next day was the show, and I have all this back stage stuff too. Paul was dating Samantha Fox at the time — I just filmed everything. It was unbelievable, but it had rained the day before and the site was really like a mud fest. Earlier in the day, on the day of the show, two people got trampled to death during Guns N' Roses' set. There was a little bit of weird vibe going on, but once we went on stage, we had to put it aside. It was quite a large mass of people and they didn't really do enough from a safety standpoint. There were no barricades; it was just one large mass of people. Today, they would never allow an audience that size to be one large crowd. They would have to separate the audience with multiple fences to keep it from being such a large mass. They start surging, when the bands came on stage, and I remember during our set, having to motion to security people and pointing out people in front to pull out. They had to be pulled over the barricade because they were getting

crushed by the people behind them. There was nothing that anybody could do about it. And unfortunately, like I said, during Guns N' Roses' set, two people had slipped in the mud and were trampled to death. It was just pandemonium. From the standpoint of being a musician on stage in front of an audience like that, it was incredible, you know. It was the biggest audience I had ever played in front of up until that point.

You made the news during this initial British visit, didn't you?
(Laughs). Eric and I went down to the site the day before. While we were in LA rehearsing for the "Crazy Nights" tour was when "Welcome to the Jungle" had just come out. It was everywhere you turned in the LA clubs on the Strip. Every time that song came on, the dance floor immediately was packed and people loved it. We were fans of it and I bought the album when it was released. So Eric and I were down at the site the day before and they were sound checking that afternoon. Eric and I walked out into the middle of the empty field and sat down on the grass. They were playing, and I was filming with my video camera. While they were playing, Eric noticed that there were two guys that were crew guys on the side of the stage and they were pointing at us.

So Eric said, "Hey, I don't think they want you filming. You better turn off your camera." So, I wasn't going to turn off my camera but I acted like I did, and just put it down on the ground next to me. I kept it running, and nothing was ever said. When we got back to the hotel that night, I walked in my room and the phone rings, and it was Paul. He says, "You guys made the news." And I said, "What are you talking about." He says, "Well, when Guns N' Roses were playing, the reporter was standing on the side of the stage and they pointed out at you and Eric sitting there in the middle of the field by yourselves. And the reporter said, 'Guns N' Roses played to a very small audience today...'" So, that's what the

guy was pointing at us about. It wasn't about the fact that I was filming.

Oh, that's absolutely brilliant. Hilarious!
Yeah, because that was such a huge show the following day and there's 100,000 people. But at this point, there's only two people dead in the center of the grass, and nobody else. I imagine that looked pretty funny, you know. We're sitting out on the ground like we're part of an audience. I never got to see the news report, but Paul made sure he told us about it. He thought it was pretty funny.

That's something I want to see if I can track down now. A week later you're in Schweinfurt and that's notable for being a pro shot for TV where you show up with a bit too much camera time, right from the first song. You're where you're supposed to be, stage left under scaffolding with a tarp around you, but I guess the camera crew hadn't been told to not film you. And you're certainly mugging for the camera! Any response to that? Was that kind of like one of those moments of sweet justice, to a certain extent that you'd been off stage all these times and now, here you are on a TV broadcast and you're getting exposure like a full band member?
Absolutely! I didn't encourage the guys to come over, so they couldn't hold me responsible or get mad at me. They weren't happy about it, and it was kind of funny to me that that kind of stuff bothered them. Every country has a KISS Army branch and every one of them had a fan magazine, after 20 years of the band's existence — or whatever it was at that point — to put out a monthly magazine and have content, Sometimes they'd do a "few degrees of separation" and you know, interview someone silly like Peter Criss' mailman or whoever had a connection to the band — just to be able to put out a magazine. So needless to say, it started getting to the point where they wanted to interview me, and it became a bit of a problem to them that I was getting that much attention.

There was no chance I was going to steal any spotlight from anybody, but they just didn't want me to get that much attention. I guess I was supposed to be a secret. They did give me permission to do one or two interviews, though.

Yeah, there's no right or wrong with that at the time. It was always a matter, at that time particularly, that the focus in KISS is on Gene and Paul as the original members. Same to this day, it's their band.
Yeah, it's their band and they can do whatever they want.

Wrapping up "Monsters of Rock," you're on tour bands like Iron Maiden, Megadeth, Anthrax, Testament, and Great White. Did you interact with any of the members of these bands, or was it just very businessman-like atmosphere? I would think Iron Maiden were utter focused pros, and just come out there and do their thing and not really be hanging around. Was there interaction between at least yourself and anyone else outside of KISS?
There wasn't much. You know, those shows were so huge and the sites were so huge, and the back stage areas were so separate and everybody's trailers so far apart. So there really wasn't much time or a place for that sort of thing. But there was a little. You know Anthrax had been an opening act on the "Crazy Nights" tour, although it was after I had left. Eric was a huge Anthrax fan. When I went through my videotapes recently from backstage, there's a whole piece where we're all sitting there with Frankie [Ed. Bello], Danny [Ed. Spitz], and Joey [Ed. Belladonna], and everybody's goofing off. But as far as hanging with Iron Maiden, I don't think that happened much, aside from Nicko, who was also a friend with Eric. It was basically anybody that I hung out with was because I was friends and hanging with Eric. He had been in the band for nearly 10 at that point. He was also a fan of Iron Maiden. Everybody loved Eric and he had many friends, so that was how I met a lot of them. I can't remember really talking much to David Lee Roth. Maybe Brett Tuggle and I talked a little bit.

Gregg Bissonette was a really nice guy. Iron Maiden was the headliner on the "Monsters of Rock" tour, so they were even more isolated than the KISS guys were, so there were no opportunities to really interact with them.

So, during this time, KISS are also doing some solo shows. I'm not going to dig into every single one of these, but I did want to ask you particularly about Iceland and playing in Reykjavik. What do you recall of that gig because that, in looking at the venue, it looks basically like a glorified barn?
Yeah, is that the one that looks like an indoor tennis court, like a big long garage basically?

Yeah, the only pictures that I've seen of it, it has dirt on the floor. I guess without the dirt, it might've not looked that way. It's certainly not the kind of traditional European type of venue!
It looked like one of those temporary kinds of metal buildings. What I remember about that gig was how strange the terrain of Iceland itself was. It really looked like you were on the surface of the moon because it was just the weirdest looking rock and that's all you could see for as far as you could see, except for the road that we were on. Driving and driving and driving, you would see nothing but this weird rock, and then all of a sudden in the middle of nowhere, there's a Hard Rock Café, and then there's nothing for miles again. And then we pull up, and we're driving down the road that leads into the venue and we thought no, please tell me that's not the place! I remember that at that gig, it was so strange because I'd never seen this before, but because of the climate, inside as opposed to outside, there was literally a cloud that formed inside the building above the audience because of the heat and the cold, and whatever it takes to make a cloud! But there was literally a cloud inside the building floating over the audience that looked really, really strange while we played. I remember that my keyboard rig's

main power supply blew up at that gig because the power in the building was not stable. That was a strange one.

Did the band do the, did the band do the full set for the Icelandic audience, or was it like a scaled back job.
No, they never would do that. They would never scale the show down if there was less people, or do less of a show because for them, the show is what KISS is about. They would never do anything other than 110 percent for the audience.

Well I'm going to call you "pusher man" now, one of the best stories I've heard from this tour — though it may not be the best for you personally — occurs when the tour reaches Holland. Let's talk Amsterdam.
Oh, gosh, that's a videotape that I'm looking to find because I have about 45 minutes of Eric in that place.

I think his family would certainly like that footage, wouldn't they? (Laughs).
When we were talking a few months back because I sent some of my personal video footage to his sister, she wasn't sure if she wanted to see that stuff. I assured her, there was nothing, you know, bad about it. The fact is the guy had never done anything else like that in his life. He had never tried smoking. He had never tried any drugs of any kind. He'd occasionally like a glass of wine. What happened was, the band took his drum solo out of the set for the "Monsters of Rock" shows because they were not the headliner. In that format they simply didn't have the time slot to do the full KISS show. So, that was one of the things that had to be sacrificed, but after the "Monsters of Rock" shows were over and we continued on and Eric completely expected the drum solo to be put back into the show. He was working it up in his head, and getting ready for that and looking forward to it because that was a really big deal to him.

He was told that they weren't going to put the drum solo back in the show once we were out on our own, regardless. He was really bummed out about it. Because of the nature of the shows, the "Monster of Rock" shows were always either Saturday or Sunday, so wherever we played, we would get there and we'd have a whole week off, which was very unlike any other tour. You know, usually you don't get to see the town you're in other than the venue, and that's it, but on these shows, because we had the whole week in between, we ended up with a whole week in Amsterdam. My sister was living in Switzerland at the time, so when I originally got the tour booked, I had made plans to visit her. So after Amsterdam, we were going to Italy, I believe, so my sister said why don't you come and spend a couple of days in Switzerland with me. So I looked at the schedule. I said, "Okay, you know what, I'm going to be in Amsterdam for a week. I'll stay like 3 or 4 days and then I'll fly to Switzerland, and then I'll meet back up with everybody in Italy." And so Eric was really upset and pissed off about the drum solo, and he comes to me and he says "I want to get high." I'm a smoker, and I was fully taking advantage of the legal things Amsterdam had to offer.

I said, "are you sure you want to do it?" He said, "Yeah, I want to do it." So we went to the coffee shop and he ordered a couple of bonbons that were laced with weed and he ate them. He didn't feel anything, as a lot of people do the first time they do it, you know. Sometimes it doesn't affect you at all, so he was kind of disappointed. The next day, I get a phone call from Bruce who said to me, "I found a coffee shop that's not a tourist place, but a place where the locals go and they'll make some really good "space cakes." they were really strong and unbelievable. So, when I saw Eric, I said, "Hey, you know, Bruce told me about this place and if you still want to try it, if we go there, you should feel something." So he agreed and we went to the coffee shop and Eric ate a bunch of space cakes and he smoked up. I rolled this big spliff with

hash in it and he was pulling it out of my hand and taking hits, eating brownies, and all kinds of crap.

Then we left and started walking around the canals, and there was this little outdoor café where we ran into the rest of the band as it was starting to hit him. He started getting very paranoid and very agitated because he was very insecure anyway, especially around Gene and Paul. And he was mad at them about the solo, and didn't want to be around them. So, he said to me, "I've gotta get outta here. Let's go back to the hotel." So we go back to the hotel and we get back to my room, and he started to freak out a little bit. He said he couldn't breathe, that he was going to die because he had forgotten how to breathe. So I called up Bruce and I called up Nite Bob, who was our sound guy, and I said, "Guys, you've got to come over and give me a hand!" The scene looks like one of those bad '70s "Don't Do Drugs" movies because I've got the music cranking on my CD player and a pile of weed on the table. I'm turning the camera sideways and doing all these strange zoom-ins and all this weird stuff, and then I would pan over to the chair where Eric was sitting frozen. He'd just have this strange look on his face, and would say these weird things. And that went on for hours. I was like, "Dude, you know, maybe you should just close your eyes for a little while and lay down on the bed and take a nap. We'll all stay here with you." He was like, "No way, man! I know if I go to sleep, I'm never gonna wake up!" And I said, "Well, listen, maybe if you eat something, you'll feel better. Maybe some food will bring you down a little bit." So we ordered room service and he took one bite of the food and threw the fork down. "I'm gonna choke, if I eat, I'm gonna choke." I mean it was just unbelievable. It was really, I think, aside from the fact that he was actually going through something traumatic to him, it was kind of funny. So, that went on for the rest of the night. My flight to see my sister was the next morning, so at the end of the night, he left and he went back to his room, and I got up the next morning and left to go to

Switzerland, and never thought another thing about it. I assumed he woke up the next morning and felt fine.

Then I fly back to meet the band that weekend. I get to Italy and I get to the hotel, and I go down to eat something by myself. I'm sitting in the restaurant, and then Paul comes into the restaurant by himself and he's sitting at the table, a few tables away, and that's where, where I started hearing it... "Hey, it's the pusher man, goddamn the pusher man" and he's singing the Steppenwolf song. And I say, "What are you talking about?" Paul says, "Oh, Eric confessed." Confessed? And of course, he threw me under the bus as the instigator. I didn't do anything wrong! I mean he wanted to do it and it was legal where we were, so what's the problem, you know? But yeah, Paul wasn't mad. It was just another opportunity to bust Eric's balls. Basically, because of the way Eric handled it, it became a thing. They weren't really mad, they just kind of thought it was funny. So, that's where "Pusher Man" comes from.

Never ever miss an opportunity to put some heat on someone, right?!
Well that that was the KISS way. They were relentless, but it was hysterical, especially when someone else was the target.

After Italy you're, you're in Paris and before the Zenith show there's a couple of days of rehearsals. What was the purpose of those rehearsals, do you recall?
Right, it was the beginning of the non-"Monsters of Rock" leg of the tour and we were rehearsing the stuff that we were going to add to the set for the rest of the shows. That was fun.

Once you're on a regular tour did the vibe change since it's pretty much just a regular European tour with Kings of the Sun opening. You guys did a lot of shows in Scandinavia on

this leg and in the British Isles. Any overall thoughts about this part of the tour?
In Newcastle, Paul was still dating Samantha Fox. I used to travel with my golf clubs so I was going to play golf because here we are going close to the birth place of the game. So I was really looking forward to going and playing, and Paul decided he wanted to come along and play. So Paul, Samantha, Samantha's assistant and our security guy who was named Graham, all went to the local golf course. Of course, we were turned away because Samantha and Paul were not dressed in appropriate golf clothes. Paul ended up having to go into the club shop and buy appropriate golf clothes for them! They sent a golf pro out to give us a lesson before they let us out onto the course. Which of course got videotaped ... We ended up playing a round of golf and that was hilarious because none of them had ever played before. It was the first time any of them had swung a golf club and to watch Paul and the rest of them all try was great. They couldn't hit the ball. It was hilarious.

I'm trying to get an image of Paul Stanley, circa 1988, wearing golf gear and holding a golf club. I mean that is almost a priceless image to try and conjure.
I wish I could send you a video clip! It's so funny, because Paul used to love to mug for the camera every time the camera came on him. I have footage of us in Budapest walking the streets and, he was hilarious when he was "on" like that, ya know? And at the golf course, although he started out that way, it ended up becoming, "Get the camera off me!" He didn't want to look bad on the camera, but it was really funny to watch him try to swing and miss the ball. He didn't have a very nice looking golf swing, I'll say that. And I doubt he ever played again.

Some golf aficionados will be happy you did this in Newcastle and not in Saint Andrews! That would have been morally wrong to have Paul Stanley on a golf course in

Scotland at the birth places of golf. I won't tell you my story of what I did at the Royal & Ancient one Hogmanay as I'd have to edit it out! Let's talk about the last show of the tour at the King's Hall in Belfast, Northern Ireland. Bruce has made plenty of comments about this show and I've nicknamed it the "Gobs of Thunder" show. From your vantage point, was this the one show where you were very thankful to be behind stage and not within spitting distance? Tell us about the show.

Absolutely, I don't know what I would have done. I've never been in a situation like that. Because you know the problem with those things, like that or the piss bottle at Donington. You're briefed about this before the shows by the promoters. They tell you that the worst thing that you can do is react to it. If you do anything, or act like you're mad about it, it's going happen ten times worse. So you really can't even try to dodge it or do anything because then you're just going to get it worse. I don't know how anybody could do it and deal with it the way they did. Paul, especially, because he was getting nailed constantly with gobs of spit from the crowd, and it was just disgusting. I mean, there was spit dripping off his knuckles on the guitar, it was dripping off the guitar, it was just absolutely disgusting. Towards the end of the show he had had enough, and he did his little dance up to the front of the stage. I guess there was one guy in particular who had been nailing him all night long and Paul goes up the front of the stage and, with his right hand he kind of motions to the people around the guy, like you move that way and you move that way, and then he just leaned over and spit right in the guy's face.

Fantastic! Go Paul. You can actually see that on the video of the show. It's brilliant when you understand the context of the barrage the band had been under for the whole show. It's another thing that reminds me why I adore Paul!

It was great.

You've got to love Paul. He knows how to work the audience and take care of them as well sometimes.
Yeah. That was the best part of the show for me, and that's probably one of the most vivid memories of that show. That and the amount of spit that came on the stage...

I'm surprised the band gave them the full end of tour show. There was full set that night including "Whole Lotta Love." One thing I noticed on these sets is, "Oh Suzanna" obviously comes in now and then, "La Bamba", "Stairway to Heaven", "Whole Lotta Love", the whole of that one. How did that section of the show work? Was it just you're briefed before the show that they may or may not do a jam section, and just adapt? Was this set up that they knew what they were going include each night they did these little jam sections?
Paul was such a huge Zeppelin fan and you know, sound checks for that band were always a jam session of Led Zeppelin's greatest hits. That's what we would do every afternoon. So it certainly wasn't the first time we ever played the songs but, you know, we never played them in front of an audience so. When a song like that gets called out there's no discussion really necessary, and it wasn't planned — it just happened. Being the last show and everybody, you know, there's that feeling of letting go because the tour is over and you're going home. They just did a couple of spontaneous things and everybody just jumped on and followed along. But it wasn't anything that was talked about or specifically rehearsed or anything.

You mentioned earlier that for the show you were briefed about not reacting to the audience or you'd get even more back from them. As a quick side note, were you guys briefed about the troubles that were occurring in Northern Ireland at the time? Safety and such?
Oh absolutely. Throughout the entire summer that show was cancelled and not cancelled then cancelled then not cancelled because it was a dangerous show. Our security guy

was ex-SAS, the equivalent of like a Navy Seal — a trained killer basically. We had heavy security because of the show and we weren't really thrilled with the idea of going. Most bands that put that show on their schedules ended up cancelling it before they got there, so I guess the guys kind of felt bad for the kids of the country there. They felt like they're so deprived of any international entertainment and probably really need a break. Plus it was an opportunity to ensure a sell-out crowd, so they decided to go ahead with it, but took some precautions.

We had a meeting and I remember them sitting in the room and having them warning us like not to walk too close to the cars parked on the curb if you're walking down the street because of car bombs. Not to stay on the top floor of hotels because of people repelling off roof. We're like, "Where the hell are we going!?" The hotel that we stayed at looked more like Folsom Prison or Alcatraz with the razor wire around the top of the fence and huge gates. We must have gone through five or six armed military check points, in our vehicle going from the airport. It was really a scary feeling. There were very few people, aside from the band's party, in the hotel that we stayed at. It definitely was eerie. We couldn't wait to get out of there. We didn't fly in until 4 or something like that in the afternoon and we went straight to the venue, did our show, went to the hotel, got a few hours' sleep, and then got out of there. It was really a little bit tense. A lot of the crew guys didn't really want to be there. They were a little nervous because if things went wrong that would have been a very bad way to end the tour.

I think knowing that the period of time and the troubles, a great deal of respect has to be given to KISS to actually play in that show and finishing the tour there.
Yes.

Fortunately, it was, other than being spat on all night a good show and a strong finish to the tour. If you had to pick a single "one," what would be a high point from working with the band on this tour?
I would say Donington. It was a very well received KISS show. The reviews of the band at that point were good, because of the changes they had made in the set and bringing back a lot of the classic stuff that we added back in at that point. You know, the reviews in magazines such as Kerrang! and "Metal Hammer" and whatever, the reviews of the show were really positive, which wasn't the case for everything that was going on the prior year. There was a lot of negative stuff written because of the "Crazy Nights" record. It was a really successful show and like a lot of bands, KISS were very competitive guys, so the fact that they were not the headliner and we were going on during the day, all of that combined to totally light the fire under them to go out and play a great show. We didn't have the pyro and the show to lean on, so they simply went out and played their asses off. I would say that was definitely the highlight for me.

As an English guy, it was a good time to be a KISS fan in Britain. It's my memories of KISS seeming to be everywhere in Britain during "Crazy Nights," which is why I'm doing this whole 30th anniversary celebration for it. It's just one of those strange things. You come off this tour and four months later, in February 1989, Paul heads out on his solo tour. You're a member of that touring band. Was there any discussion about the solo tour during the "Monsters of Rock" leg? At what point did you get invited to be a part of that band with Eric Singer, Bob Kulick and Dennis St. James?
That didn't happen until probably 2 or 3 weeks before we started the rehearsals for that tour. It was kind of a last minute thing. It was just a whirlwind it seemed more than anything else. Paul called me up and said, "Listen, you know I'm thinkin' about going out and doing a solo tour ..." He had never gotten to do any shows around the solo record that

they had all done back in the day, so there were songs that he wanted to play from that. He just wanted to go out and have fun and play some clubs and get back to feeling like a young up and coming band again. So we played all these clubs, like HammerJacks, Toad's Place, and it was a blast. I mean we were still staying at Four Seasons and we still had a bus and a tour manager, an accountant and everything. But the venues were clubs and very intimate and every one of them was like an event, ya know? They were packed way beyond capacity; people were really excited about them. Paul was in a very relaxed state of mind at that point because it wasn't KISS; he didn't have to compete for the spotlight with Gene. He didn't have to compromise with anyone on anything that he wanted to do. Not that that's a bad thing, but it was just an opportunity for him to go out and do his own thing and he seemed to really enjoy it. He was more fun on that tour than any other time I spent with him because he was so relaxed and it was just about having fun. And the band was great too. It was a really killer band. Eric Singer is a great drummer. Bob, he's a great guitar player who was the perfect guy for that band. He was a perfect fit, as was Dennis. So it was great!

Were you given any different instructions about the keyboards or it was just a matter of you did it before, come and do the same thing on this tour?
I was on stage so that was different. On the songs that we had played with KISS, I played them pretty much the same as I played in with the band. All I wanted to do was what was best for the music, not to show off my keyboard playing skills. So my parts didn't change though I might have gotten some new keyboards at the time, but as far as the approach, it was still the same, except on the big ballad we did, "I Still Love You."

That's an epic song!
Yeah. So, I got to play a little bit more on that one and the keyboard parts in that were a little bit more "keyboard-ish" than normal, as far as a KISS song goes. Whenever I play with bands like KISS or Cinderella, or bands like that, I always approach my part that way, where they are fitting in as though I'm the rhythm guitar player, as opposed to playing twinkly sparkly stuff that sits on top like a lot of keyboard players do. I was very into John Lord and Deep Purple and the way he played the organ was very much that way. It wasn't about showing how fast you could play or how many notes you could play; it was making the keyboard sound as mean as possible and compete with the guitarist in that way. That was always the way I approached it.

What are you up to currently musically?
I'm just recovering from three shoulder surgeries so I took the last 2 years off to deal with that. I recently got involved in a new project with the Nelson twins. We're just finishing up a record now actually and it should be pretty interesting. There are plans to go out and support it, so I'm really looking forward to that. There's also some talk of me doing some shows with Mark Slaughter who's just released a new solo record as well.

Many KISS fans are raving about Mark Slaughter's new album.
Yeah. It's a great record. The Nelson Project is called the Stone Canyon Band, which was actually the name of the band that was their Dad's backup band when he passed away. So it's a bit of a nod to what their dad was doing at the time he passed. It's definitely not a continuation of the Nelson thing. It's very exciting for me to be a part of something from this early on as opposed to being hired on after a record is completed.

Absolutely, it must be nice to be invested in a band project from the ground floor rather than being a go to person after the fact when a band remembers, "we need a guy to play keys!"

Exactly. I got to thinking about and it dawned on me that during my entire career I've never done something like that. We started working on this project and I was originally contacted by Gunnar to just play keyboards on some recordings. They started sending me the tracks, and I'd been working in my studio at home and then sending the tracks back. So at first, they were just hiring me to play some keyboards on the recordings, but I guess what I was sending back was exactly what they were looking for and, everything started to really mesh. After the third song he said, "Would you be interested in being a part of this and being an actual member and help get this thing going?" And for me, that sounded really, really inviting. At this point in my life and career, I'm goin' for it. The collaborative process is really fun because I can try something, send it to them; and they'll be honest and give me their opinion. If they have an idea, I'm totally open to it. If I have an idea about something they're doing I could suggest it, which is very different than anything else I've ever done. So I'm actually really enjoying it.

Bruce Kulick

KissFAQ: Bruce, let's start with the end of the "Asylum" tour in April 1986, your first tour supporting an album you were fully involved with. How had that tour compared with the "Animalize" outing and what kind of head space were you in as it finished?
Bruce Kulick: I very much felt by the end of the "Animalize" tour that the word was out that KISS had a new guitarist. It was very confusing period, there had been such a revolving door [of guitarists]. They got Mark St. John for the album and then of course he had his illness and the next thing you know I'm filling in and doing all the dates. There was a short period there where Mark was kind of given the shot when he got well in America, and that was pretty weird, but you know, it was probably something that KISS needed to do contractually. And then the gig was mine, but we didn't share information back in '84 the way we do now so it took a long time for people to really know what was going on. That was the great thing about moving forward from "Animalize," a very successful album and tour.

There's always been a bit of a feeling that "Asylum" has been judged unfairly due to its cover art and associated image rather than the contents of the music; which was definitely in the sort of the hard rock vane you'd expect from KISS at the time. As a band, had you discussed the album's reception on the road, considering, "Maybe this isn't the right image for us. We need to start thinking about the next change for how we approach our next album?"
I don't think we ever really just pointed a finger at the artwork, even though we were aware there might have been a little bit of a disconnect. I thought Paul was being very creative. If you think of the colors, it was in touch with what was happening then with the neon style of that era. We do

know one thing, fashion changes all the time of course. It has to! I noticed lately that John Varvatos — who are connected to KISS of course — started offering all this Animalize-like print stuff, the leopard print and everything. Duh! I looked at that I went, "Wait a minute!" Not that it ever went completely out of fashion; but you get my point here, that there are cycles in style.

I didn't think the cover was *that* crazy! I thought the faces looked so large and the biggest thing that the band had stress, and we had to laugh, about was that Eric Carr got the smallest part of square footage on the cover. But I thought the record had some great tracks on it. In some ways I think it could have been mixed even a little heavier, but we didn't just point a finger at the cover or image. When the tour did start we did have some drop in sales with the attendance. When we tried some new songs from that album they didn't always go over [with the audience]. That was always a big thing with KISS: What the set should have when we're out there for a new tour, how many new songs, but sadly new songs never really survive that much unless they have teeth like "Crazy Crazy Nights" did. It was a big hit in Europe, so of course it was always going to be in the set. I still think that it was a little confusing why "Asylum" didn't do at least as well as "Animalize." I really don't know.

You know what, you guys didn't look that much different than say Mötley Crüe or W.A.S.P, or so many of the bands at the time. Even Bon Jovi...
It was the thing. I think maybe the market got saturated back then with a lot of good bands doing a lot of good stuff. I'd hate to in any way think that a KISS fan was turned off to by the record because of the cover. I'm not going there.

So the tour, the "Asylum" tour ends; what's your recollection of the band's plans at the time? Was there an initial plan just to do the usual rinse and repeat of take a

little break and then be in the studio by the summer or was it always planned that there was going to be a substantial break between the end of the "Asylum tour and hitting the studio with Ron Nevison to start work on "Crazy Nights?"
You know, the details that you're asking about, I don't really remember if there was a conscious decision that, "Oh, we need a break here." But looking back, the "Asylum" tour did present some struggles for Gene and Paul. I'd be a fool to think I really knew what happened in between the two, but first off the stage had to change a lot. The initial floor, the one with our faces, was too slippery. The first three weeks of "Asylum" tour was tumultuous. The lightning bolt staircases were a hazard. Then, the attendance was not 100 percent or as big as "Animalize." All of a sudden, financially Gene and Paul looked at, "How can we make this more efficient?" That's smart. Who wants to go in a hole over an overabundance of stage components that weren't really working?

Absolutely, tours are challenging and you have to adapt to the market and work out the kinks. Did that play into a shift in thinking for the next album?
So things kept changing. I think the smartest link from "Asylum" to "Crazy Nights," was it was probably more Paul than Gene's decision to seek out someone like Ron Nevison, a proven hit rock record producer of that era. But I wouldn't be surprised if some of that direction came from the feeling that, "We're not invincible." Perhaps there was some licking the wounds from "Asylum." Even though there great songs and it's still a well-received record in KISStory, things didn't go as well we hoped; they maybe went down a notch. So, maybe we have to come out of the gate with something better on the next album, which was "Crazy Nights."

Do you remember a change of direction being communicated to you that you were going to basically try

and do a KISS version of "Slippery When Wet," by becoming more radio accessible material with "Crazy Nights?"
I really think the only thing discussed was that Ron Nevison, the successes that he had with Ozzy and Heart, I don't remember all of his resume, but it was decided, "Let's go in that direction." I did learn from KISS, and Gene and Paul were the people that are successful. Most of the time the reason why they're successful is because they understand how to do something well. During my years, Paul always played a larger part in many things than Gene; because he was the most uncomfortable without the makeup and got involved with the Hollywood thing —movies and acting. Paul continued to be more the decision maker of the band, but Paul didn't have a lot of other aspirations and Gene did. Paul worked really hard.

With Gene's external activities taking up so much time, and maybe more importantly artistic energy, it's not surprising perhaps that Paul felt he had to take the load on his shoulders more.
I have a "Crazy Nights" demo cassette, pre-studio sessions with Ron Nevison, that had nine songs on it. What's ironic about it is that a lot of the songs did wind up on the record. Not all nine, but the point is, as far as Paul was concerned, he didn't care if nine of them were on the album, and then just let Gene have one. That was very clear from Paul. It was not out of disrespect to Gene, it was just that he was really dialed in. He was going to work with hit songwriters.

What sorts of songs were included at that time?
I do have a scan of that cassette cover. I can't remember exactly probably "Time Traveler" was on it and some of the other songs that you've known about, but didn't make "Crazy Nights." I don't even know if "Sword & Stone" was on there. Paul was very driven to use Ron and have Ron guide us to success and in many ways I think Ron delivered.

There's a certain impression that for the parameters that Ron was given, he certainly more than delivered in terms of the finished product, and that Paul (in particular) was not unhappy with what the resulting product was.
No and even if Gene was, it certainly fit that era. I was happy to work with a producer. I thought left to their own devices, even though it's always more Paul that decides things in the studio. He'll let Gene do what he wants to do on his songs, but in the same way, he's still going to play more of the bigger "producer" role from what I've seen with KISS. But Paul was very happy with Ron. Gene was petrified, he thought Ron was going to water it down and I think that even Nevison had said he wished there was a little more bottom end on the record.

Yes, he has.
Maybe if it was mixed a little differently. But, again, for that era it sounds fine. Look, hindsight's always 20/20 — we know that! I thought it was appropriate and most importantly, he allowed me to be very well featured. You know, he was sometimes a little crusty in the studio. He didn't really know me that well and he was clearly working more for Paul and Gene than me. So we had some an interesting relationship and dynamics, but Ron delivered a solid record in his vision. I think it holds up very well 30 years on.

When I think about you in KISS, and reaching the high point with your guitar playing, I often think "Revenge" and the really aggressive guitars very much in forefront of the sound. Going back and listening to "Crazy Nights," there's a lot of guitar work on that album, Bruce, an amazing amount of texture and variety on there. So, as a guitarist how do you approach working with Ron and also having keyboards more present in the mix to make sure that you're still in the picture?
I was never really concerned once I heard the way Ron always featured the lead player of some of the other bands that he

had success with. Keyboards were very much a part of that era. I was always a huge Van Halen fan, in some ways I was a "1984" on. "Jump" was just such a killer track to me and Eddie was playing keyboards, which was very new for them. But like Journey, there were so many other bands that used keyboards effectively that still had a stellar lead guitar player. I didn't see the keys as a threat. I knew that Ron still needed powerful solos.

And that sort of Van Halen-esque power was very much present in songs like "No, No, No." How did that one come about?
I don't really remember how and why I wound up doing a solo guitar introduction to "No, No, No," but I certainly welcomed it. Maybe it was because Van Halen was known for a solo guitar, but he posed no threat that way to me. It all seemed natural. That record is a lot of guitars and textures, but a guy like Ron Nevison is going to really work with everybody and get the best out of them. Just because you have keyboards there doesn't mean the guitars take a backseat.

I was just kind of wondering if the keyboards was something that motivating you, not really as a threat, but whether you thought that you had to work even harder in conjunction with the keyboards since they add an extra dynamic in the song's musicality?
I think really the keyboards were just another kind of pad. I laughed one time "No, No, No" was mentioned in a review in a stereo magazine. It was pretty cool that they were actually discussing a rock record, when most of the time they just get into more like classical or maybe jazz, the guy said that the "synthesizer" introduction of "No, No, No," with the hammer-on part, obviously, was very creative. I was like, "Wait a minute, that's just my guitar with a little chorus effect on it." It just showed their ignorance. I think it all worked together.

I have to tell you the story of Gene's face during mixing when we were adding a sample to the snare, whenever the snare was played of the drums. It was kind of a strange sounding drum machine sample that he just added in. It was just blended in so that it wouldn't be like, "Oh yeah, I hear *it*." If we had the multi-track tapes, then probably I could point it out, but I remember Gene's face. It was as if he was crying and cowering in the corner of the room. You know, "What are you doing!?" Gene's probably responsible for the big drums on "Creatures," so I get it. But it was just the texture that Ron wanted to add that was probably part of his radio rock friendly formula that put many gold and platinum records on the wall for him. What Ron was doing, I understood Gene's concern, but it wasn't so excessive. Gene's grimace was horrifying! Even Eric Carr wasn't that freaked out about it, you know. Paul was probably smiling because he's putting the "Nevison" magic on it.

Eric was probably used to that sort of studio "magic" by that point anyway, because Allan Schwartzberg had previously come in to do drum overdubs like that on both "Animalize" and "Asylum."

I don't remember about "Asylum" anything different for Eric, but definitely "The Elder." There were a lot of things going on for Eric, so who knows? Everyone should know who's a big KISS fan, Gene and Paul always looked at KISS the way the Beatles looked at the Beatles. McCartney played a lead guitar solo if needed. McCartney might have played drums on some tracks that we think are Ringo. Or even a session guy who was involved in the very beginning [Ed. Andy White] because George Martin wasn't so sure Ringo had the right swing. In other words, nothing was sacred. It was about the song and the performance. Of course, to be replaced by a drum machine later on "Hot in the Shade" on a couple songs; I thought that was not necessary. But yeah, Eric was used to a little bit of drama that way, sadly.

I do want to talk about some of the songs, and "Sword & Stone" is the first one that comes to mind. It didn't make the album, and was mentioned in Billboard in January 1987 that it'd been given to Loverboy to record. Paul Dean did later record it for his "Hardcore" solo album so I can understood why it might not have been used for "Crazy Nights" if it was promised to another mainstream band like that. What do you recall about writing that song with Desmond and Paul? Ron has said that he can understand people being disappointed with it not being on the album.

Yeah, my bank account was disappointed! I think that Ron didn't love the song that much and then it was easy to say, "Hey, I got it covered by somebody else," even though I was not there for any conversation. What I'm sure about is that I had a great idea for a song. I remember coming up with the chords in the dressing room of one of the shows. I'd usually have a guitar room for practice on tour so I could warm up, which is one of the luxuries of being a headliner on an arena tour. I just remember having those chords and I remember recording it and playing it for Paul. Paul liked it, and I remember we [Ed. Paul and Desmond Child] all jumped in on it and I was pretty happy that Paul responded to the basic chords and that I was able to have a co-write with the two of them.

Both of them were so successful in song writing, so for me it was a blessing and then we recorded a full blown demo. Back then it wasn't a big deal to do something like that at the studio. So we're at Electric Lady Studios doing a demo so I have a pretty decent cassette copy of it. I know I offered it to Tommy when he was putting the box set together. Anything I have of KISS I've shared with them just in case they didn't have a good copy of something. But it didn't wind up in the box set so it hasn't been properly released with the version that Paul sang. So, Paul Dean covered it I was very proud that it was the first song from his solo record. A German band also covered it for some soundtrack.

Yeah, Bonfire covered it for the "Shocker" soundtrack in 1989.
When I did some sort of interview regarding that horror flick, I remember it came up. So, you know, it's kind of cool that it got covered a few times. It's a good song, you've got Paul and Desmond's names attached to it, so that's an attractive thing. I really think Paul singing our version was the best. That's another one of those little gems that is unfortunately hidden from the masses, in a good way. But I just think that Nevison just didn't think he needed it for the record or didn't want to record it. I thought it was an obvious choice for "Crazy Nights," but I think I have four co-writes so I wasn't really crying. It could have been worse!

You do have four co-writes on the album; two with Gene and two with Paul. The first one of those I want to talk about is, "I'll Fight Hell to Hold You." I believe that was initially based on a Paul riff. Do you remember anything about how that song came to be?
That whole climb (sings the section) that was something I came up with and then I had some chord ideas for the verse. The rest, really Adam and Paul ran with and I was happy if that's all I sparked. Although they're important pieces it's not the entire song. I was pretty excited about that track, but man, is it a high vocal! What a crazy vocal on that! I liked Adam Mitchell a lot, we still stay in touch and I thought he worked really well with Paul as well at that time. I probably had some ideas and got together with Paul at his house when in the zone working with Adam as well. So, that's how that came about.

Back in 1987, this was one of the songs that kind of stopped me in my tracks with how high Paul was singing on this album. He really had range and power that's absolutely incredible. When you were writing for "Crazy Nights" with Paul, or coming up with your own riffs and ideas on your

own, were you writing in that range in mind or was Ron and Paul trying different keys in the studio?
Most of the vocalists in bands at that time were in that range. So it was kind of where you were expected to sing; way up there in the stratosphere. It wasn't so much decided, "Let's put 'em way up there," you know. Paul was comfortable there and that era just produced a lot of that kind of stuff. I can't really remember if "Crazy Crazy Nights" was down a half step, I don't think it is, but I prefer KISS' music when we're down tuned a half step. It's closer to the Hendrix thing and it makes stuff a little heavier sounding but some of the pop stuff is 440, which is regular concert pitch. That record's probably more concert pitch than it should have been, but it doesn't matter, Paul could pull it off. It's great stuff that definitely represents 1987 for sure.

He certainly pulled it off. Someone recently posted a version of the song that was detuned half a step, which made for a really weird listening experience. All of a sudden the song becomes broader, more powerful and Paul's voice takes on a little bit more of a David Coverdale tone. What I think is interesting is, a good song is a good song is a good song. It doesn't ultimately matter where it's being sung.
There's a lot of times I have to manipulate the tuning of a track too. When I want to show guys that are going to perform with me a song that I only have a version that's in concert pitch, I can manipulate it does change the vibe a little bit, but it's still the same song and it works. I will add that with Bob Ezrin on "Revenge," there were no issues with anyone's vocal range. The point is, he did sometimes adjust keys just to make it feel more comfortable for what he felt the song needed, but it was not so much about the singer. "Domino" is in 440 and on "Alive III" we're down a half step. On that tour, Gene, and that low stuff doesn't sound as good as it does on the record. But we cut it in concert pitch cause it sounded best there. I think there are also songs on "Revenge" that are a whole step down because it felt better for the

song. So experimenting with that is important, but back in the "Crazy Nights" album days with Nevison, we didn't really look at changing a key as long as the singer sounds like that era.

I'm curious, have you ever heard the Rod Gonzalez disco version of the song that came out in 2000? For me it kind of proves the point about a song being a good song regardless of how it's interpreted.
I think someone did share that recently. It's very odd.

During the recording of the album, what sort of guidance were you given for the solos, if any? Were you just said, "You're Bruce, you know what to do?" Or did you ever get any, "No, no, no, that's the wrong direction?"
By then I was very comfortable in the band and I don't remember being micromanaged like I was on "Asylum." Both Gene and Paul had very specific approaches with things. With Ron producing the record, they took a bit more of a back seat. The only thing that was interesting, was what you do solo wise. Everybody that records knows that sometimes you take one, two, or three stabs at the solo, and then you can combine them. They call that comping. You do it with vocals, and you could do it with lead guitar especially. Anyway we were comping between a few solos, and I knew where I wanted him to switch — because I'm very critical of my playing and I always want me to sound the best — and he didn't understand where I wanted him to do the switch and it was getting him a little frustrated. So he just said, using a bad word, "You do it!" Back then it was a magnetic tape machine and you have to anticipate a little bit — Pro Tools cut and paste didn't exist. So I did it, and then he looked at me and he just said, "Why didn't you tell me that?" That kind of thing was a joke. When you're talking guitar riffs and talking measures and beats, it's not like I gave him bar two on the second beat of bar two! I didn't do that, maybe I didn't explain it well enough.

Certainly, he'd be capable, but I wasn't communicating it well enough to him. So I did it and then he was a little bit of a snarky reply. But and it was kind of funny because Paul was watching this whole thing. He knew what happened. Later on, he said, "Don't take that to heart. Nevison respects you, don't worry about it." I didn't take it badly, I'm glad I stood for myself and he challenged me. If I wasn't able to show him what I wanted, then I'd look like the fool! But I wasn't trying to make him look foolish, I just wanted to show him this move to this track right at this moment would be the better switch of going from track one to track two. It was a funny stressful moment, but it turned out all good in the end. Actually, I am very positive that Nevison told Gene and Paul very good things about me and didn't have to suffer through much with me. That album and working with Nevison gave Gene and Paul even more confidence in me, and appreciate me more. And that meant a lot to me, of course.

The overall impression I get from what Ron has said about the album is that the experience working with KISS was overall a very positive experience for him. It was not a painful, even if things didn't quite live up to expectations. The process, the function, the business was all as good as you could want from a band.
The things that stand out the most about that album is the story I just told you about comping a solo and then Gene's face when Ron was adding that sample. Otherwise, it was just hard work and to do a record, I was on pins and needles when the songs were going to be chosen, because, like we just discussed "Sword and Stone" didn't make it. But I was happy with the record. You know Ron did a good job working with us and I liked when the band used an outside producer. It was less about the way Gene and Paul can get in the in the sandbox as brothers in business can do. They're like brothers, but they fight sometimes and they don't always see things eye to eye. And yet they love each other and totally respect each other. So having that other person there, ultimately in

charge it, takes off some of that stress. If you look at a band like a family, I'm happier as one of the kids! It's managed in a different way, how the creative process happens.

Paul's described some of his personal challenges with Gene at this time in his autobiography. Gene has also described some negativity towards the album and the keyboards in particular. Both Philip Ashley and Gary Corbett have also described that negativity towards keyboards. How do you appraise how Gene coping with his role at the time? You co-wrote two songs with him, was he "Well, if Paul wants keyboards, then I have to do a certain thing?"
I don't think Gene was trying to compromise the record in any way or even compete differently. If it did inspire Gene to work a little harder, good, but I don't think he was trying to overcompensate. There was no, "These songs are going to have keyboards, so mine are going to be such-and-such." I don't remember that sort of attitude. With a lot of Gene's material, you couldn't imagine a keyboard anyway with his musical point of view or style. Paul wanted to be broader. I liked the way Van Halen was using keyboards and I always enjoyed bands like Journey, and I'm a big fan of Yes. There's probably ten other examples of great keyboard parts in melodic rock music so I didn't have an issue with that.

Let's talk about some of your co-writes with Gene for the album?
One was "Hell or High Water," which was an AC/DC-ish vibe meets RATT. That's the way I looked at that song; it had the big chorus and the verse was very indicative of that era. It was something I came up with in one of the rehearsal rooms.

"No, No, No" was you, Eric, and Gene.
That was really a coordinated effort with Eric Carr because he loved that double bass drum exciting thing and needed some flashy guitar. We all worked hard together on that. That's a good balance, if you think about it, to a song like "Reason to

Live." If you think we're all going to be syrupy and pop, listen to "No, No, No!" I think that's Gene just being in his zone and not trying to overcompensate or anything, or do something different. Let's not forget that Paul wrote "God of Thunder." So he's certainly capable of the heavy dark song too, but it was sometimes better for Gene to deliver the message.

Without a doubt, it seemed more natural coming from Gene whereas Paul best presented the soaring anthems and power ballads. "Hell or High Water" is one of my favorite Gene vocals from the unmasked era. To my ears, he seemed really comfortable singing and the vocal seems totally natural. You mentioned in your 25th anniversary feature that Gene plays bass on the song. Did you play any bass on the album?
I do not remember any bass playing for "Crazy Nights." With "Hell or High Water," there was an interesting thing about the demo that we did which was very similar to the track we cut with Nevison. Of course, it sounds more professional and tighter with Nevison and there might have been a couple of little changes, but it was basically the same. It's funny how I always heard the title being "Come Hell or High," followed by riff, riff, riff, riff, riff, riff, right, and then "water," going over that. It was a different timing in that section and Gene actually heard it in a different spot. When we were doing the demo, I did understand where he was putting it and I didn't like it at all. I was really grateful that he didn't persistent about where he heard when we were working on the demo. Fortunately, the demo came out the way I heard it originally. Otherwise, that song was pretty straight ahead and it's a fun track to play.

It even got played a couple of times during the tour, just a couple of times, but didn't seem to last.
Like I said about "Asylum," we would try new songs and they don't go over with the audience well enough, well... That should have or could have been a great concert track, but it

wasn't. There was sometimes a disconnect with our fans that I could never understand why they didn't react to the new songs from new records.

You guys never know how the audience is going to react to new songs. Songs that fell good in the rehearsals might leave blank faces in the audience regardless of the quality of the performance or energy. They just don't resonate. On the "Crazy Nights" tour, you played six songs from that album live, which was certainly impressive. One of the other songs performed during the tour was another of your co-writes, "When Your Walls Come Down." What do you remember about that song? That started with some of your ideas that were finished off by Paul and Adam. Again, the song has the big anthemic choruses expected for the era. I think you've mentioned that they kind of took your idea, ran with it and completed it. So did the song realize your initial vision?
I remember mostly contributing some verse movements in that song and I don't remember any big riff contribution. I thought the direction that Paul and Adam took it was quite exciting because it definitely seemed that *this* is definitely where Paul wants to be with Ron Nevison. That made me happy it got picked up. If anything, at that era of KISS, I will admit that I was very influenced by Eddie Van Halen, which was not inappropriate. I had respect for Richie Sambora, but he certainly wasn't an idol to me like Eddie was who the next guy after Clapton and Hendrix and Jimmy Page who turbo charged rock 'n roll. I've talked about this in some books that discuss that era — Eddie was the guy. I could tell that he listened to Eric Clapton. I could tell that he loved the stuff that really inspired me to be a lead player. But he had made it his own and then it's like he became the Super Charged Camaro! He just ran with his finger tapping and whammy bar stuff that Hendrix couldn't do. There was no device like a Floyd Rose then. But I really feel like even the chordal way, the ways that Eddie played he was very knowledgeable.

There was no mystery why he wound up on a million guitar magazine covers. Eddie is a real a real icon of rock 'n roll.

Bruce, with you just mentioning Eddie, where did players like Randy Rhoads fall for you? And did they have any influence in how you approached your playing?
That's come up in a lot of interviews and actually I think to be honest I kind of feel with Randy, I respected him, but I didn't have the same passion for him like I did with Eddie Van Halen. Randy's amazing technique and double and triple tracking things was based more on a classical point of view. I thought what he created for Ozzy was incredible and perfect, but Eddie's thing was based more on Eric Clapton and the British sound; there was more string bending and it was coming from a different root. That was more what I responded to. So it's not like I didn't respect Randy, I did, but I more wanted to learn how did Eddie do *that*!

In the mid-1980s, it's a time where you've got the George Lynches and all sorts of guitar warriors. Were there any of these like guitarists within that period that when their band came out with a new album, you'd be down to the store to get that to check out what they were doing on the guitar?
I really would hear it on the radio first usually. I always though Warren Demartini was a great guitarist. There were so many bands at the time. A lot of the bands that opened for us had really terrific players. Slaughter had a great guitar player [Ed. Tim Kelly]. When we had Winger open on the "Hot in the Shade" tour, those guys were also doing great guitar playing. I thought John Sykes was great on that Whitesnake album. Sadly you know, those guys didn't continue to work together. So a lot of those players... Every player that Ozzy had was great, from Jake E. Lee, who also worked with, with Eric Singer. You know, all those guys could play. Even when Brad Gillis, the Night Ranger guy, first filled in... Just tremendous guitar players. There was a lot of that very flashy and exciting lead guitar work going around. But then some of

the bands that were the biggest, C. C. DeVille wouldn't be an influence, even though I know he was a big fan of people like me and other people. But Poison was huge because they had these great songs and with Brett Michaels being the perfect front man. Mötley Crüe always had great stuff too.

Mick Mars is vastly underrated; he remains one of my favorite players from the time.
I was friends with Nikki through that year and we'd talk about Mick. All these guys back then, they wouldn't make me run out and buy something. I heard what they were doing, because for me what started it all were the players I just mentioned, Hendrix, Clapton, Page and Jeff Beck. Those original guys — that was really it for me.

"Crazy, Crazy Nights" obviously the big anthemic chorus song, has come back into the KISS' set in recent years. What do you think about that happening? Did you ever see that song becoming a KISS classic and them playing it 30 years later?
It deserves to be a classic, but it was always bigger in Europe than it was in America, very big in the UK apparently and then throughout Europe too. So for some fans that's the big track that means the most. I'm not surprised that they've revisited it — I think it's smart, especially with KISS, when they tour nearly every year overseas, they've got to do a song that's a big hit. So, no, I'm not surprised that it's so important. I remember Adam and Paul providing a demo of that track and I knew right away, "Wow, this has really got all the elements of a great pop tune, a great rock track." I was pretty excited about it. The only difference in the demo is it kept modulating towards the end. We didn't do that in the studio, so maybe Nevison didn't think that that was necessary. I bet you've probably read the interviews that either Adam or maybe even Paul have given where they say that they thought the demo was better than the track. I don't think it's all that radically different though to state the demo being

better than what we put out. But the spark and all the excitement of the track was in the demo, for sure. There's no mystery to me why the album is named after that song and it's still valid and important for KISStory even 30 years later.

I think the impression I get from the demo is that it's just not as polished. So the chorus feels bigger and it's got that original urgency, or energy, which you often lose when you take a demo into the studio to be recorded. You can't recapture that, as you said, initial spark. I guess one of my favorite songs on this album is "Turn on the Night," which I always felt to be pure power-pop perfection. Did you guys ever rehearse that one to perform it live? I know you did mime to it for the video shoot in Worcester, MA.
The video's pretty exciting, it's cool. That was a bummer that we didn't include it, and I don't know why and I don't ever remember us getting that serious with it. Of course, I remember playing it a million times for the crowd that we had for the concert that night, but we were miming it. It was a great song. Who did he write that with again?

That one was with Diane Warren...
She proved to be a formidable pop hit writer. It's a great song that I try to include that in my sets when I do dates. The reaction's always terrific. Ironically, that one I think on the record is down a half step. Maybe because of the vocals... Who knows, you know.

It's got great tempo, and again is just a very well-crafted pop song. Diane couldn't remember much about writing it, unfortunately, but Diane is DIANE in capital letters is Diane, so she's had so many hits she won't remember the misses.
Oh yeah.

I know sometimes fans get a kick out of Gene's writing, but he recycled all of "Thief in the Night" that had been recorded by Wendy O. Williams in 1984. Were you aware

that he was digging into his back catalog when that song gets on the album?
I think I was and maybe Paul didn't, but it didn't matter. I know Gene always does that and there's nothing wrong with that. There are many, many bands where a terrific song on a record that just never saw the light of day was actually on another album in some different form. I didn't see any negative about that. Maybe that was one of the ones that Paul was really surprised about, but there's nothing wrong with taking a song and just digging it out from the past. Nothing wrong at all...

Another one of Gene's song is "Good Girl Gone Bad." A lot of the stuff in the mid-80s by Gene is often considered to be not quite up to standard. I think there's an improvement to his contributions on "Crazy Nights" over the previous two albums in particular. What did you think of his contributions to the album? Did you think, "Ooh, this is better than 'Asylum'," or was it more simply, "this is a good song?"
We did talk earlier about whether or not because of Nevison and the keyboards that Gene maybe changed his game. Maybe he was just working harder because Nevison was involved. I don't really know or he was tired of the kind of back seat attitude from Paul. Because he was so driven to do other things that had nothing to do with KISS product, but I can't really put my finger on why Gene might have come up with some better songs for "Crazy Nights" than he did in other years. But he certainly did and that's what's important.

"No, No, No" is a song that I did not like back in 1987. Surprisingly, it's grown on me over the years watching all the tour bootlegs and seeing how important it was to the performance and show. How fun was song that for you to perform? You look like you're having a good time, just letting fly on the guitar and doing your thing. Then there's the also the jam section you perform with Eric. Was it a fun song for you to do on the tour?

I know the essence of recording it in the first place was always Eric really liking double bass drum Van Halen kind of thing, and then Gene making one of his tongue in cheek statements throughout, and it's got those riffs that stop and start up in the verses. It's very much a perfect vehicle for Gene. And even if Paul didn't like it, now imagine that we're taking that to live shows and putting it on stage and making it a spot where I can be featured. Then I'm turning it over to Eric, which really made the song even more valuable in the KISS catalog — it became something of a centerpiece in the live concert. So, of course I would look like I was having a good time! Here's the guitarist and the drummer, not the two original guys, having a good time with a song from a current record. It's just another valuable thing that I helped contribute that I think turned into even a better thing live.

Another thing you did onstage during the tour was play some keyboards. Were you actually playing keyboards while Gary was with you on the tour?
Gary was featured, but I actually did play and I could hear myself a bit. But it was more to show, "All right, this is where it's coming from." I took keyboard lessons when I was younger and it's kind of funny, I remember Nikki Sixx being very impressed when I sat down at his grand piano in his house and played a couple of things. I used to know the standard "Misty" on piano and I could play a little bit of a Beatles song. Stuff like that, but I only really knew how to play a few songs well. I did understand the mechanics of a keyboard, but I worked with so many amazing keyboard players that I could never represent myself as a keyboard player. It was helpful to have Gary there, especially for a song like that, but also he could let Paul perform a little more. We used to have a great sample on the keyboard that sounded very guitarlike and he knew what notes to play to make it seem as if he's also playing rhythm guitar on the keyboard.

That was the beauty of Gary's contribution offstage. There was another tour where we had a different guy, Derek Sherinian. That's the role that keyboards would play offstage for KISS. We did feature a keyboard onstage for "Reason to Live," and there I was with a guitar slung around my side and there I was playing keyboard chords. Then I would switch to the guitar. It was kind of cool, but I'm not representing to anyone that it was mostly me they were hearing. I did know how to play those chords, but I had enough pressure holding and switching to the guitar. Gary was the one with the burden of having the big keyboard pads be featured in the in the house.

It always surprised me; "Reason to Live" went Top 40 in the U.K. As an English guy it was a really cool thing to see because with Donington, the band in Kerrang, 12" singles and picture disks everywhere, it really seemed to me that KISS was everywhere! Paul's power ballads through the 1980s seemed to get stronger and stronger with each album. You got "Who Wants to be Lonely" and "Tears are Falling "on "Asylum" followed by "Reason to Live." What do you think of that song?
I think "Reason to Live" is beautiful, it's a great track. I cannot tell you what an amazing reaction I got from my wife, Lisa, and I performing it in New York. It went over incredible. We did that one in Indy also, but New York had a really huge crowd. We had a real good audience at the end of the day at the New York Expo, the one that Peter Criss was at, and the P.A. showed up a little late so things got started a little late. But "Reason to Live" was our first number and it went over great. People loved that, but, it was a challenge just playing it solo on an electric acoustic guitar with my wife. I realized it's well written and it's got a great vocal. It's just a great song.

It has certainly held up well and does not sound dated. When you were on tour were there any special effects that were part of your setup for the guitar?

I think during that era I actually might have had just to complement the Marshall head that I was using. I might have had even a Rockman set up, because I do remember something about a gig with Ted Nugent and him seeing that and us talking about it. Otherwise, I didn't do much effect wise. I might have had the opportunity to add a little chorus thing in, not on the Marshall but onto the Rockman, because that's a line in and out. So you could add an effect to it very easily from the rack. Then you can just press a button and there it is. Maybe I had a little chorus effect when I did the intro of "No, No, No." But most of the time with KISS, it was pretty straight forward where I was just loud through a Marshall. I'd have fun switching guitars. I was playing a lot of those ESPs but the gear was straight ahead. You know, I'd go, usually go center stage, go loud for the solo and then run around like a maniac. That was the era where you ran around the stage; just don't bump into Gene or Paul!

It doesn't look like you're doing a lot of guitar switching in concert videos. Did you keep it pretty simple, or were only doing a switch here and there for a song in a different key rather than any other consideration?
Now you have me wanting to go look at an entire "Crazy Nights" concert on video! I remember with Tokyo it was mostly a red Horizon and I always really liked those. I still play some. But that red one, I also had a Sunburst one I remember taking to Europe. Obviously the Floyd guitars worked the most because that was that era. Remember we were talking about Van Halen too, so I probably focused more on that. I also had my "Banana" guitar made, the yellow ESP, which made some appearances too, like at the Ritz show. I can remember the "Asylum" guitars, but I'm trying to remember with "Crazy Nights" though I'm pretty sure it was a lot of the Horizons and the "Banana" guitar, which was an M1. I'm not even sure if I had anything that was really Gibson-related on that tour or not.

I don't remember seeing anything. I do to recall a wood grain ESP...
I'm glad you mentioned that one. That one probably only had one pickup in it though.

That's right.
I do remember that. That was a natural ash body that eventually did get painted and put together differently. Then it didn't sound good, and I wound up donating it for a big charity called the T.J. Martell Foundation, which was very popular back in the day. That had a gold Floyd Rose on it too, so that was like an M1 from ESP guitars.

Would you generally just play a guitar on stage until it went out of tune?
No. I thought I liked certain guitars for certain songs. I got a little worse with it later on where I switched more often, but some of it might have been comfort. That whole era I was very much into the ESPs and having a Floyd Rose, so if there was one that was sounding right I'd stick with it. Fortunately I still have that Sunburst one that I still really love. The red one I got rid of years ago, sadly, but I think I like the Sunburst one better. But it's funny, you do get attached to certain instruments and it's very hard for me to explain why. It's funny.

The some guitarists sand the back of the neck and some scallop the frets out or fiddle with the pickups. Did you do anything like that with your guitars?
No, my ESPs were all stock. I would get a little bit specific about a certain Seymour Duncan guitar pickup, but most of the time I didn't have to get too nuts with anything.

Let's jump back to the album for a minute, specifically "My Way." Even with the high vocals, I love the positive message Paul has often put into his songs. That's the one song where

I really like the keyboards, the guitars, and all of the elements that represent "Crazy Nights" coming together.

"My Way" was really interesting. It's not my favorite track from "Crazy Nights," but I always thought the title was funny because I was very aware that was also the title of a Frank Sinatra song. But of course the song is rock, and it doesn't sound anything like Frank's thing

Is there a song in this period that just makes you think that is the quintessential Paul Stanley?

To me it's "Crazy Crazy Nights." Whenever Paul's just embodying that whole rock and roll spirit that is so indicative of what KISS represents to so many fans, he's hitting a grand slam. There's no doubt that a song like "Crazy Nights," and then on the softer side something like "Reason to Live" just fits perfectly. The tongue in cheek, "Bang Bang You" and stuff like that is always fun on a KISS album. But I do think "Crazy Crazy Nights" really sums up that album the best.

I'm glad you've briefly mentioned "Bang Bang You," because I did not mention that song all throughout this interview, and I do apologize. My reaction in 1987, I'm sitting at a bus stop and that song comes on, with the "Shoot you down with my love gun" lyric. Even at 15 I just shook my head a little bit on that one...

Me too and we used to do it live. I was really kind a surprised, but look, I did whatever we did. I enjoyed playing all the KISS songs. I rarely had any kind of issue with any of them, so it was just part of the tongue in cheek KISS thing. Just remember we used to do "Fits Like a Glove," with the breakdown that Gene sang, "like a hot knife through butter!" When I watch that stuff now, I really giggle. There was a time when I was maybe a little embarrassed watching it later, but now I enjoy it. I enjoy it all. It's not a big deal.

Oh, I'd agree now. I'm not 15 anymore so I can appreciate it a bit more for what you were trying to do. So, are you going

to do anything to celebrate the 30th anniversary of "Crazy Nights?"

Ultimately I've been at work on this concept for over a year now, so on my website (www.kulick.net) and on all Social Media like Facebook, I'll be announcing two special Platinum and Gold packages. The Platinum package will be limited to twelve actual "Banana" guitars made by ESP from the Korean World LTD factory — which makes it much more affordable. That's a replica of my "Banana" guitar known from the back cover of "Crazy Nights." It's kind of ironic, my wife and I realized that if you Google "banana guitar," my guitar shows up, which is really cool! It got that nickname over the years from it being yellow, and probably being a non-vintage Gibson instrument. It's my most important guitar and one of the best sounding Floyd Rose-style rock guitars that I have in my collection. I'm very proud to offer a limited replica of that. Every detail is as close as possible to the original. Only twelve of those will available in the limited platinum package in 2017. They'll be signed, with a COA, and there will be an 8 x 10 color photo and double-sided photo pick pack included. Also included will be a mini "Banana" guitar replica made by Axe Heaven.

That's a company that you may or may not be familiar with, but they've done a lot mini versions of iconic guitar players' instruments. It's a miniature replica of the banana guitar. The mini guitar is also the gold package. That will come with the photo pick pack as well and is limited to just a hundred worldwide, with a signed and numbered COA. So, those are the two things that are my commemorative 30th Anniversary "Crazy Nights" offerings for the fans that I've been planning that's finally going to be a reality. I don't do a lot of stuff like that. You know, I've always offered my albums, CDs and 8 x 10 photos on my website or at expos, but I've never really put together something that's specific to a particular milestone in my career. So I wanted it to be done right! Everybody that has a "Crazy Nights" album knows I'm holding

my "Banana" guitar on the back cover and they can find videos of me playing that guitar. There are many photos of me the studio and it's probably one of the most identifiable with my career with KISS, even though I probably played about 50 guitars. But I really do love that, that instrument, and I'm really excited to offer these packages because of the 30th Anniversary of "Crazy Nights."

That rear cover photo is an iconic image. You're not holding that guitar, you're embracing it!
Yes, I am!

One final question I have to ask, relates to the Gene Simmons' Vault coming out. Do you have anything of interest on there that he's come to you about?
There are co-writes with me, and of course there's some performances from me besides the songs that I may have co-written. Gene did have me up to his house and he played me a little snippet of every song. Of course the ones we talked about the most were the ones that I was involved with, but he wanted me to hear a little bit of everything, which was some ways exhausting, but exciting. It's a fascinating offering so I'm happy but when we went over it he didn't have all the details of how he was going to sell it exactly, just that he was going to be putting it out. I wish him the best with it. It is very interesting and it's quite immense, the amount of music on there to digest. I'm obviously real excited that I'm part of it of course.

So you feel well represented on it?
Actually there are some other songs that I reminded him of, that we worked on that didn't make this box set. But I'm fine with what's on there. I think it's really cool.

What about yourself in terms of music? It's been quite a while and since you released the stunning BK3 album. I've never got to tell you in person, thank you so much for that

album. What's next for you musically? Do you have any plans or intend to do another solo album?
It's a great question and I have thought about it many times. I have been so busy making music live which is the best way to make a living. And I think everyone's aware that physical sales are very bad for even the biggest bands in the world. Digital streaming doesn't pay and a lot of people listen to music that way. So that's why you see a big disconnect in many artists going into the studio and recording new product. Part of the problem is the fact that if I actually spent the amount of money I usually need to do a record up front, I very possibly would not recoup even a third of it. That is really sad. So it's not something that makes good business sense. My idea was that I could do pledge music or one of those things where you raise the funds first. But I'm the kind honest, polite person that would never want to ask anybody for money unless I had the ten songs ready. So I have songs that I like that could be used for a BK4, but I don't have ten ready. I also don't have a clear direction and haven't completely formulated what and how I would want to do it. So that's the long story. The short story is, yes I do have a desire to do that. A lot of people now just put out songs, or singles; and anyone that's followed me on social media would know that I put out a single back in April with my wife Lisa.

That was "If I Could Show You," which Lisa sings lead on. It's available on iTunes?
I put it as her name, Lisa Lane Kulick featuring Bruce Kulick, but I wrote the song and am playing all the guitars on the song and the bass. I was real excited to do it, but I don't have a physical version of it yet. I will do some more things with Lisa in the future, but it doesn't necessarily mean that's my BK4. I want to do it all! I have this love for standards and pop music and lots of things, acoustic music and jazz music! I should go on record in saying it's the biggest year for Grand Funk — in the sense of how many dates we're doing — which keeps me on the road, besides the fact I went to Australia

and have a trip to Finland and Norway coming up later in the year. So you see, I stay pretty busy and it's hard to be in the studio. I've done sessions for people, because that's easy — that's just an afternoon where I'm recording. I don't want anyone to think that I'm not interested in putting out new music. It's just been hard to logistically do it and then to make the plan. The way the music business has changed has probably been another big factor in keeping it a little frustrating for me to figure it out. I will say that brother Bob just put out a solo record. It's officially come out today, so I think everybody should go check that out.

You're on it, aren't you? It's titled "Skeletons in the Closet" and features four new songs, a cover, and five of Bob's favorite songs from his back catalog. You play bass I think on a track or two.
Yes, I play bass and co-wrote a song. It's only a minor way I'm on it. I think there's one of the other tracks I might have done some dueling guitars.

Yes, "Guitar Commandos" from Skull is one there.
It's got a great reaction in the press so I'm wishing him the best, you know. Of course we're going to be on the KISS Kruise together, and we'll be performing lots of cool songs on that.

Here's the million dollar question: Are you going to jam with Gene, Paul and Eric, for a "Revenge" era lineup reunion?
I know that's the big question that everybody asks me, so...

You're not going to answer it!
No, I can't answer it because I have no idea outside of knowing that I'm committed to be on the "KISS Konfidential World Panel" and I do a set with my brother, which I'm really gearing up for. I don't know what else could happen. I have no idea!

This is KISS. Anything could happen. Everything is possible, but nothing is promised.
Exactly.

Ron Nevison

By Tim McPhate

Just months after the "Asylum" tour, in summer 1986, Paul Stanley was already mulling the direction of the next KISS album. Though the in-house produced "Asylum" crept past gold status, Stanley was taking note of bands such as Bon Jovi, Poison, Heart, and Ozzy Osbourne, who were all racing up the charts with hit singles and multi-platinum albums. He wanted KISS to get in on the action. He knew he needed a hot producer to help him toward this goal. He wanted Ron Nevison.

Nevison's discography reads like a who's who of classic rock royalty, including work with the Who, Led Zeppelin, Bad Company, Thin Lizzy, and the Rolling Stones, among others. By the time the calendar turned to 1987, he was fresh from resuscitating the career of Heart, who sold millions on the strength of four hit singles from their 1985 Nevison-produced self-titled album. Nevison was in such high demand throughout late 1986 and early 1987, KISS (read: Paul Stanley) chose to hold their new album until his schedule was clear. The resulting fruit of Nevison/KISS' labor was "Crazy Nights." True to 1987-style rock, there are big guitars, shout-along choruses, shredding solos, ample keyboards, well-crafted songs, and polished production. The album finds Stanley's powerful voice in fine form, particularly on the singles "Crazy Nights," "Reason to Live" and "Turn on the Night." After recording was completed on "Crazy Nights," the band thought they had hit a home run. "Everybody was really excited," recalls Nevison.

While "Crazy Nights" would ultimately yield platinum-plus sales, the hit single to catapult the album to multi-platinum status in the United States eluded KISS. The aforementioned

"Reason to Live" only managed No. 64 position on the Billboard Hot 100. Fan opinions of "Crazy Nights" varied across the board, with detractors criticizing Nevison's polished, keyboard-friendly mix. Even Stanley put on a pair of hindsight headphones. "I think it's a bit plastic-sounding," he once remarked. "The material, and what it could have been, was better than what it turned out to be."

When peppered with questions on "Crazy Nights" a quarter century later, Nevison stands by the album and offers no apologies. Nor should he. The fact is that "Crazy Nights" cracked the Top 20 in five countries, hitting No. 4 in the UK, KISS' highest-charting album there ever. The title track matched the album's performance, climbing to No. 4 on the UK singles chart. As far as Nevison is concerned, he delivered exactly what was asked of him. And the only thing that got in the way of that home run, multi-platinum album was ... KISS.

Tim McPhate: Before we get to "Crazy Nights," can you share your first recollections of KISS? Do you remember the first time you became aware of KISS?
Ron Nevison: I don't think I remember the first time. When did KISS start?

Their debut album was released in 1974.
1974. I was in England until about 1975. But in the late '70s I did have an interview to do Paul Stanley's solo album so I was obviously aware of their impact by then.

Do you recall anything about the interview and why you didn't end up working on the album?
I remember the interview was at Casablanca with Neil Bogart. And I had just done an album with Dave Mason. And I remember Neil showing me what they had planned, a Mylar album cover, and they were going to cost like a $1 each. I don't remember if it was that much, but it was a lot. And I

remember going to Columbia and fighting with them to do a laminate on Dave's record for like 5 cents each. (Laughs) So it's the irony in the way things were marketed by the old establishment Columbia and the upstart Casablanca. But as to why I didn't end up working with Paul at that time, I don't know.

Fast-forwarding to 1986, who was it that approached you in terms of working with KISS?
I think they contacted my manager, Michael Lippman — it may have been either Mercury or Paul. I was just working on the Heart "Bad Animals" album and I had this girlfriend, and she was a model. And around Labor Day, she had a film shoot in Aspen. So I went there with her because it's a beautiful place. While she was working I was nosing around, and I rented a house for Christmas and New Year's. And we broke up around Halloween and I was stuck with this house. And I asked Paul, and Paul said, "Yeah, I'll share it with you. I'm not doing anything special for the holidays." So we went up there for a couple of weeks and shared a house and had a real good time getting to know each other and hanging out. That was cool. Then the album we did, probably, the following spring.

While in Aspen, was it confirmed that you were producing the next KISS album?
I don't remember if it was a done deal. I think it was. They had decided they were going to use me and they had to wait until I was finished with whatever I was doing. We actually went halves on a private plane home. We had a great time.

Getting into the album, what was the process of going through the material and deciding what would be recorded or worked on during the sessions?
Gene just gave me everything. (Laughs) He loaded me up with 20, I don't know, 25 songs. And Paul was much more discerning in terms of what he let me hear. Gene just let me hear everything. And I told him what I liked and what I didn't

like. There were some odd songs — there was one song I remember called "I'm Going To Put A Log In Your Fire Place." (Laughs)

Paul, to my recollection, wanted to make a different kind of album. You know, with the success that Bon Jovi was having in writing with Desmond Child and other bands — I had taken Ozzy down that road with his first hit single in years, if ever, "Shot In The Dark," in 1986. And of course, Heart. I was actually very pleased with the material on ["Crazy Nights"]. And I took some heat after that album because of the keyboards.

Can you describe the recording process for the basic tracks on "Crazy Nights?"
Well, we laid down drums, bass, guitar and a vocal [guide track]. Now, I don't remember exactly that Bruce played rhythm or Paul played the rhythm. I think I probably had Bruce play so Paul could sing his songs. That's how I usually do it. You know, I've had 45 albums since then ... (laughs) I think we used One and One [Recording], which had a good drum room, but we didn't stay there long. We went to Rumbo Recorders out in the [San Fernando] Valley. And [then] it was Captain & Tennille's studio. It had a big lounge, and had a lot of room in the studio for guitars and a full Neve board. It was just a comfortable place to work. So that's we did a majority of the recording. During that period of time, I did lots of albums there.

Ron, you touched on one of my questions. In 1987 rock acts such as Heart, Poison, Def Leppard, Bon Jovi...
They saw what they were doing with "Livin' on a Prayer" and all that. And I wanted to get KISS that same level of — you know, instead of selling 500,000 to 700,000 records, which is respectable, especially these days — I wanted it to be bigger than that. I was impressed with the stuff that Paul [brought in]. You know, Gene's stuff was Gene's stuff. Gene wrote rock

stuff, but not commercial really, but KISS fans love Gene's songs.

Do you think Paul was coming from an angle where he wanted to write songs that were in line with what other bands were writing?
Yeah, I think so. I think that was the goal. And I think it was a great album. My favorite songs are "Crazy Nights," "Reason to Live" and "My Way." Those are my favorites. The Diane Warren was a good song.

A lot has been said over the years about Gene's acting career and outside interests during this time. Do you recall him being focused or were his outside projects a distraction in terms of his commitment?
Well, this was the only album I did with them. I do know that Gene wasn't there all the time. Obviously Bruce was, and to some extent, Eric. Mostly, a majority of the work on that album I did with Bruce and Paul. The bass tracks were cut initially, and Gene was only needed for lead vocals. I must say that most of the time he was there, he was in the back of the studio reading "Variety."

Did Gene play bass on all of the tracks on "Crazy Nights"?
From what I remember, yes, he played. I must say, having a master player like Bruce Kulick made it easy for the entire band...

Guitar-wise, Bruce really shines on this album. Do you recall any songs in which you helped guide Bruce's solos? Or did he pretty much have carte blanche with his ideas?
Total carte blanche. You know, I don't guide people. I don't sit down with a guitar player and say, "I want you to play this," because that blows whatever thoughts they might have in their head. I was that way with everybody. If I have a really good idea for a part, I shut up and I see what they do, because I want them to blow my mind. If somebody fumbles

around for 15 minutes, I'll say, "Why don't you try this?" You know, I have the idea but I don't have to ever tell anybody I've got the idea. I don't use the idea unless I have to. Basically, I'd let them go. Then I'd do comps. Comps of vocals and comps of guitars. Then I'd take six or eight takes and comp a "best of." Sometimes somebody plays it the first time. A lot of times they play a good guitar solo the first time, right out of the box, because they're warming up and they're not thinking too hard. Thinking hurts you.

What about Eric Carr? How does he rank in terms of the drummers you've worked with?
I don't like to rank people, because they're all too different. But Gene and Paul, once they disbanded the original lineup ... I mean Eric and Bruce; you couldn't find two greater, nicer guys. In fact, all of them ... Gene, Paul — they're the most wonderful, professional band to work with. No drugs. No alcohol. No bulls***. I have to say, it was just a pleasure to work with them.

Paul was really singing at the top of his range on "Crazy Nights." In listening to songs such as the title track, "I'll Fight Hell to Hold You" and "My Way," he really stretched himself. How did you approach recording Paul's vocals for the album?
I actually wasn't that happy with all the keys that Paul chose. But he wanted to sing it as high as he could sing it.

Really?
Yeah, he thought that was the way to go. And in listening back to a little bit of the album today, especially "Crazy Nights" with the modulation ...

That goes up a step and a half ...
He got up there. And there was no Auto-Tune in those days. It was like 10 years before Pro Tools and all that stuff. And there was really no other way but to keep recording it. I

would have felt more comfortable if a couple of the songs had been a half-step down, or something to make it easier on him. But he wanted it like that and the songs were written like that and demoed like that. That's the way he wanted to do it. I went along with it, and as far as performance goes, he did a great job.

And it was the most successful album that they did in the '80s. It was big in England; it was big in Scandinavia. I expected more out of "Reason to Live." As you know, to get a hit single in those days, you had to have some kind of ballad. There was no other way. I thought "Reason to Live" was that ballad, and it did ok, but it didn't quite catch on. I think there was still a reluctance amongst CHR stations, which was Contemporary Hit Radio in those days, to play a song by KISS. Not based on the merit, but based on the fact that their listeners didn't listen to KISS.

In hindsight, it seems like "Reason to Live" should have fared better. I've always felt it was as good, if not better than many of the ballads that were hits at the time.
It's gorgeous. I was very disappointed. I was happy with how it came out, but it didn't become a hit. And if we had a big hit, ["Crazy Nights"] would have sold another couple of million records. I thought "Reason to Live" was the right single. It was a passionate, emotional song. It rocked a bit. It was perfect.

This reminds me of a quote I've read from you in which you said that you had the name "KISS" going against you in terms of pop radio success.
Certainly. I know how they operated then. I know how the system worked. I know how the promoters promote. I knew how all those people got artists on the radio in that time period, 1985 –1990. And suddenly that formula didn't work with KISS. Look, "Shot In The Dark" wasn't a huge smash. The fact that he had never had a single was a big factor. Something like "Crazy Nights," I don't know it was Top 5 in

the UK. Obviously it did affect some kind of playlists and some stations.

When AOR radio was big in the U.S., there [was] nothing like pop radio for selling albums, if you had a hit single. That's why I was really happy with the material. Because I thought "Crazy Nights" was a single. And I thought "Reason to Live" was a single. I also thought "My Way" was a single. But it was out of my hands. It's the vaunted record company promotion guys and what they want to do. Having said that, Paul and Gene have taken KISS a very, very, very long way. You know coming up with the concept. And then with taking off the makeup, changing players, putting the makeup back on. They've really reinvented themselves over and over again. And having one of the biggest grossing tours. They have lots and lots of things to be proud of.

I'm curious, when you hear "Reason to Live," do you hear elements of Foreigner's "I Want to Know What Love Is"?
Huh. There is a little bit. (Sings melodies of both choruses) I've never even thought about that. That wasn't the intention.

What do you recall about "Turn on the Night"? That was co-written by Paul and Diane Warren, who typically writes all of her own material. Were you the catalyst in getting them together?
I don't recall. I had hits with Diane after that with Chicago.

"Look Away."
Right, "Look Away." And "I Don't Want To Live Without Your Love." I think that predated that.

"Turn on the Night" was the third video/single from the album. It really seems like that song should have performed better as well.

Oh yeah. I think it's a great album. You know, Tim, I tried to do what was right for 1987 for that band. And I think I succeeded.

In terms of the album's sonics, I think you've admitted, in hindsight, that you would have mixed the synthesizers down a bit and that it might be too "slick" or "soft" sounding.
I wasn't that happy with the final mix. But I wasn't that unhappy with it. I have to tell you, Tim, I'm not happy with any mix that I've done. I think I could have made it a bit more powerful sounding.

Some of the album's detractors have commented that the sonics are too similar to Heart's 1985 self-titled album and Ozzy's "The Ultimate Sin" album.
There you go. That's [the type of album] I make. That's what I do.

Exactly. In that sense, you delivered. KISS wanted Ron Nevison. They wanted that sound at the time and you gave it to them.
Yep. I have to say that I think as time goes on it will be more accepted and more liked because it has great songs. I think, song-wise, it really stands out as one of the best KISS albums ever, song-wise.

On their most recent tour, KISS actually added "Crazy Crazy Nights" to their set list. It was the first time they'd played it in 20 years.
I didn't know that. You know, I've actually never seen them live. I've just never been in the same city. Or when they're on tour, I've been somewhere else.

They did tune the song down. On the album, it's in the key of G, and they played it in F. Ron, is there one song, in

particular, that you would take off the album or replace, in hindsight?

I think we probably recorded more songs than we needed. I think there was another ballad. But I thought it would be suicide to put two ballads on the record. "Reason to Live" was a better song, I don't remember the title of the other one.

Let me run through some song titles of songs that were demoed around this time that didn't end up on the album. Do you have any recollections of these tracks? "Sword and Stone."

I think I remember that one.

Bruce has said he thinks you left a "great song" off the record.

Yeah, that's probably because he's one of the writers, and writers always think that. [Ed: The song was co-written by Paul, Desmond Child and Bruce.]

(Laughs) "Time Traveler."

Don't remember that one.

"Are You Always This Hot" — this song is purported to have been fully recorded for the album.

Well, I think we had to juggle how many of Paul's songs we had on the album and how many of Gene's. I don't think that song was finished though. I can't be sure of this, but I think we made decisions fairly early on in the recording about what was going on and what wasn't. I don't think we finished a bunch of tunes and then decided what was going to be on the album.

Do you recall any creative differences or arguments over songs between Gene and Paul?

You know, it's a process that goes on. It's not something that comes down to that ever. The process is [a band] sends me all the material and I listen to it all and we decide pretty

much ahead of time what's happening. It's not decided when we get in the studio, it's decided before we get there. And if there's a couple of extra tracks, we'll do those. I don't remember that part of it [with KISS]; I'm just giving you what I usually do.

I don't remember any situation where there was any disagreement between the two of them over anything. But certainly I am there to give my opinion, and they're there to say yes or no on that opinion. That's how it all works. I'm working for them.

Do you recall the general atmosphere as you completed the project? Were spirits high that you had something "big" on your hands?
Oh yeah. We were in New York with the management company, and I remember we had a playback party. Everybody was really excited.

It's tough to word this next question because a platinum album is nothing to be ashamed about. But obviously KISS sought you out because they were looking for a home run like the 1985 Heart album, which eventually sold five million copies...
Yeah, well because we had No. 1 singles. That's where I was trying to go. KISS was their own worst enemy as far as singles go. I have to tell you, by ignoring pop radio for 20 years, you just don't turn up and they let you on. By saying that we had keyboards, by saying, "We're not selling out," you don't work your way into those kind of radio spots. As far as it goes, if "Reason to Live" had done what "These Dreams" did, we would have sold five million. So how can you call a platinum-plus album anything but successful?

That's a very good question.
It was their most successful of the '80s, worldwide. That says it all right there.

Ron, did you ever have a thought of bringing complete songs in from outside writers for "Crazy Nights"?
I did not bring any outside material. Paul is the one who hooked up with Desmond. Paul is the one who hooked up with other writers. I did not bring any of those songs in.

Ron, what would be your message to KISS fans?
I hope they appreciate the reason I was hired and the position I was put in to make this [album]. I fought hard to get those kind of things played. And they did pretty good compared to other KISS singles. But it wasn't a home run in terms of Contemporary Hit Radio, and it never will be for KISS. But I tried.

Would you ever be game to remix the album?
Yeah. I would love that. I have to tell you, Tim. I got an email from Pete Townshend last year telling me that they were re-releasing the "Quadrophenia" album as a box set and they were going to use my original mix that sounds so much better than the remix in the '90s they had done. And I was thrilled they did that. And he emailed me to ask if I would be available for a BBC interview. So I came down to Los Angeles last November and went to Steakhouse Studio in North Hollywood. And I sat there and I thought they were just going to play me the "Quadrophenia" tracks and I was going to talk about them. But what they did was, they had the 16-track stems. In other words, I had all 16 tracks on the console so I could solo and listen to each individual track, and talk about the vocal or the guitar and bass parts, and drums. It freaked me out. I didn't know until I got there that they were going to do that. So that was really cool. But yeah, I would be open to it.

On Tour: Crazy Nights

With nearly 20 months passing between the end of the "Asylum" tour in April 1986 and the start of the "Crazy Nights" tour, KISS had enjoyed their longest break in their history. However, "enjoyed" may well be a completely inappropriate word to describe the circumstances the band faced during that interim period. While the situation is very well detailed, first hand, in C.K. Lendt's excellent "KISS & Sell," some other words fall into play, "urgency" and "hope" foremost among the many choices. "Crazy Nights" was a gamble. Wait for a producer and hope that he is able to replicate with KISS what he had successfully done with act such as Heart and Ozzy Osbourne. Hope for a hit single to drive album and concert ticket sales. And urgently prepare for that success with a stage-show worthy of the album. Also taken into consideration was the need to pair the band on the road with an appropriate opening act, one that could pull patrons to the show on their own — something that was becoming more important in the touring business and certainly something that had been missing from the opening acts of the previous few tours.

The idiom, "don't count your chickens before they're hatched," comes to mind. KISS were preparing for a "Slippery When Wet" success. While the band rehearsed in San Bernardino, CA, the tour initially planned to start in early November, with Paul commenting in Billboard, "We'll be out until every arena's been played and every ear has been deafened" (Billboard, 9/12/87). Commencement dates varied with Paul mentioning Nov. 5, and a brief mention in Billboard noting a date in Pensacola, FL on Nov. 3. Whatever the case, as final routing and scheduling was put together, the band hoped that the tour would be as mammoth as the album was expected to be; and planned to commence support with an

85-city schedule. With scheduling there was simply no way for the success of the album to be ascertained before the band hit the road. Therefore, the perceived necessary investment was being made for success at a time when the band were struggling financially. According to C.K. Lendt, "There was a kind of eerie calm to everything. KISS may have been teetering from all the bills that had piled up, but you'd never know it from the outside. KISS was rolling along, hoping that Crazy Nights would strike a vein of gold and bring them a mother lode of riches. But money was still tight" ("KISS & Sell").

While the album may have been born out of a desire for the band to, as Paul succinctly put it, "raise our standards to another level," the same really could not be side of the tour staging. While he suggested, "'It'll be the biggest show we've ever done. We're thinking about parking the cars in the arenas and taking over the parking lots for the shows" (Orlando Sentinel, 9/27/87), the show could hardly be considered much more than a natural progression from the previous tour — even while being visually striking and impressive. While the omnipresent "KISS" logo was suggested to have grown to some 50' in height, the reality was quite different. Such exaggerations had been a hallmark of the band's career so should never have been particularly surprising or insulting. One can't sell sizzle without superlatives. According to Paul, "This is by far the biggest show we've done. The stage is 88 feet wide, 60 feet deep. If I want to talk to Gene now, I use the telephone. It's fun; it's based on total chaos in some kind of framework. It's like controlled anarchy or something" (Charlotte Observer, 2/5/88). Perhaps one benefit in the extended layoff from the road was that memories of the "Asylum" and "Animalize" tours would have dimmed enough for the patrons to fully embrace the illusion of the "show of shows" when it visited their town. Even before the band set foot on the road visits to both Japan and Europe were planned as follow-ups to the

initial North American leg. 1988 would mark a decade since the previous visit to Japan, and Europe had been skipped during the 1985/6 touring cycle meaning that it was approaching 4 years since the band started the "Animalize" tour there in September 1984.

The planned benefits of switching from ICM to CAA for tour booking didn't result with an improved pairing with quality opening acts. It nearly did... Timing was only slightly "off" with White Lion, who opened the first run of shows before Ted Nugent took over. He would be replaced by Anthrax for the final U.S. dates in early 1988. In some ways the band were simply unlucky with White Lion. While their "Pride" album would later climb to #11 on the Billboard 200 album chart, it was languishing around the middle of that chart as the band concluded their run with KISS. Their first major hit single, "Wait," was released in December and was soon in heavy rotation on MTV aiding its rise to #8 on the Billboard Hot 100 singles charts. For White Lion guitarist Vito Bratta the exposure was useful for the "Pride" album: "With KISS, we played the secondary markets, which really helped make people aware of us. You can't beat that kind of exposure" (Billboard, 12/19/87). How different things might have been for the tour had that success come slightly earlier. Whatever the complaints with opening acts during the previous tours, Paul was enthused by Ted: "He's got what we like — energy and real kick-butt rock 'n' roll. Our roots are the same, too. The first time we played with Ted was in the 2,200-seat Tower Theatre in Philadelphia. He was our opening act and (angry) about it, also. At one point during his set, he had the place going crazy, and then he just snickered and said, 'We'll have young KISS coming out in a little while.' Ted knows that being together on tour is a good idea. Everybody wins because of it; people see more than one good band, and it makes both of us look good" (Houston Chronicle 1/24/88).

Unfortunately, Ted's "If You Can't Lick 'Em… Lick 'Em" album missed the mark scrapping to a mediocre #112 on the Billboard 200 U.S. charts — hardly the blockbuster he or KISS would have wanted. This was a marked decline from his previous album, "Little Miss Dangerous," that had reached #76, and was indicative of his march towards ~~artistic irrelevancy~~ musical reinvention as part of the Damn Yankees. As for Anthrax, as the lesser of the "big-4" the crossover appeal of their somewhat niche act is questionable. According to guitarist Scott Ian, "Even though I wasn't a fan of the record — or any eighties KISS — it was mind blowing that they were interested in touring with us. We went over well but the best memories weren't onstage. I'd sit with Gene in catering for hours every day, and he told me everything I ever wanted to know about KISS from 1975 to 1978. He would eat his dinner or sip his coffee and let me ask anything a superfan would want to know" ("I'm The Man: The Story of that Guy from Anthrax").

Harkening back to the 1982/3 "10th Anniversary" jaunt, the tour was immediately faced with religious and other protests — which while generating some press didn't have the teeth of previous tours. It was almost too perfect of a coincidence. Groups in Jackson, MS, and Lake Charles, LA, were at the forefront of efforts to keep the band from performing. Paul addressed the controversy in the latter location, commenting, "We've had problems (from anti-rockers) because sometimes what you don't know about something is more dangerous than what you know. These people don't take the trouble to learn what we really are. I'm as proud of our enemies as I am our friends. Some of these people I wouldn't want as friends" (Jackson Clarion-Ledger, 11/13/87). In Lake Charles the protest was veiled against the band being "vulgar, obscene and that KISS advocates the use of alcohol and encourages teen-agers to have sex" (Lake Charles American Press, 11/11/87). Gene's response was equally straight-forward to the absurdity of the accusations: "What's

rock 'n' roll without a protest? What's rock 'n' roll if you can't cause something, some controversy... They [the protestors] are knuckleheads" (Lake Charles American Press, 11/14/87). However, the show in Lake Charles would be cancelled... In Jackson, the first date of the tour, press reports suggested the show the issue hadn't prevented fans from turning out for the show. Paul had faced the furor head-on and showed up at a local meeting, the day before the show, to defend KISS against one of the religious groups, Citizens for Decency, who were protesting the band's scheduled concert using the time-honored grounds that the show represented Satanism. He commented, "The people who listened to Elvis consider themselves as upstanding citizens... KISS stands for nothing" (Jackson Clarion-Ledger, 11/13/87). As a parting shot, when a protestor told him that he'd pray for him, Paul retorted with an offer to pray for the protestors too...

The tour attendances being a roller-coaster, Paul became somewhat fatalistic about the tour as it became apparent that the grand plan was a failure: "You can't expect to always be on top. Anybody who's in this business just to be on top should get out. That's crazy. When you are not on top anymore is no reason to quit" (Fayetteville Observer, 2/3/88). But while issuing a challenge, he also reiterated a threat, particularly at a time when he was carrying the weight of the band on his shoulders: "I think there will always be a KISS. I hope so. I may not always be in it, but I think there will always be a KISS. I can be replaced just as anybody in the band can be replaced" (Fayetteville Observer, 2/3/88). The underlying threat could equally be seen as a veiled message directed at Gene, that he too was at risk. That Paul suddenly decided to embark on a solo tour the following year is illustrative of the stress on the dynamics within the band at the time. However, Paul wasn't going to go down without a fight. He commented, "There's always somebody who sees some kind of fatal writing on the wall. But those people have seen fatal writing on the wall for 14 years. It's interesting, for

whether it's touring or records, there's usually vultures overhead that ultimately have to go, 'Well, not this time,' and they fly away... There certainly is a certain segment that wants to ask, 'What's next? Is the ship going down?' No. This ship will pull into port when we're ready. And it won't be because it's on the bottom of the ocean" (San Diego Union-Tribune, 4/1/88). So, on the one hand Paul was threatening bleak possibilities and then spitting in the face of the same old adversity he'd built a career on.

Gene saw the situation more prosaically, that the band had a history that was more important than perhaps retaining the same group of fans: "There's a safety valve in rock 'n' roll. Sometimes something lasts too long. Then the older brother and sister and what they liked aren't cool to the younger brother and sister... We go from one generation to the next. Very few groups been able to do that, and 15 years proves that we have... You remember a group called Quiet Riot? You remember a group called Twisted Sister? They did very well and then they died" (Fayetteville Observer, 2/1/88). KISS, on the other hand, continued — even at a time when Paul was carrying the load. It might be a reach to suggest that Gene's tone represents complacency in his mindset, though Paul certainly felt, in hindsight, that the band had become lazy. He commented in his autobiography: "Complacency had developed in KISS, especially once we had a stable lineup again for a few years. We played everything a million miles an hour — Gene equated that with excitement, but it caused a loss of groove. On the Crazy Nights tour we'd even had people on the side of the stage playing keyboard sound pads — to enhance the rhythm guitar so I could slack off and jump around more, and to fortify the background vocals for that big eighties 'gang' vocal sound. Looking back, I can see there was no mystery about why the audience dwindled" ("Face the Music").

Even with the negativity, the "Crazy Nights" era did result in the band returning to Japan (for the first time in 10 years) and touring Europe as part of the festival circuit. The short run in Japan would at least result in one of the best pro-shot videos with the stunning Budokan show becoming the definitive visual documents of the era, even if the staging was not the same as had been used during the U.S. legs of the tour (documented professionally in Philadelphia). Also missing from the show was any pyro leaving the band's musical performance to do the talking. Compared with the previous set used in the U.S., the band added "Reason to Live" and "Black Diamond" for the Nagoya show. The following night in Osaka, the set was further expanded with "Calling Dr. Love," "No, No, No," "I Was Made for Lovin' You" and "Strutter" being performed. As had previously done with release of "The Originals II" for the 1978 tour, the 1988 visit was commemorated with the release of the "Chikara" CD, a greatest hits package notable for its inclusion of the 8-minute remix of "I Was Made For Lovin' You." At the rain-soaked 1988 "Monsters of Rock" festival in Donington, England, KISS had to play second on a bill to the band that had opened for them in 1980: Iron Maiden. Playing under them were acts including David Lee Roth, Helloween, and the upstarts Guns N' Roses. What should have been a triumphant day, in front of 100,000 music fans, was marred by the death of two members of the audience in a crowd crush during G N' R's set. The tragedy resulted in the festival being cancelled for the following year. Paul Stanley spent part of his time in the U.K. recording vocals for the new tracks that would be used on "Smashes, Thrashes, and Hits" later in the year. The songs had been mentioned as early as June for the band's next album.

August 8 - Olympic Auditorium, Los Angeles, CA
Promoter: The Company
Other act(s): None — Promo Video Shooting
Reported audience: ~2,000
Set list: Cold Gin / Lick It Up / Detroit Rock City / Whole Lotta Love
Notes:
- Produced by Steven Brandman and directed by Jean Pellerin and Doug Freel, KISS filmed the audience/performance sequences of the "Crazy Crazy Nights" video at this venue in a session that started around 9pm and lasted 4 hours. The band performed a 30-minute mini-set as a reward for the patience of the crowd who endured sweltering conditions in the boxing arena after being admitted at 6pm for the "Crazy Night."

November 11 - Mississippi Coliseum, Jackson, MS
**REHEARSAL
November 12 - Mississippi Coliseum, Jackson, MS
**REHEARSAL
Notes:
- The band conducted two days of final production rehearsals at the venue.

November 13 - Mississippi Coliseum, Jackson, MS
Promoter: Be-Bop / Mid-South Productions
Other act(s): White Lion
Reported audience: (10,000 capacity)
Set list: Love Gun / Cold Gin / When Your Walls Come Down / Bang Bang You / Fits like a Glove / Hell Or High Water / No, No, No / Reason to Live / War Machine / Heaven's On Fire / Tears Are Falling / I Love It Loud / Lick It Up / Detroit Rock City / Crazy Crazy Nights / Black Diamond / Rock And Roll All Nite
Notes:
- First night of the tour with the public live debut of six songs from the new album. In press leading up to the tour Paul

suggested, "It'll be the biggest show we've ever done... We're thinking about parking the cars in the arenas and taking over the parking lots for the shows."

- Atlantic Records act White Lion had been on tour with Frehley's Comet immediately prior to their "Crazy Nights" run with KISS.

- From a local review: "Guitars screeched, drums boomed, lights flashed and a few swear words flowed freely as a heavy-metal rock groups KISS and White Lion rocked and rolled Friday night the Mississippi Coliseum. Despite attempts earlier in the week from about 50 ministers and Jackson residents to get the Mississippi Fair Commission to ban the performances and similar acts, only a handful of protestors appeared Friday night... During performances, both White Lion and KISS members reminded the almost packed house of this week's protests" (Clarion-Ledger, 11/14/87).

November 14 - Civic Center, Pensacola, FL
Promoter: Cellar Door Productions
Other act(s): White Lion
Reported audience: ~5,250 / 8,500 (61.76%)
Set list: Love Gun / Cold Gin / Hell Or High Water / Bang Bang You / Fits Like A Glove / Crazy Crazy Nights / No, No, No / When Your Walls Come Down / War Machine / Reason To Live / Heaven's On Fire / I Love It Loud / Lick It Up / Detroit Rock City / Tears Are Falling / Rock And Roll All Nite
Notes:
- Press reports suggested the show attendance was about half-capacity.
- A generally poor AUD recording circulates from this show.

November 15 - Mid-South Coliseum, Memphis, TN
Promoter: Mid-South Concerts
Other act(s): White Lion
Reported audience: (9,931 capacity)

November 17 - Civic Center, Lake Charles, LA **CANCELLED
Promoter: Pace Concerts
Other act(s): White Lion
Reported audience: (8,000 capacity)
Notes:
- This show was cancelled on the day of show due to poor ticket sales. According to press reports, "Their promoter said the momentum in sales just didn't warrant the tour, and he had to cut his losses" (Lake Charles American Press, 11/17/87). Additional dates in Texas may have also have been cancelled around this time. The show had also been assaulted by a healthy round of protests against the band by the usual sort of suspects with more anger than common sense.

November 18 - Memorial Coliseum, Corpus Christi, TX
Promoter: Jam Productions
Other act(s): White Lion

Reported audience: (5,000 capacity)

November 20 - Bell County Expo Center, Belton, TX
Promoter: Jam Productions
Other act(s): White Lion
Reported audience: (9,076 capacity)

November 21 - Municipal Coliseum, Lubbock, TX
Promoter: Pace & Stardate Concerts
Other act(s): White Lion
Reported audience: (8,000 capacity)
Set list: Love Gun / Cold Gin / Bang Bang You / Fits Like A Glove / Crazy Crazy Nights / No, No, No / When Your Walls Come Down / War Machine / Reason To Live / Heaven's on Fire / I Love It Loud / Lick It Up / Detroit Rock City / Tears Are Falling / Rock And Roll All Nite
Notes:
- A very poor AUD recording circulates from this show. Audience filmed VID also circulates, the only currently known visual capture of "When Your Walls Come Down."

November 22 - Britt Brown Arena @ Kansas Coliseum, Wichita, KS
Promoter: Contemporary Productions
Other act(s): White Lion
Reported audience: (10,000 capacity)
Set list: Love Gun / Cold Gin / When Your Walls Come Down / Fits Like A Glove / Bang Bang You / War Machine / No, No, No / Crazy Nights / Heaven's on Fire / Reason To Live / I Love It Loud / Lick It Up / Rock And Roll All Nite / Tears Are Falling / Detroit Rock City
Notes:
- A partial AUD recording circulates from this show.

November 24 - Expo Square Pavilion, Tulsa, OK
Promoter: Little Wing Productions
Other act(s): White Lion

Reported audience: (8,000 capacity)

November 25 - Lloyd Noble Center, Norman, OK
Promoter: Contemporary Productions
Other act(s): White Lion
Reported audience: (9,600 capacity)
Notes:
- From a local review: "KISS was lewd, provocative, loud and destructive — and their fans would have it no other way. It's been a long wait for the return of this group, and the crowd, although fairly small, was not disappointed... The opening song was the raunchy, thumping 'Love Gun,' which set the mood for the rest of the concert. Of course, the band played songs from their numerous albums, but they did more than that — they truly entertained. For starters, Paul Stanley still looked terrific after all these years. Then during the drum solo, Eric Carr nearly 'blew the roof off' when the sound he produced caused a small part of the ceiling to come loose and drop on the stage. Gene Simmons spit fire, of course, for it couldn't be a KISS concert if he didn't. Plus, during his bass solo, his ax-shaped instrument shot off fireworks like Roman candles, blowing up two of the speakers hanging from the ceiling. There were lots of flash pods, fireworks and the like, and the occasional piece of lingerie flung up onto the stage, where it was either hung on a guitar, a microphone stand, or in the case of one tiny red bra, around Paul Stanley's neck. Unfortunately, most of the monologue can't make it into print. Sum it up as being colorful and imaginative" (The Oklahoman, 11/28/87).

November 26 - Landon Arena @ Kansas Expocenter Center, Topeka, KS
Promoter: Little Wing Productions
Other act(s): White Lion
Reported audience: (7,800 capacity)

November 27 - Civic Auditorium Arena, Omaha, NE
Promoter: Rose Productions
Other act(s): White Lion
Reported audience: 2,592 / 9,000 (28.80%)
Set list: Love Gun / Cold Gin / Bang Bang You / Fits Like A Glove / Crazy Crazy Nights / No, No, No / War Machine / Reason To Live / Heaven's on Fire / I Love It Loud / Lick It Up / Rock And Roll All Nite / Tears Are Falling / Detroit Rock City
Notes:
- There was no "You Wanted The Best" introduction for this show due to technical challenges. 26 fans were cited for drugs and other offences during the show.
- On this night KISS' appearance on MJI Broadcasting's "Metalshop" radio programming was scheduled.
- From a local review: "KISS launched an all-out assault on the senses Friday night at City Auditorium and the 5,184 ears of the 2,592 in the audience may never be the same again. The elaborate light show added damaged vision to hearing loss, and as for taste, well, never mind. The heavy metal band led by guitarist and lead singer Paul Stanley launched into one scorching song after another, pushing decibel levels ever higher along with teen-age excitement. After New York's White Lion loosened up the crowd with its run of the mill hard rock, KISS came out and put on a show that would have unsettled the likes of Tipper Gore, to say the least. Expressing every violent emotion imaginable, inundating the audience with explicit sexual material, the band put on an aggressive show. Their showy leather costumes, stunning stage presence and use of pyrotechnics captivated the crowd... They started off shaky, with a sludgy sound system and shaky rhythm. The band was unbalanced and the vocals weak. But soon they warmed to the crowd and began to show why they're known for their live shows. The band came alive with sizzling guitar riffs and rough vocals by Gene Simmons. KISS showed a high level of instrumental proficiency despite the distortion and feedback so basic to their playing. After about 10 minutes the

rhythm clicked and the intensity level climbed" (Omaha World-Herald, 11/28/87).

November 28 - Palmer Auditorium, Davenport, IA
Promoter: Jam Productions
Other act(s): White Lion
Reported audience: (4,800 capacity)
Set list: Love Gun / Cold Gin / Bang Bang You / Fits Like A Glove / Crazy Crazy Nights / No, No, No / War Machine / Reason To Live / Heaven's on Fire / I Love It Loud / Lick It Up / Rock And Roll All Nite / Oh Susannah / Tears Are Falling / Detroit Rock City
Notes:
- The day following this show the band were scheduled to drive to Moline and then fly to Minneapolis where they'd spend a few days off before the next show.

- An audience filmed VID circulates from this show.

December 1 - Civic Center, St. Paul (Minneapolis), MN
Promoter: Rose Productions
Other act(s): White Lion
Reported audience: (15,406 capacity)
Set list: Love Gun / Cold Gin / Bang Bang You / Fits Like A Glove / Crazy Crazy Nights / No, No, No / Reason To Live / War Machine / Heaven's On Fire / I Love It Loud / Lick It Up / Rock and Roll All Nite / Whole Lotta Love / Tears Are Falling / Detroit Rock City
Notes:
- During the show, Paul was hit by a bottle thrown from crowd.
- This show circulates as an AUD recording.

December 2 - Taylor Arena @ Mayo Civic Center, Rochester, MN
Promoter: Rose Productions
Other act(s): White Lion
Reported audience: (6,600 capacity)

December 4 - Veterans Memorial Auditorium, Des Moines, IA
Promoter: Contemporary Productions
Other act(s): White Lion
Reported audience: 5,795 / 7,500 (77.27%)
Notes:
- From a local review: "While other hard rock acts have come and gone, the heavy metal monster that is KISS keeps rolling along... An evening with KISS is like nothing else in rock 'n' roll. To the crowd at Vets, it was a decadent religious experience. KISS' main attractions are vocalist/guitarist Paul Stanley and bassist/vocalist and 'lead tongue' Gene Simmons. Blasting onto a large slanted stage with a giant, lighted logo behind the band, KISS brought enough lights and hardware to build a battleship. Lead guitarist Bruce Kulick's lightning licks

and Eric Carr's throbbing drums helped launch the band's assault on the senses, but it was Stanley and Simmons who provided the sex appeal... Simmons strutted like a rooster through song after song and Stanley pranced like a wild stallion, inciting the crowd to a near-riot" (Des Moines Register, 12/5/87).

December 6 - Prairie Capital Convention Center, Springfield, IL
Promoter: Jam Productions
Other act(s): White Lion
Reported audience: (8,900 capacity)
Notes:
- The KISS itinerary for Nov/Dec lists this show as the final one with White Lion opening. However, ads in the Toledo Blade for the following night's show still include them on the bill. Unfortunately, the review of that show makes no mention of the opener.

December 7 - Sports Arena, Toledo, OH
Promoter: Belkin Productions
Other act(s): White Lion
Reported audience: ~3,000 / 7,500 (40%)
Partial set list: Love Gun / Cold Gin / Bang Bang You / Fits like a Glove / Crazy Crazy Nights / Heaven's On Fire / Lick It Up / Rock And Roll All Nite
Notes:
- Last show with White Lion opening, who headed for Europe and a headlining club tour.
- From a local review: "The KISS Army is not nearly as strong as it used to be, but some 3,000 fans still showed up last night at the Toledo Sports Arena to see this heavy metal band that just refuses to die... During its 90-minute show last night, KISS exhibited a few flourishes of showmanship, but for the most part, the foursome offered a muddy mishmash of overpowering, barely distinguishable music... The members of KISS made sure that everybody in the crowd knew exactly

who they were. Behind them, a 25-foot-high backdrop of lights and lamps which spelled KISS continuously flashed in varying colors and intensities throughout the show. It was far more impressive than the weary pyrotechnics from countless previous KISS tours. While many have kissed off the band long ago, it continues to defy its critics, pumping out record and drawing meager yet diehard crowds. It's a band that just won't die" (Toledo Blade, 12/8/87).
- Video circulates from this show.

December 9 - Civic Center, Erie, PA
Promoter: Belkin Productions
Other act(s): Ted Nugent
Reported audience: (7,500 capacity)
Notes:
- A protest group, the Erie County Citizens Coalition against Violent Pornography, attempted to have parents keep their children from attending the concert on the grounds that the groups had previously violated state law.

December 10 - Maple Leaf Gardens, Toronto, ON, Canada
Promoter: Concert Productions International (CPI)
Other act(s): Ted Nugent
Reported audience: 8,832 / 10,000 (88.32%)
Reported gross: $152,979
Set list: Love Gun / Cold Gin / Bang Bang You / Fits Like A Glove / Crazy Crazy Nights / No, No, No / Reason To Live / War Machine / Heaven's On Fire / I Love It Loud / Lick It Up / Rock And Roll All Nite / Tears Are Falling / Detroit Rock City
Notes:
- From a local review: "If you were one of those music fans who was glad to see the end of the 1970s, the last two nights at Maple Leaf Gardens were a distressing spectacle. Last night's KISS/Ted Nugent concert and Wednesday's Yes show demonstrate that seventies rock, if not very much alive, is still kicking. The continued success of KISS is, in a way, most surprising. When they first appeared, dolled up in kabuki-

style make-up, they looked like a novelty act. Yet 15 years later, they forge on, plying their brand of pedestrian, bump-and-grind hard rock to large crowds. KISS's durability can be traced to a couple of factors, but mostly to good old fashioned marketing. The KISS philosophy is to give the fans — no, the customers — what they want: escapist, soft-porn fantasies about the teenage party life; lots of bright lights and a reassurance that for that moment, they are the most important people in the world.

Throughout the show, Gene Simmons and Paul Stanley thrust crotches forward, wagged tongues, told "dirty" stories and sang songs like Lick It Up. Hustler magazine publisher Larry Flynt hasn't gone broke; neither will KISS. And Flynt doesn't even spit fire (Simmons does) or shoot out speakers with his bass (ditto). While KISS might find comparisons to a pornographer flattering (or at least commercially advantageous), the real secret of KISS comes down to a simple rule of salesmanship: make the customer feel important. Throughout the show, band members shone lights or pointed fingers at the audience. At the end of each song the big KISS sign lit up, illuminating the audience. Thank you. Here's your change. Please come back soon" (Toronto Globe & Mail, 12/11/87).
- From another local review: "*Pow / Right here and now / Right between the eyes...* The lyric came about midway through last night's show at Maple Leaf Gardens, and it was as pointed a summation as KISS would make of the evening's proceedings. For the 14 thou plus who came to be KISSed, it was just the promise of instant gratification they were hoping for... Paul Stanley remains the consummate sage storyteller and rates high as one of rock's most engaging front men. Even at his most salacious, there's an element of the little kid known just how naughty he's being and loving it. Simmons seemed very casual with his sinister image, flicking very little tongue, blowing only one desultory fireball, and offhandedly shooting out the lights above the stage with his guitar-gun.

He wasn't going through the motions, but he wasn't far off either. It was only by comparison with the all-out effort of Stanley that it was noticeable" (Toronto Star, 12/11/87).
- This show circulates as a below average AUD recording.

December 11 - Civic Center, Glens Falls, NY
Promoter: Magic City Productions
Other act(s): Ted Nugent
Reported audience: (8,000 capacity)
Notes:
- From a local review: "To borrow the title of the band's latest album, it was one of those 'Crazy Nights' with KISS. As the only two remaining original members, Gene Simmons and Paul Stanley led the assault, alternating the lead vocal assignments. Neither are stellar musicians, but both perfectly captured KISS's entertainment-first ethic. Guitarist Stanley was in constant motion, dancing across the stage and wiggling his behind to the cheering crowd. In his skin-tight pants and long, curly, bouncing black hair, the bare-chested singer looked like the quintessential pretty-boy rock star. While Stanley made the little girls pant with his tales of sexual prowess, Simmons played to the boys, dishing out the darker side of rock 'n' roll. Still dressed completely in black and silver, the horror-rockin' bassist stomped and stalked the stage, flicking out his long and lascivious tongue and striking cartoonishly macho poses" (Schenectady Gazette, 12/14/87).

December 12 - Civic Center, Providence, RI
Promoter: Gemini Concerts
Other act(s): Ted Nugent
Reported audience: 10,106 / 12,300 (82.16%)
Reported gross: $166,749

December 13 - Cumberland County Civic Center, Portland, ME
Promoter: Gemini Concerts
Other act(s): Ted Nugent

Reported audience: (9,400 capacity)

December 15 - The Centrum, Worcester, MA **POSTPONED
Promoter: Gemini Concerts
Notes:
- This show was postponed until Jan. 27. A show at the Springfield Civic Center had originally been rumored, which was scheduled for Jan. 28.

December 16 - War Memorial, Syracuse, NY **CANCELLED
Promoter: Magic City Productions
Other act(s): Ted Nugent
Reported audience: (8,000 capacity)
Notes:
- This show was cancelled due to a snow storm that "prevented the bands from trucking their equipment" (Syracuse Herald Journal, 12/17/87) to the venue and there wasn't scope in the schedule to change the date.

December 18 - The Spectrum, Philadelphia, PA
Promoter: Electric Factory Concerts
Other act(s): Ted Nugent
Reported audience: 10,294 / 14,080 (73.11%)
Reported gross: $163,641
Set list: Love Gun / Cold Gin / Bang Bang You / Fits Like A Glove / No, No, No / Crazy Crazy Nights / War Machine / Reason To Live / Heaven's On Fire / I Love It Loud / Lick It Up / Rock And Roll All Nite / White Christmas / Detroit Rock City
Notes:
- This show was also professionally filmed. A brief selection from the show was included on the main section of "KISSology" Volume 2 in 2007: Love Gun / Bang Bang You / No, No, No / Crazy Crazy Nights / Reason To Live. An average AUD recording also circulates.
- Bruce was interviewed for a feature that was published in the May 1988 issue of "Guitar for the Practicing Musician."

December 19 - Veteran's Memorial Coliseum, New Haven, CT
Promoter: Cross Country Concerts
Other act(s): Ted Nugent
Reported audience: (9,900 capacity)
Set list: Love Gun / Cold Gin / Bang Bang You / Fits Like a Glove / No, No, No / Crazy Crazy Nights / War Machine / Reason to Live / Heaven's on Fire / I Love It Loud / Lick it up / Rock and Roll All Nite / Tears are Falling / White Christmas / Detroit Rock City
Notes:
- Average audience filmed VID circulates from this show. While there's a bit of zoom and panning the filmer does an admirable job of capturing the show from a high vantage point.

December 20 - Brendan Byrne Arena, East Rutherford, NJ
Promoter: Monarch Entertainment Bureau
Other act(s): Ted Nugent
Reported audience: (18,014 capacity)
Set list: Love Gun / Cold Gin / Bang Bang You / Fits Like a Glove / No, No, No / Crazy Crazy Nights / War Machine / Reason to Live / Heaven's on Fire / I Love It Loud / Lick it up / Rock and Roll All Nite / Tears are Falling / White Christmas / Detroit Rock City
Notes:
- From a local review: "If KISS ever decides to pack in its arena-rock shows, a home awaits the band in Las Vegas. We're talking SLICK. This is a group that relies on the spectacle, and last night at the Brendan Byrne Arena, the four-man band seemed to spare no expense in staging one of the glitziest and campiest shows to hit town in a long time. Music is secondary when it comes to discussing KISS. Led by lizard-tongued bass player Gene Simmons and hip-swiveling guitarist Paul Stanley, who trade lead vocals, Kiss is your average macho heavy-metal outfit. Translated, that means KISS relies, in large measure, on suggestive lyrics to arouse its

largely teen-age fans. And while KISS is fueling its fans sexual fantasies, the group bludgeons them with sound. Driven by Eric Carr's thunderous drumbeats and filled with piercing guitar chords provided by the tandem of Stanley and Bruce Kulick, songs such as 'Heaven's On Fire,' 'Fits Like a Glove,' 'Crazy Nights,' and 'Bang Bang You' were turned into ear-shattering rockers.

Where KISS, which first stormed up the record charts in the mid-Seventies, has always excelled is in the staging of its shows. And last night's 90-minute extravaganza complete with a movable drum stand, fireworks, shooting flames, and a marquee spelling out the group's name in blinking lights was no exception. KISS even saw fit to help the audience get in the holiday mood with an *acappella* rendition of 'White Christmas.' (No, don't throw out the Bing Crosby version for this one.) With Carr's massive silver drum stand tucked into a slightly angled horseshoe, the open stage, complete with two side ramps, allowed ample room for the lithe Stanley to prance, spin, and bump-and-grind his way around the stage. Undoubtedly, Stanley views himself as the band's sex symbol, and his constant fluffing of his long dark mane of hair and his slightly off-color stories of his off-stage escapades were certainly meant to underscore that image. Not quite as spry as Stanley, the barrel-chested Simmons favored posing at the edge of the stage and on the side platforms. But he had a few tricks up his leather sleeves. Wielding his bass like a rifle, Simmons took aim at the speakers above the stage and fired off several rounds of ammunition. He also did a fire-breathing sword bit" (Hackensack Record, 12/21/87).
- A decent AUD recording circulates from this show.

December 26 - Allen County War Memorial Coliseum, Fort Wayne, IN
Promoter: Sunshine Promotions
Other act(s): Ted Nugent
Reported audience: (10,000 capacity)

December 27 - Market Square Arena, Indianapolis, IN
Promoter: Sunshine Promotions
Other act(s): Ted Nugent
Reported audience: (17,500 capacity)
Set list: Love Gun / Cold Gin / Bang Bang You / Fits Like A Glove / Crazy Crazy Nights / No, No, No / War Machine / Reason To Live / Heaven's On Fire / I Love It Loud / Lick It Up / Rock And Roll All Nite / Tears Are Falling / Detroit Rock City
Notes:
- This show was billed as the "Holiday Festival Jam '87."
- This show circulates as an AUD recording.

December 29 - Freedom Hall, Louisville, KY
Promoter: Sunshine Promotions
Other act(s): Ted Nugent
Reported audience: ~8,500 / 18,700 (45.46%)
Notes:
- This show was also billed as the "Holiday Festival Jam '87."
- From a local review: "For the teenagers, the event was more than historic. It's rare enough for a heavy metal band of KISS' stature to come to Louisville. To have KISS and Ted Nugent on the same night — well, that was almost more than the crowd could stand. More than 8,500 people gathered in Freedom Hall last night, and more than a few actually were younger than the bands, which have been recording for about 15 years... For nearly two hours, Paul Stanley and his veteran team — Bruce Kulick on lead guitar, Eric Carr on drums, and the indomitable Gene Simmons on bass — relentlessly pounded out old stuff and new stuff, all of which the audience loved, some deservedly... New cuts from 'Crazy Nights' are better live than on vinyl, but don't cut it against the older material. Without the legendary makeup and fake blood, KISS has to compete on the strength of its music. Sometimes it manages, and sometimes it doesn't" (Louisville Courier-Journal, 12/30/87).

December 30 - Roberts Stadium, Evansville, IN
Promoter: Sunshine Promotions
Other act(s): Ted Nugent
Reported audience: (13,600 capacity)
Notes:
- This show was also billed as the "Holiday Festival Jam '87."
- From a local review: "New Year's Eve came early to Evansville this year as Roberts Stadium hosted a Wednesday night party featuring some of the city's favorite rockers. There was enough sound and energy produced in the stadium to mistake it for Times Square at 11:59 p.m. on Dec. 31... KISS ran onstage to an ovation that never really subsided. The foursome's members have learned to be complete entertainers. Not content with being musicians only, they have learned how to bring an audience to a happy and comfortable frenzy... It has been said that metal and rock music are not so much music as an attitude. It was a positive attitude Wednesday night" (Evansville Courier, 12/31/87).

December 31 - Hara Arena, Dayton, OH
Promoter: Belkin Productions
Other act(s): Chastain
Reported audience: 6,715 / 8,000 (83.94%)
Reported gross: $107,440
Notes:
- Ted Nugent was still being advertised (Dayton Daily News) as the opening act on the day of show, but did not perform. Cincinnati group Chastain replaced him on the bill at the last moment.

January 1, 1988 - Freedom Hall, Johnson City, TN
Promoter: Sunshine Promotions
Other act(s): Ted Nugent
Reported audience: 9,058 / 9,200 (98.46%)
Reported gross: $140,399

January 2 - Civic Coliseum, Knoxville, TN
Promoter: Sunshine Promotions
Other act(s): Ted Nugent
Reported audience: 6,810 / 7,500 (90.8%)
Reported gross: $105,555
Set list: Love Gun / Cold Gin / Bang Bang You / Fits Like A Glove / Hell Or High Water / Crazy Crazy Nights / War Machine / Reason To Live / Heaven's On Fire / I Love It Loud / Lick It Up / Rock And Roll All Nite / Tears Are Falling / Detroit Rock City
Notes:
- This show was also billed as the "Holiday Festival Jam '88."
- An average AUD recording circulates from this show.

January 5 - Lakeview Arena, Marquette, MI
Promoter: Stardate Productions
Other act(s): Ted Nugent
Reported audience: (6,500 capacity)
Notes:
- "Hell or High Water" was reportedly also performed at this show...

January 6 - Brown County Arena, Green Bay, WI
Promoter: Stardate Productions
Other act(s): Ted Nugent
Reported audience: 5,005 / 7,044 (71.05%)
Reported gross: $75,005
Notes:
- From a local review: "Poof, zap, BAM! — and another speaker high above the stage exploded in smoking ruin. Gene Simmons of KISS wasted it with his weapon, a bass guitar. Hugh cheers erupted from the crowd of 5,235 teens (mostly)... That's rock 'n' roll, KISS-style — spectacular, gimmicky, eye-filling and outrageous. It was one of the few times KISS didn't aim directly at the groin... KISS' encore opened weirdly — bits of 'Oh Suzannah' and 'My Way' and a full, a cappella White Christmas. Then came a couple of

closing blasts, including Tears Are Falling and booming fireworks" (Green Bay Press-Gazette, 1/7/88).

January 7 - MECCA Auditorium, Milwaukee, WI
Promoter: Stardate Productions
Other act(s): Ted Nugent
Reported audience: ~5,000 / 8,700 (57.47%)
Notes:
- From a local review: "In the '70s, KISS was a living cartoon, cranking out party hard-rock classics while breathing fire, vomiting blood and stalking stages in high-glitter costumes and psycho-Kabuki makeup. But sans makeup and two original members, KISS' in-concert impact was reduced to run-of-the-mill metal posing and narcissistic prattle. Clad in leather, spandex, glitter and chrome, lead vocalist Paul Stanley still had the pout, and bassist Gene Simmons' immense pointed tongue still flicked the air like a giant reptile. However, their old muscular rockers like 'Cold Gin' reeked of oldies revivalism and newer numbers seemed routine and mediocre" (The Milwaukee Sentinel, 1/8/88).

January 8 - U.I.C. Pavilion, Chicago, IL
Promoter: Chicago Jam Productions
Other act(s): Ted Nugent
Reported audience: (10,595 capacity)
Notes:
- Kerrang writer Steffan Chirazi and photographer Joe Giron attended this show for a feature that ran in issue #172 of the magazine.

January 9 - Kiel Auditorium, St. Louis, MO
Promoter: Contemporary Promotions
Other act(s): Ted Nugent
Reported audience: 8,184 / 10,522 (77.78%)
Reported gross: $125,808
Set list: Love Gun / Cold Gin / Bang Bang You / Fits like a Glove / Shout It Out Loud / Crazy Crazy Nights / War Machine

/ Reason To Live / Heaven's On Fire / I Love It Loud / Lick It Up / Rock And Roll All Nite / Oh Susannah / Tears Are Falling / Detroit Rock City

Notes:

- From a local review: "A rock 'n' roll circus came to town when the rock group KISS brought its 'Crazy Nights' tour to Kiel Auditorium on Saturday evening. The veteran glam-rock outfit reignited the legendary 'KISS Army' with its bombastic musical style and spectacular stage production. KISS has been thrilling audiences with its top-notch rock spectacles since it first appeared on the New York music scene in 1974. But the last few years and most recent albums have brought about a success approaching the band's peak years in the late '70s. While the hairline of the band's sex symbol, Paul Stanley, recedes further with each passing tour, the singer's non-stop enthusiasm propels both him and the audience through the program with an almost juvenile abandon. While Stanley still peppers each and every song introduction with an inevitable plethora of four-letter words, his role as rock cheerleader takes on an almost comic book appeal. Bassist Gene Simmons may have moved on to a healthy career in the movies, but his heart still appears rooted in his rock 'n' roll. Simmons contributed his bare-bones instrumental approach to the quartet's thud-infested barrage and brought the house down with his fire-breathing antics during his theatrical bass solo. Both drummer Eric Carr and lead guitarist Bruce Kulick have been in the band long enough to inject their own personal trademarks to the band's style. Kulick, in particular, has pressed his musical fingerprint on the group's sound with inventive, fleet-fingered melodic excursions" (St. Louis Post-Dispatch, 1/11/88).

- Audience filmed VID circulates from this show. Filmed from a distance center-stage the video often becomes blurry and unfocused though the audio is more than acceptable.

January 11 - L.C. Walker Arena, Muskegon, MI
Promoter: Belkin Productions

Other act(s): Ted Nugent
Reported audience: 6,706 / 7,501 (89.4%)
Reported gross: $108,973
Notes:
- A crowd crush was reported at this show with 6–12 fans having to be rescued from the stage barrier.
- From a local review: "The sellout crowd of about 6,600 vented frustration and excess energy by screeching and thrashing throughout the acts... KISS, a teen favorite since the mid-1970s, pleased the crowd with their acrobatic showmanship and pubescent sexual humor" (Muskegon Chronicle).
- Gene was interviewed via phone by David Perry of the Lowell Sun while in town for the show. An article appeared in the Lowell Sun on Jan. 23 to promote the band's Jan. 27 concert at the Centrum.

January 12 - Wendler Arena, Saginaw, MI
Promoter: Belkin Productions
Other act(s): Ted Nugent
Reported audience: 6,141 / 6,586 (93.24%)
Reported gross: $98,256
Set list: Love Gun / Cold Gin / Bang Bang You / Fits like a Glove / Shout It Out Loud / Crazy Crazy Nights / War Machine / Reason to Live / Heaven's On Fire / I Love It Loud / Lick It Up / Rock And Roll All Nite / Tears Are Falling / Detroit Rock City
Notes:
- Audience filmed video, from an elevated stage left position, circulates. Visually it's a bit jumpy in places, but the audio is decent enough.

January 13 - Ohio Center, Columbus, OH
Promoter: Belkin Productions
Other act(s): Ted Nugent
Reported audience: 5,536 / 7,500 (73.81%)
Reported gross: $88,576
Notes:

- From a local review: "Wednesday night the circus came to town — a rock 'n' roll circus circa 1975. The almighty party animals known as KISS and self-proclaimed Motor City Madman Ted Nugent played to a capacity crowd in the Ohio Center. KISS, Nugent and the kids — a fun-filled three-ring circus. Essentially, neither KISS nor Nugent has changed since either began more than a decade ago. Well, KISS has replaced two original members, and the musicians no longer wear the superhero face paint. Other than that, both acts still perform — and excel — at what they were born to do: boogie excessively and go crash, bang, boom... The KISS men bash out exuberant teen anthems through basic 4/4 rock 'n' roll. Bassist Gene Simmons, guitarist Paul Stanley, guitarist Bruce Kulick and drummer Eric Carr make a thunder similar to 100 OSU marching bands.... While Carr pounds his mammoth drum set, guitarist Stanley struts his Technicolor outfit. Kulick, dressed like a court jester, plays guitar riffs into a numbing oblivion. And Simmons, who's dressed like an over-the-hill burlesque queen from a Catskills motorcycle hangout, flicks his tongue lewdly and constantly. It's long enough to be a necktie... The band is kicking out the jams royal, and everybody's high on the power of live rock 'n' roll. No one wears a long face at the circus" (Columbus Dispatch, 1/15/88).

January 15 - Richfield Coliseum, Richfield (Cleveland), OH
Promoter: Belkin Productions
Other act(s): Ted Nugent
Reported audience: 14,935 / 15,522 (96.22%)
Reported gross: $246,427
Set list: Love Gun / Cold Gin / Bang Bang You / Fits like a Glove / Shout It Out Loud / Crazy Crazy Nights / War Machine / Reason To Live / Heaven's On Fire / I Love It Loud / Lick It Up / Rock And Roll All Nite / La Bamba / Whole Lotta Love / Tears Are Falling / Detroit Rock City
Notes:

- Gene tricks the audience into singing "Happy Birthday" to Paul.
- From a local review: "It would be tough to top KISS' finale Friday night. It 'blew up' the Coliseum stage. Well, almost. First, showers of sparks shot into the air. Then came a series of deafening explosions that ripped open the runway behind the drum kit. And that was the only gimmick from the same band that once gave us fire-eating, spitting up 'blood,' wild black-and-white makeup, medieval armor and seven-inch heels... But four years ago, the band gave up its makeup. Then it gave up its outrageous clothing. It also gave up on its prepubescent following... Now, if the band could give up a bit of its rude and lewd patter. ... Sexual innuendo and even a little raunch seem to fit in with hard rock and heavy-metal music, but guitarist Paul Stanley's stories got a little repetitious and were a bit of a drag. Enough is enough" (Plain Dealer, 1/17/88).
- Audience filmed VID, from an extreme right position, circulates from this show. The audio is very good.

January 16 - Civic Arena, Pittsburgh, PA
Promoter: DiCesare-Engler Productions
Other act(s): Ted Nugent
Reported audience: 8,808 / 12,500 (70.46%)
Reported gross: $147,645
Notes:
- KISS' show wasn't reviewed independently, but was mentioned in a Def Leppard review (they played the venue the night following KISS): "KISS cleaned up after Ted Nugent died a slow and (boringly) painful death onstage Saturday night before about 9,500. If heavy metal's dead, there sure are a lot of people breathing life into the corpse" (Pittsburgh Post-Gazette, 1/18/88).

January 17 - Cobo Arena, Detroit, MI
Promoter: Belkin Productions
Other act(s): Helix

Reported audience: (12,199 capacity)
Set list: Love Gun / Cold Gin / Bang Bang You / Fits like a Glove / Shout It Out Loud / Crazy Crazy Nights / War Machine / Reason To Live / Heaven's On Fire / I Love It Loud / Lick It Up / Rock And Roll All Nite / Tears Are Falling / Detroit Rock City
Notes:
- Ted Nugent was scheduled to perform a headlining show at the Cincinnati Gardens resulting in his replacement by Canadian band Helix (who had previously opened shows for KISS in 1983) for this show.
- Partial choppy audience filmed VID circulates from this show. During a brief jam following "Rock And Roll All Nite," Paul plays a bit of "Stairway To Heaven" on an out of tune guitar (his defense) and a brief bit of the opening to "Black Diamond."
- Two audience filmed videos circulate, one complete and the other partial. A separate AUD recording also exists.

January 18 - Civic Center, Huntington, WV
Promoter: Southern Productions
Other act(s): Ted Nugent
Reported audience: (11,000 capacity)

January 20 - The Scope, Norfolk, WV
Promoter: Cellar Door Productions
Other act(s): Ted Nugent
Reported audience: (13,800 capacity)
Notes:
- From a local review: "Wednesday night at Scope, the group barked best when bass player Gene Simmons bounded into the spotlight. At 6 feet, 2 inches, Simmons is the epitome of rock 'n' roll sleaze. Squeezed into an ornate leather outfit, tongue flickering in and out, Simmons played off male dominance fantasies with lewd delight. His aggressively obscene gestures and wolfish eyes could have left even Joan of Arc faint with fear. Needless to say, Simmons was having buckets of indecent fun... KISS' other main man, rhythm guitarist/vocalist Paul Stanley, could muster none of Simmons' bravado. For much of the show, Stanley came across like Eddie Murphy doing an impression of Richard Simmons having a bad day at work. Toward the end of the evening, for example, Stanley cut his thumb. For the remaining two songs, he sucked and stared at his injured digit with more attentiveness than he strummed his guitar" (Newport Daily Press, 1/22/88).

January 22 - Auditorium, Utica, NY
Promoter: Magic City Productions
Other act(s): Ted Nugent
Reported audience: ~3,500 / 6,000 (58.33%)
Notes:
- From a local review: "The fans came 3,500-plus strong for a rock concert, and that's what they got. They were in good hands. KISS, the main attraction, has been making the rounds since before a fair number of those fans were born. But

though they may be old enough to be many of their rooter's parents, it doesn't stop them from celebrating those 'crazy, crazy nights' of their recent release. The band's longevity is not hard to explain. They know what its crowd wants — a rock concert with all the trimmings. That they don't provide much in the way of substance or challenge is beside the point. Whoever criticized the music on a pinball machine? So here's what KISS delivered: Its name in lights. Lots of them. Blinking in rhythm, giving the stage the look of an amusement park car ride. And don't forget the sequins and many-colored pants. Guitar picks dispensed generously among the faithful in front of the stage.

In the middle of his solo, lead man Bruce Kulick paused several times to toss a few picks like Santa in a Christmas parade pitching candy to the kids along the route. More than a few glimpses of bassist Gene Simmons legendary tongue. Front man Paul Stanley's numerous invocations of the name 'Utica.' These guys might say they never mess with politics, but the way Stanley kept dropping the name of their current stop was pure campaigning. An awesome electronic arsenal that emitted a rumble measuring at least four on the Richter scale. Some pyrotechnics, notably from Kulick's solo. Some teasing during drummer Eric Carr's stop, when he kept stopping waiting for the applause, then starting again until he was trading note for note with the crowd. And a few solid rock anthems" (Utica Observer-Dispatch, 1/23/88)...

January 23 - War Memorial Coliseum, Johnstown, PA
Promoter: Magic City Productions
Other act(s): Ted Nugent
Reported audience: (6,000 capacity)

January 24 - Memorial Auditorium, Buffalo, NY
Promoter: Magic City Productions
Other act(s): Ted Nugent
Reported audience: (18,000 capacity)

January 26 - Mid-Hudson Valley Civic Center, Poughkeepsie, NY
Promoter: Magic City Productions
Other act(s): Ted Nugent
Reported audience: (3,000 capacity)
Set list: Love Gun / Cold Gin / Bang Bang You / Fits like a Glove / Crazy Crazy Nights / Shout It Out Loud / War Machine / Reason to Live / Heaven's On Fire / I Love It Loud / Lick It Up / Rock And Roll All Nite / Whole Lotta Love / Detroit Rock City
Notes:
- Close-up VID filmed from the audience circulates. Audio quality is average, but the filmer's position makes up for that — even with the heads and arms in front of the lens.

January 27 - The Centrum, Worcester, MA
Promoter: Gemini Concerts
Other act(s): Ted Nugent
Reported audience: (12,768 capacity)
Set list: Love Gun / Cold Gin / Turn On The Night / Turn On The Night / Bang Bang You / Fits Like A Glove / Crazy Crazy Nights / Shout It Out Loud / War Machine / Reason To Live / Heaven's On Fire / I Love It Loud / Lick It Up / Rock And Roll All Nite / Turn On The Night / Tears Are Falling / How Many More Times / Strutter / Detroit Rock City
Notes:
- Rescheduled date from Dec. 15.
- Live segments for the "Turn on the Night" video were filmed before and during this show with the album version of the song being played over the PA multiple times — the band did not perform the song live. The band rewarded the audience for their patience with a performance of "Strutter."
- An average AUD recording circulates from this show.

January 28 - Civic Center, Springfield, MA
Promoter: Cross Country Concerts
Other act(s): Ted Nugent
Reported audience: 5,440 / 10,500 (51.81%)

Set list: Love Gun / Cold Gin / Bang Bang You / Fits like a Glove / Crazy Crazy Nights / Shout It Out Loud / War Machine / Reason to Live / Heaven's On Fire / I Love It Loud / Lick It Up / Rock And Roll All Nite / Detroit Rock City

Notes:
- Numerous fights and arrests were reported at this show with local police representative complaining that there had not been enough security staff. One fan was later fined $300 after being found guilty of throwing M-80 firecrackers into the audience, injuring one person.
- From a local review: "Amid rockets' red glare, bombs bursting in air and brassieres being tossed on stage, KISS turned the Springfield Civic Center into something of a cross between Beirut and ancient Rome Thursday. It was the kind of night that would send shudders through one unaccustomed to such rock 'n' roll debauchery. And while not exactly good clean fun, it was — as all KISS shows are — something that had to be seen to be believed... The highlight of the entire concert had to be guitarist Paul Stanley's 'Crazy, Crazy Nights,' the power pop title track off the group's latest album" (Springfield Union-News, 1/30/88).
- An audience shot VID circulates from this show.

January 29 - Nassau Coliseum, Uniondale, NY
Promoter: Ron Delsener Enterprises
Other act(s): Ted Nugent
Reported audience: 10,000 / 14,000 (71.43%)
Reported gross: $160,452
Notes:
- Both AUD and VID exist from this show.

January 30 - Memorial Auditorium, Rochester, NY
Promoter: Monarch Entertainment Bureau
Other act(s): Ted Nugent
Reported audience: 5,404 / 11,000 (49.13%)
Reported gross: $74,632

Set list: Love Gun / Cold Gin / Bang Bang You / Fits like a Glove / Crazy Crazy Nights / Shout It Out Loud / War Machine / Reason to Live / Heaven's On Fire / I Love It Loud / Lick It Up / Rock And Roll All Nite / Detroit Rock City

Notes:

- From a local review: "All of us get older, it's a fact of life. Rock and roll is getting older, too, and some of its best talent is reaching 40. Some grow into it with grace; others try to fool the young with what they believe the crowd wants to hear. Never was a case in point so evident as the recent Ted Nugent/KISS show in Rochester... KISS, on the other hand, could take some lessons in the 'Remember rock and roll?' department, because it was obvious they have a short memory. The stage was well lit with a Hollywood KISS background as Gene Simmons, Paul Stanley and company bounded onto the stage. Almost immediately, the show began its downhill descent. Opening with the tune 'Cold Gin' off the 1976 live LP, this song lacked the fire of the original. Gene Simmons no longer looks like a cool rocker, though he's still trying to be one. Poured into a leather outfit, he looked more like an overweight businessman than a bass player. Paul Stanley at least looked the part, but his onstage demeanor was condescending. The poor guitar player and drummer, not the original members when KISS was in their made-up heyday, might as well have been non-existent, for they had no identity at all onstage.

Drummer Eric Carr had a drum set so ridiculous; no kid would ever believe it could be played correctly. Mammoth in proportion, its artificial construction made it look downright silly. Topping this off, the kit was on a moving riser that didn't even move well. Simmons brooded and sneered at the audience, and spent half the evening calling security guards to the stage while he pointed into the crowd with a large flashlight, looking for 'troublemakers.' There weren't enough people there to make trouble, Gene. The entire show had the feel that it was geared to make money, not to entertain or

really rock. Guys like these give rock a bad name. They have forgotten their roots (if they ever had any) and their contrived version of a rock show was an insult to every adolescent that paid money to see them. Kids aren't stupid, and they can spot phonies a mile off" (Auburn Citizen, 2/4/88).
- A partial SBD and full AUD recording circulate from this show.

February 1 - Capital Centre, Landover (Largo), MD
Promoter: Cellar Door Productions
Other act(s): Ted Nugent
Reported audience: (15,000 capacity)
Notes:
- From a local review: "KISS and Ted Nugent dispelled any thoughts Monday night at the Capital Centre that they are dated dinosaurs destined for the scrap heap. Although neither act has approached its mid-1970s superstar status lately, both have continued in the '80s to produce a steady stream of basic, glitter-free, barebones '70s-style rock... In concert both groups showed the advantages of maturity, experience and lots of studio time. Both were clear, polished, fast, and all performers possessed a stage presence. Except for some well-timed pyrotechnics during the KISS show, there were no cheap stunts, phony lightning or excessive prancing. It wasn't needed" (Washington Times, 2/3/88).
- From another local review: "Paul Stanley certainly couldn't have picked a more crowd-pleasing garment to wear for KISS' encore Monday night at the Capital Centre. When the band reappeared to play 'Strutter,' Stanley came out wearing a Washington Redskins jersey, a wily move that of course received a roar from the audience. Not that Stanley needed a show of burgundy and gold to grab audience approval. There were plenty of other gimmicks to please the fans at the half-full arena... The sound mix turned KISS' raunchy tunes into even harsher slabs of hard rock. Stanley's vocals were much too high and became increasingly annoying, especially since

he persisted in screaming his braggadocio song introductions. Simmons' bass was a muddled, muffled thump. Old tunes like 'Detroit Rock City' and 'Rock and Roll All Night' were entertaining enough because of their sheer velocity and basic pop structure, but the newer material from the 'Crazy Nights' album was repetitive and lacked all of the studio sheen that makes music like this palatable in small doses" (Washington Post, 2/3/88).

February 3 - Memorial Auditorium, Greenville, SC
Promoter: Cellar Door Productions
Other act(s): Ted Nugent
Reported audience: (6,500 capacity)

February 4 - Civic Center, Savannah, GA
Promoter: Cellar Door Productions
Other act(s): Ted Nugent
Reported audience: (8,532 capacity)

February 5 - Coliseum, Greensboro, NC
Promoter: Cellar Door Productions
Other act(s): Ted Nugent
Reported audience: (15,587 capacity)
Set list: Love Gun / Cold Gin / Bang Bang You / Fits like a Glove / Crazy Crazy Nights / Shout It Out Loud / War Machine / Reason to Live / Heaven's On Fire / I Love It Loud / Lick It Up / Rock And Roll All Nite / Tears Are Falling / Detroit Rock City
Notes:
- An AUD recording circulates from this show.

February 6 - Cumberland County Civic Arena, Fayetteville, NC
Promoter: C&C Entertainment
Other act(s): Ted Nugent
Reported audience: (6,300 capacity)

February 7 - Coliseum, Charlotte, NC
Promoter: C&C Entertainment
Other act(s): Ted Nugent
Reported audience: 7,728 / 10,000 (77.38%)
Reported gross: $127,677
Set list: Love Gun / Cold Gin / Bang Bang You / Fits like a Glove / Tears Are Falling / Shout It Out Loud / War Machine / Reason to Live / Heaven's On Fire / I Love It Loud / Lick It Up / Rock And Roll All Nite / Crazy Crazy Nights / Detroit Rock City
Notes:
- An AUD recording circulates from this show.

February 9 - Municipal Auditorium, Nashville, TN
Promoter: Concert Promotions/Southern Promotions
Other act(s): Ted Nugent
Reported audience: 6,431 / 9,900 (64.96%)
Reported gross: $106,112
Notes:
- There was no mention of KISS in a minor news feature in the Tennessean paper, the day following the show, which focused on local bass player, David Kiswiney, a member of Nugent's band at the time.

February 10 - The Omni, Atlanta, GA
Promoter: Concert Promotions/Southern Promotions
Other act(s): Ted Nugent
Reported audience: 7,526 / 17,023 (44.21%)
Reported gross: $131,705
Set list: Love Gun / Cold Gin / Bang Bang You / Fits like a Glove / Crazy Crazy Nights / Shout It Out Loud / War Machine / Reason to Live / Heaven's On Fire / I Love It Loud / Lick It Up / Rock And Roll All Nite / Detroit Rock City
Notes:
- An average AUD recording circulates from this show.

February 12 - Sportatorium, Hollywood, FL
Promoter: Cellar Door Productions

Other act(s): Ted Nugent
Reported audience: (11,400 capacity)
Set list: Love Gun / Cold Gin / Bang Bang You / Fits like a Glove / Crazy Crazy Nights / Shout It Out Loud / War Machine / Reason to Live / Heaven's On Fire / I Love It Loud / Lick It Up / Rock And Roll All Nite / Oh Susannah / Tears Are Falling / Detroit Rock City
Notes:
- A reasonable audience filmed VID circulates from this show.

February 13 - Bayfront Center Arena, St. Petersburg, FL
Promoter: Cellar Door Productions
Other act(s): Ted Nugent
Reported audience: (8,300 capacity)
Set list: Love Gun / Cold Gin / Bang Bang You / Fits like a Glove / Crazy Crazy Nights / Shout It Out Loud / War Machine / Reason to Live / Heaven's On Fire / I Love It Loud / Lick It Up / Rock And Roll All Nite / Medley / Tears Are Falling / Detroit Rock City
Notes:
- An AUD recording circulates from this show. The medley included bits of "Cat Scratch Fever," "Calling Dr. Love," "La Bamba," "Wipeout," and "Stairway to Heaven."

February 14 - Coliseum, Jacksonville, FL
Promoter: Cellar Door Productions
Other act(s): Ted Nugent
Reported audience: (11,000 capacity)

February 15 - Municipal Auditorium, Columbus, GA
Promoter: Colson Brothers Promotions
Other act(s): Ted Nugent
Reported audience: 5,263 / 5,500 (95.69%)
Reported gross: $76,905
Notes:
- Gene was arrested following this show for allegedly mooning the audience.

February 16 - Carolina Coliseum, Columbia, SC
Promoter: Cellar Door Productions
Other act(s): Ted Nugent
Reported audience: ~3,000 / 12,352 (24.49%)
Notes:
- 30 patrons were arrested during the show for drugs and other offences. Following this show the Richland County Sheriff's Department narcotics patrol weren't invited back to police the USC venue with police and venue officials disputing the size of a drug use problem at area concerts. By comparison, some 75 had been arrested at a Jan. 25 Def Leppard show; and 17 at a Hank Williams, Jr. show on Feb. 25.
- From a local review: "There's just no recapturing the past. KISS and Ted Nugent proved that during their concert at Carolina Coliseum Tuesday night. These veteran rock 'n' rollers, who some would argue have long since outlived their usefulness, delivered a laborious and deafening three-hour show sorely lacking in freshness and precision. Their sets were identically formatted — start with a gut-churning rocker, swoop into a new song, reach back for one or two chartbusters, try another new song, promote the new album, dive into another group standard and then go for the blowout finale. They were embarrassingly predictable. No surprises. No innovation. No life. On top of that were the interminable and sloppy solos, the unimaginative banter between songs, [and] the juvenile sexual references. It wasn't long before it became irritating. Even so, the audience of 3,000 stuck with the performers throughout — flicking lighters on command, chanting back and forth, punching the air. Paul Stanley, KISS's frontman, veiled, however thinly, his disappointment at the meager turnout by saying, 'Sure, we could have canceled the show. But we thought we'd come out and (the rest unprintable).' Unfortunately, the show went on — and on" (The State, 2/17/88).

February 18 - I.S.U. Hulman Center, Terre Haute, IN
Promoter: Sunshine Promotions
Other act(s): Ted Nugent
Reported audience: (10,000 capacity)

February 19 - Five Flags Arena, Dubuque, IA
Promoter: Contemporary Productions
Other act(s): Ted Nugent
Reported audience: (5,200 capacity)

February 20 - Municipal Auditorium, Kansas City, MS
Promoter: Rose Productions
Other act(s): Ted Nugent
Reported audience: ~8,000 / 10,300 (77.67%)
Notes:
- From a local review: "Right, there were no surprises at the KISS and Ted Nugent concert Saturday at Municipal Auditorium. The construction workers of rock 'n roll jack-hammered their loud, repetitive chords into the ears of more than 8,000 fans for 2 1/2 hours... Now the music is more sedimentary than ever, and all that remains of the stage show is the giant lighted KISS logo and a few fireworks during the opening and closing numbers... The band pounded out 90 minutes of old and new material with an equal lack of imagination... Even the group's lone enjoyable performance of 'Reason To Live,' one of the few musically original tunes from the band's latest album, 'Crazy Nights,' was tarnished by Stanley's plea for fans to call MTV every day to ensure the song remained No. 1 on the cable network" (Kansas City Times, 2/22/88).

February 21 - Barton Coliseum, Little Rock, AK
Promoter: Mid-South Concerts
Other act(s): Ted Nugent
Reported audience: 7,365 / 10,000 (73.65%)
Reported gross: $110,475
Notes:

- From a local review: "Tickets for Sunday night's KISS-Ted Nugent concert at Barton Coliseum should have come with a warning label from the Surgeon General: 'Tonight's concert may be hazardous to your hearing.' KISS, the band that has worried millions of parents and thrilled even more fans for more than a decade, turning in one of its patented 'loud and fast' performances for which it has received recognition, if not praise. Guitarist Paul Stanley, whose version of the bump-and-grind thrilled a legion of female fans, put on his own brand of stage Olympics, running from side to side and leaping atop banks of speakers to address the adoring throng. Stanley, with his jokes and waggling, provided and interesting contrast of bassist Gene Simmons, a shining knight in black leather, commanding attention his own unique way atop the rows of speakers... Minus the heavy makeup and special effects that made them famous early in their career, KISS proved that they deserve a place in the heavy-metal hall of fame" (Arkansas Democrat, 2/22/88).
- From another local review: "KISS hasn't changed its musical approach too much — still utilizing the 'wall of sound' overkill — but the group has updated its stage show and personal appearance to keep it in touch with today's trends. Thankfully, that means no makeup, no platform heels, less posturing, a cleaner stage and crisp, clean lighting. Musically, KISS doesn't sound much different than it always has... KISS' music, although loud and a tad monotonous, was fairly melodic, was filled with good guitar hooks and solid drum work and featured enough harmony work to soften it just a bit" (Arkansas Gazette, 2/22/88).

February 23 - Kiefer U.N.O. Lakefront Arena, New Orleans, LA
Promoter: Concert / Southern Promotions
Other act(s): Ted Nugent
Reported audience: (18,000 capacity)
Set list: Love Gun / Cold Gin / Bang Bang You / Fits like a Glove / Crazy Crazy Nights / Shout It Out Loud / War Machine

/ Reason to Live / Heaven's On Fire / I Love It Loud / Lick It Up / Rock And Roll All Nite / Tears Are Falling / Detroit Rock City
Notes:
- A partial AUD filmed VID exists. The filmer was sadly busted during Bruce's solo, which is a shame due to his close-up stage position (even with obstructions and camera movement at times). A second VID is also known to exist.

February 24 - The Summit, Houston, TX
Promoter: Pace Concerts
Other act(s): Ted Nugent
Reported audience: (9,600 capacity)
Set list: Love Gun / Cold Gin / Bang Bang You / Fits like a Glove / Crazy Crazy Nights / War Machine / Reason to Live / Heaven's On Fire / I Love It Loud / Lick It Up / Shout It Out Loud / Rock And Roll All Nite / Tears Are Falling / Detroit Rock City
Notes:
- An AUD recording circulates from this show.

February 25 - Convention Center Arena, San Antonio, TX
Promoter: Stone City Productions
Other act(s): Ted Nugent
Reported audience: (8,700 capacity)

February 26 - Frank Irwin Center, Austin, TX
Promoter: Stone City Productions
Other act(s): Ted Nugent
Reported audience: (11,600 capacity)
Set list: Same as Feb. 24
Notes:
- An AUD recording circulates from this show.

February 27 - Tarrant County Convention Center, Fort Worth, TX
Promoter: 462 Inc.
Other act(s): Ted Nugent

Reported audience: (9,020 capacity)
Set list: Same as Feb. 24
Notes:
- Final show with Ted Nugent opening.
- An incomplete AUD recording circulates from this show.

March 1 - Dane County Expo Center, Madison, WI
Promoter: Stardate Productions
Other act(s): Anthrax
Reported audience: ~4,100 / 8,000 (51.25%)
Notes:
- From a local review: "Perennial metal-heads KISS took the Dane County Coliseum stage Tuesday night. They didn't take it to the limits. But they could have taken it to Akron, Ohio, and few people would have missed it. An audience of 4,100 filled less than half of the venue... 'This definitely isn't the biggest crowd,' noted guitarist Paul Stanley, stepping up to the microphone. On the other hand, KISS really isn't the biggest band anymore, either. Funny how these things work out. Why the band's comeback seemed less successful than, say, Aerosmith's probably has more to do with the fact that Run-DMC has yet to cover a KISS song than that the band has shorn its makeup in a dubious attempt to remain fashionable... Musically, KISS is stuck in the days when people still thought bellbottoms and 'Happy Days' were neat ideas. As far as spectacle goes, Tuesday night's show was pretty darned tame... If obnoxious was your bag, though, opening band Anthrax was more fun than a barrel of monkeys" (Madison Wisconsin State Journal, 3/2/88).

March 2 - Holiday Star Theater, Merrillville, IN
Promoter: Holiday Star Productions
Other act(s): Anthrax
Reported audience: (3,400 capacity)
Set list: Love Gun / Cold Gin / Bang Bang You / Fits like a Glove / Crazy Crazy Nights / War Machine / Reason to Live / Heaven's On Fire / I Love It Loud / Lick It Up / Shout It Out

Loud / Rock And Roll All Nite / Tears Are Falling / Detroit Rock City
Notes:
- An AUD recording circulates from this show.

March 3 - Carver Civic Center Arena, Peoria, IL
Promoter: Jam Productions
Other act(s): Anthrax
Reported audience: ~5,000 / 11,277 (44.34%)
Set list: Love Gun / Cold Gin / Bang Bang You / Fits like a Glove / Crazy Crazy Nights / War Machine / Reason to Live / Heaven's On Fire / I Love It Loud / Lick It Up / Shout It Out Loud / Rock And Roll All Nite / Strutter / Detroit Rock City
Notes:
- From a local review: "More than 5,000 young concertgoers voiced their enthusiastic approval of KISS, the ageless quartet of heavy metal entertainers who Thursday brought their sensory assault to Carver Arena. Those in the mostly adolescent audience who were adults had to endure an unpleasant evening of mixed messages in the music: excitement and emptiness. They — or any nonfans — probably sneered as much as bassist Gene Simmons or mumbled as much as singer/guitarist Paul Stanley. KISS no longer dons its rock clown make-up, but they put on a terrific circus of show-biz pizzazz and searing pyrotechnics: an active stage presence of kicking and prancing like dancers or athletes; flash pots and flames, fiery explosions and furious fun. Furthermore, their individual craftsmanship had bursts of creative brilliance, highlighted by drummer Eric Carr's impressive solo and too-brief showpieces by guitarist Bruce Kulick. And their song list had occasional value, such as 'Reason to Live,' a hard-edged, loud ballad with a memorable melody.

But most of the time, the four men seemed to find joy in blind rage and ignorance — a combination that tends to lend itself to hopeless chaos. They laughed as they shouted out

angry encouragement to complain to MTV, cranked up the ear-piercing volume so guitar licks drowned out sirens, thundered the percussion so it could be felt in the sternum, and ignited banks of brilliant lights pointed at the crowd's defenseless retinas. In fact, if any entertainer comes up with a way to threaten an audience's sense of taste, KISS will do it. Strike that. Maybe it has. The dramatic and meaningless state of KISS' act survives in contrast to its high-energy beginning, which more than 20 gold albums ago promised to blend Jimi Hendrix, theatricality and a rock-solid foundation in a brash slash across the charts. As Thursday night's concert showed, Hendrix should be appreciated with breathless reverence for his positive contributions to pop music. Those who picked up his guitar gauntlet are embarrassing.

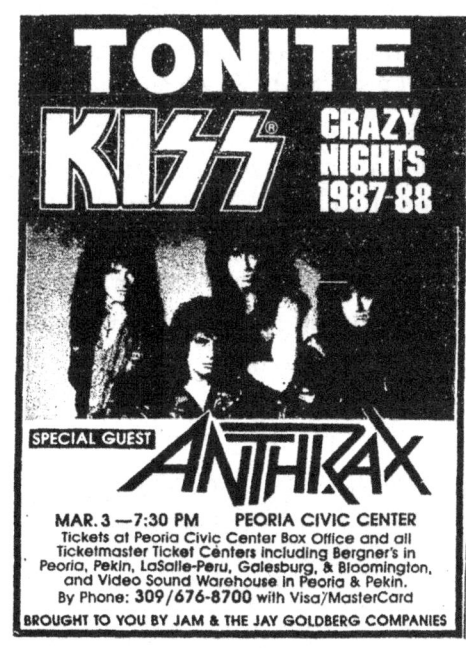

The largely innocent audience was subjected to juvenile lyrics so sexist they make Jon Bon Jovi seem like Phil Donahue. The simple-minded, mean-spirited noise bore little resemblance to the spirit and soul of rock and roll. In a few older numbers and new tunes from their current LP such as 'Crazy, Crazy Nights' and 'Bang Bang You,' they sang about mindless self-abuse and alcohol and sex with all the charm of an overloaded fuse box. It's sad that groups have to grovel for acceptance by using tired clichés to appeal to the worst — or lowest — traits in people. It's sadder to see a sea of upraised fists and hear cheers from kids who've heard so little of quality rock and roll

that they don't notice when it's bad or boring. In a couple of interesting bits such as Simmons 'shooting' out P.A. cabinets with power beams from his hands, KISS demonstrated that it at least retain its stirring professionalism. Anthrax is a group of rank amateurs — with the emphasis on rank" (Peoria Journal Star, 3/4/88).

March 5 - Arena, Winnipeg, MB, Canada
Promoter: Concert Productions International (CPI)
Other act(s): Anthrax
Reported audience: ~4,800 / 12,361 (38.83%)
Set list: Love Gun / Cold Gin / Bang Bang You / Fits like a Glove / Crazy Crazy Nights / War Machine / Reason to Live / Heaven's On Fire / I Love It Loud / Lick It Up / Shout It Out Loud / Rock And Roll All Nite / Tears Are Falling / Detroit Rock City
Notes:
From a local review: "Talk about regeneration. Here it is, 1988, and KISS draws a rapturous crowd composed mainly of fans who weren't even born when the original lineup first planted platform boots on stage. From the looks of the fans, few of the 4,800 seemed old enough to be enduring followers since the band's days of pancake makeup and kabuki visuals. Depending on how you take it, this says plenty about KISS' consistency in satisfying an audience many years the band's junior, or the improving taste of the KISS Army's original foot-soldiers.

This terminal liberal suggests both views are worthy. The 40 minutes of music heard by press time, presumably representing a crucial first thrust of recent material, sounded like heavy metal for beginners. The band played well enough, and Bruce Kulick ground out some exciting guitar noise, but the music was merely a functional, noisy soundtrack, not so much generic as miniaturized, a kind of Young Person's Guide To Arena Rock. No surprise, that. In its early days, the band was nothing less than brilliant at self-promotion, whacking

out three albums in about a year, touring extensively, following that with the obligatory two-record live set, then repackaging the first three discs in a package so inexpensive that fans who already had the originals bought the new package just to get the various trinkets sealed within. The corporate logo, the pyrotechnics, the wild makeup, all these were part of one of the shrewdest marketing campaigns since the Volkswagen people first learned about drollery.

Apart from the makeup, nothing has changed. The huge 'KISS' sign in bright white lights at the rear of the stage was as much a star as Paul Stanley, Gene Simmons, Eric Carr or Kulick. It really came into its own during Carr's drum solo. Despite a drum kit only slightly smaller than your average bungalow, and the muscle necessary to hit many parts of it in suitably thunderous manner, Carr didn't really have anything to say in his feature (well, apart from "Me!"). This, too, was part of the beginner's package — a drum solo for its own sake and Carr obliged by playing a bit, cueing applause, playing a little bit more, etc. It all made sense, though, once that huge sign started flashing while the spots bathed Carr in a variety of colors. Never forget to stress your logo.

Anthrax was more interesting for musical reasons. These five New Yorkers aren't the first to reintroduce punk to its heavy metal base, but they play with a verve and a sense of fun that do not so much goose heavy metal as give it several swift, heavy kicks up the backside. The 45-minute set included a lumpy but funny rap parody and a cover of The Sex Pistol's God Save The Queen (lessened by the singer's pointless mimicking of Johnny Rotten), neither of which are especially common in metal shows, and a frenzy that was generated by more than loudness. At first, the band was dogged by dodgy sound. The vocals, guitars and bass sounded only incidental to the drummer's massive but imaginative propulsion. Matters were sorted out somewhat by the middle of the set, though most of the lyrics were only to be guessed.

Encouragingly, Anthrax was, er, infectious with the KISS fans" (Winnipeg Free Press 3/6/88).
- An AUD recording circulates from this show.

March 8 - Northlands Coliseum, Edmonton, AB, Canada
Promoter: DKD / CPI / Perryscope Concert Productions
Other act(s): Anthrax
Reported audience: 5,057 / 7,500 (67.43%)
Reported gross: $79,565
Set list: Same as Mar. 5
Notes:
- An average AUD recording circulates from this show.

March 9 - Olympic Saddledome, Calgary, AB, Canada
Promoter: DKD / CPI / Perryscope Concert Productions
Other act(s): Anthrax
Reported audience: 5,641 / 7,500 (75.21%)
Reported gross: $85,066

March 11 - Pacific Coliseum, Vancouver, BC, Canada
Promoter: DKD / CPI / Perryscope Concert Productions
Other act(s): Anthrax
Reported audience: (7,500 capacity)
Set list: Same as Mar. 5
Notes:
- From a local review: "KISS without make-up is like a night strip without a drag queen: no camp, no glitz, no glamour. It's just another heavy metal band, tamer than most, and good nonetheless. The music performed at the Coliseum was hard, energetic and loud. But KISS was once special, full of theatrics which included a stage with a built-in elevator, flying guitar kits, and the band in full make up, all playing character roles: remember Space Ace and The Demon? Guitarist Gene Simmons, of tongue-trick fame, still practices his superhuman extension, but without the make-up he is far less delightfully monstrous. And the sporadic stage explosions feel like a stilted, awkward tribute to a more magnificent past. Lead

singer Paul Stanley still has a great rock voice, especially on the popular oldies 'Shout It Out Loud,' and 'I Wanna Rock and Roll All Night.' Guitar and drum solos given to band newcomers, guitarist Bruce Kulick and drummer Eric Carr, are out of place, and a waste of time. Stanley tells an overly long, though amusing, tale of lust in a (insert name of town) Vancouver health club. 'I don't want to offend anyone, but this story has to do with S.E.X.,' he warns. It's actually a long introduction to 'Lick It Up,' another big oldie, and a rocking success in performance.

KISS's light show is a truncated version of what it once was: spinning colors only, no lasers now. The first song ends with a brief, localized shower of light. Simmons holds a torch ceremonially above his head, [and] then plunges its base into a box at the front of the stage where it is quickly, and safely, extinguished by a roadie. No risk. No fun. But the band still engages its audience well. Those audience musicians interested in accessorizing for their next gig found guitar picks and drum sticks aplenty tossed into the writhing mass by the generous band. Simmons shoots the traditional fireworks out of his guitar neck, and the speakers and lights he aims at appear to break, fall from position, and swing crippled in the smoky air. Stanley smashes his guitar on stage. A big, fiery explosion on the surprisingly underused circular ramp behind drummer Carr provides the biggest pyrotechnic display of the evening. Though muted, KISS remains entertaining, a generous assessment perhaps encouraged by a screeching, directionless opening act called Anthrax, a band which takes its name from a boil disease of sheep and cattle" (Vancouver Sun, 3/12/88).
- An AUD recording circulates from this show.

March 13 - Jackson County Expo Park, Medford, OR
Promoter: Media One Productions
Other act(s): Anthrax
Reported audience: 5,005 / 5,700 (87.81%)

Reported gross: $74,960
Notes:
- From a local review: "KISS, minus the wild facial makeup that was the band's trademark in the 1970s and early 1980s, opened its set with an oldie but goodie called 'Love Gun.' With each song the band played, the spirit of the crowd seemed to increase... The mood was enhanced by a guitar solo, followed by a drum solo. KISS got the crowd to sing along by belting out some of its recent hit songs, including 'Reason to Live' and "Heaven's On Fire'" (Medford Mail Tribune, 3/14/88).
- Local press reported that 4,200 tickets had been sold in advance with strong walk-up sales.

March 14 - Memorial Coliseum, Portland, OR
Promoter: Media One Productions
Other act(s): Anthrax
Reported audience: 4,107 / 9,000 (45.63%)
Reported gross: $65,835
Set list: Love Gun / Cold Gin / Bang Bang You / Fits like a Glove / Crazy Crazy Nights / War Machine / Reason to Live / Heaven's On Fire / I Love It Loud / Lick It Up / Shout It Out Loud / Rock And Roll All Nite / Detroit Rock City
Notes:
- From a local review: "Follow the music. Or, some would say, the sound. Or, still others would insist, the noise. It is everywhere in Memorial Coliseum the night of a rock concert. It fills the arena; it seeps through concrete as if the thick walls were a thin membrane. Take a walk into the coliseum arena, where Kiss appeared earlier this week, along with an opening act called Anthrax, a word usually thought of, when thought of at all, in terms of an ugly infectious disease of cattle and sheep. If the KISS name is legendary these days, it is also of only moderate consumer appeal. Perhaps 5,000 eager fans joined forces at Memorial Coliseum that night to pay homage to their heavy-metal heroes, a sharp drop from the KISS crowds of the middle and late '70s.

Nevertheless, inside the coliseum those 5,000 faithful waved their arms in evangelistic fervor, the overwhelming bass flooding the ears, mind, body and emotional soul with a powerful, if mind-numbing, excitement and incessant vibration" (The Oregonian, 3/18/88).
- An AUD recording circulates from this show.

March 15 - Coliseum, Spokane, WA
Promoter: Media One Productions
Reported audience: ~3,700 / 8,500 (43.53%)
Other act(s): Anthrax
Notes:
- An audience of 3,700 was reported in the local press. From a local review: "The center ring belonged to KISS. How badly they wanted it is questionable. After playing to audiences of close to 15,000 earlier this year, the small turn-out must have been deflating... Overall the show lacked an explosive energy. The potential was there. With the exception of Simmons' black leathers, the outfits were colorful and the lighting system impressive. But the biggest efforts to please the fans included the throwing of an endless supply of picks into the front rows and the smashing of a guitar... The group's music isn't strong enough to carry a show on its own" (Spokane Chronicle, 3/16/88).
- From another local review: "Overall the show lack and explosive energy. The potential was there. With the exception of Simmons' black leathers, the outfits were colorful and the lighting seemed impressive. But the biggest effects to please the fans including the throwing of an endless supply of picks into the front rows and the smashing of a guitar... The group's music isn't strong enough to carry the show on its own... It's time for these veterans to grow up" (Spokesman-Review, 3/16/88).

March 17 - Coliseum, Seattle, WA
Promoter: Media One Productions
Other act(s): Anthrax

Reported audience: 5,945 / 14,327 (41.50%)
Reported gross: $94,661
Set list: Love Gun / Cold Gin / Bang Bang You / Fits like a Glove / Crazy Crazy Nights / War Machine / Reason to Live / Heaven's On Fire / I Love It Loud / Lick It Up / Shout It Out Loud / Rock And Roll All Nite / Detroit Rock City
Notes:
- After a drought of rock shows following Aerosmith's Jan. 16 show, Ted Nugent arrived in town (with Armored Saint) to perform the night prior to KISS. Two shows with similar artists, in such a short timeframe, may have impacted the attendance at both, though the Pacific Northwest was hardly fertile ground for the band.
- From a local review: "You'd think that the band by that name, which ruled the hard-rock world in the 1970s, would be burned out by now, consumed by its own excesses. But somehow the explosive heavy-metal show band has survived into the late '80s, still gaudy, loud and sexist, although without the trademark makeup that characterized its heyday. Although the face paint is gone, the group is still highly theatrical, with more flash-pot explosions per show than any other group and enough lights to illuminate the city of Seattle. Gene Simmons still does his fire-breathing and blood-spitting routines, Paul Stanley is still the gyrating centerpiece of the show and drummer Eric Carr still works out on an elevated platform that grows, spins and tilts. You still get a lot of bang for your buck at a KISS show" (Seattle Times, 3/11/88).
- An AUD recording circulates from this show.

March 19 - Rushmore Plaza Civic Center Arena, Rapid City, SD
Promoter: United Concerts
Other act(s): Anthrax
Reported audience: ~4,500 / 11,000 (40.91%)
Notes:

- From a local review: "The 4,500 young people who were at the Rushmore Plaza Civic Center Arena Saturday night had a gas. Bass player Gene Simmons owned the show. And anyone who tells you that KISS isn't theatrical since they washed off their faces hasn't seen them lately. With the addition of Bruce Kulick and Eric Carr, the band has become more musical while retaining the theatrical presence that has been their trademark since the 70s. Kulick's guitar work was amazing. A long solo early in the concert had the crowd roaring. Drummer Carr joined in about halfway and finished off with a solo of his own that could loosen molars" (Rapid City Journal, 3/20/88).

March 20 - Events Center, Casper, WY
Promoter: Nath / Baker Productions
Other act(s): Anthrax
Reported audience: 3,869 / 10,452 (37.02%)

March 21 - Acord Arena at the Salt Palace, Salt Lake City, UT
Promoter: United Concerts
Other act(s): Anthrax
Reported audience: 7,000 / 13,000 (53.85%)
Reported gross: $105,000

March 23 - McNichols Arena, Denver, CO
Promoter: Fey Concerts
Other act(s): Anthrax
Reported audience: 5,575 / 10,137 (55%)
Reported gross: $91,410
Notes:

- From a local review: "Wednesday night's concert at Denver's McNichols Arena by one of thud rock's reigning bands was loud, if nothing else. KISS, a rock group that has been playing heavy metal since before the phrase was coined, played to a disappointingly sparse audience in the giant arena's half-house seating arrangement... There were plenty of times in the '70s and early '80s when KISS filled McNichols to near capacity in its full-house configuration, but, even with half-house seating Wednesday, the balcony was about as crowded as a mile of Montana prairie. That's too bad. The KISS show is still as outrageously entertaining as it has been since its members donned their legendary black-and-white face paint and elevator shoes. The makeup is gone, but the pyrotechnic presentation remains intact" (Colorado Springs Gazette Telegraph, 3/26/88).

March 25 - Compton Terrace @ Firebird Lake, Chandler (Phoenix), AZ
Promoter: Evening Star Productions
Other act(s): Anthrax
Reported audience: 5,363 / 10,535 (50.91%)
Reported gross: $77,868
Set list: Love Gun / Cold Gin / Bang Bang You / Fits like a Glove / Crazy Crazy Nights / War Machine / Reason to Live / Heaven's On Fire / I Love It Loud / Lick It Up / Shout It Out Loud / Rock And Roll All Nite / Detroit Rock City
Notes:
- An AUD recording circulates from this show.

March 26 - Pacific Amphitheatre, Costa Mesa, CA
Promoter: Nederlander Productions
Other act(s): Anthrax
Reported audience: (18,742 capacity)
Set list: Love Gun / Cold Gin / Bang Bang You / Fits like a Glove / Crazy Crazy Nights / War Machine / Reason to Live / Heaven's On Fire / I Love It Loud / Lick It Up / Shout It Out Loud / Rock And Roll All Nite / Detroit Rock City

Notes:
- From local press: "KISS, a band with a reputation as one of the noisiest in the rock business, blatantly violated a noise level injunction against Pacific Amphitheatre during a concert Saturday night, the consultant for a homeowner's group said. Sam Lane, a consultant for Concerned Citizens of Costa Mesa, said KISS and opening act Anthrax far exceeded noise levels set by a court order for almost the entire first two hours of the concert. 'KISS is the loudest of any performance I've heard,' said Lane, who has monitored sound levels of amphitheater concerts for four years. 'The maximum limit that you can't go over for one second is 70 decibels, and they've gone over that a hundred times.' Lane set up his equipment in a back yard on Presidio Drive, about 2,000 feet away from the arena" (Los Angeles Times, 3/27/88).
- From a local review: "KISS has had a long, lucrative run as the Ringling Brothers of rock. But at the Pacific Amphitheatre on Saturday, the band's heavy metal circus was more like a stale old animal act than the greatest show on earth. As always, Paul Stanley cussed and showed off his chest hair. Gene Simmons wagged his tongue at everyone, did his fire-breathing routine and shout fireworks out of a bass guitar shaped like a battle ax. Behind the stage, the band's name flashed in lights. If the tricks were predictable, the beasts at least managed to show their fangs from time to time. KISS roared convincingly at the start with 20 minutes of animated, hard-pounding rock. But 'Crazy, Crazy Nights,' an anthem that should have taken the show higher, slowed it to a plodding pace while laying bare the frayed, stringy thing that Stanley is trying to pass off these days as a singing voice. Ten minutes of drum and guitar solos followed, with an effect as deadening as a tranquilizer dart. KISS showed signs of stirring again toward the end, but adjourned for the night after playing only 13 bona fide songs in 75 minutes — a skimpy show for a band that boasts of its longevity" (Los Angeles Times, 3/28/88).
- An AUD recording circulates from this show.

March 28 - ARCO Arena, Sacramento, CA
Promoter: Bill Graham Presents
Other act(s): Anthrax
Reported audience: (10,500 capacity)
Set list: Love Gun / Cold Gin / Bang Bang You / Fits like a Glove / Crazy Crazy Nights / War Machine / Reason to Live / Heaven's On Fire / Tears Are Falling / I Love It Loud / Lick It Up / Shout It Out Loud / Rock And Roll All Nite / Detroit Rock City
Notes:
- An AUD recording circulates from this show.

March 30 - Civic Auditorium, San Francisco, CA
Promoter: Bill Graham Presents
Other act(s): Anthrax
Reported audience: (8,500 capacity)
Set list: Love Gun / Cold Gin / Bang Bang You / Fits like a Glove / Crazy Crazy Nights / War Machine / Heaven's On Fire / Tears Are Falling / I Love It Loud / Lick It Up / Shout It Out Loud / Whole Lotta Love / Rock And Roll All Nite / Detroit Rock City
Notes:
- From a local review: "It's hard for a band like KISS to keep its fans. Time passes, the fans grow up, get into other things - music, for example. So who goes to see KISS in 1988? The same types who saw them in 1977, basically. Teenagers, mostly boys about 16, the kind who drink beer and leave bottles in the parking lot. These fans don't come out in as great numbers as in the old days. Two years ago KISS' Cow Palace show was half empty. Wednesday night, even worse, the much-smaller Civic Auditorium was only two-thirds filled. But KISS hangs on. 'We are here to kick your motherf----- a--,' were Paul Stanley's first words onstage. And that's the level we're dealing with here — beyond lowbrow, more like no-brow. You can picture these guys getting tossed raw meat. Some years back KISS dispensed with the white and black make-up they used to wear, and this tour, possibly a

concession to the fact that they're not raking in the money like they used to, there are no fireworks, fire-breathing stunts or bombs going off at the end of songs. All that's left is the four letters K-I-S-S in lights at the back of the stage. It would be hard to keep a straight face and tell you this was a good show, but it was definitely fun. Against all my expectations, I enjoyed KISS more than any rock band I've seen perform in the last six months. They're vulgar and silly, but then so are most rock groups" (San Francisco Chronicle, 4/1/88).
- A poor distorted AUD recording circulates from this show.

March 31 - The Forum, Inglewood (Los Angeles), CA
**CANCELLED
Promoter: Nederlander Productions
Other act(s): Anthrax
Reported audience: (18,679 capacity)
Notes:
- The configuration of the venue to be used had not been determined at time of show cancellation. Tickets had been due to go on sale Monday, Feb. 15.

April 1 - Sports Arena, San Diego, CA
Promoter: Bill Silva Presents
Other act(s): Anthrax
Reported audience: (8,100 capacity)
Set list: Love Gun / Cold Gin / Strutter / Bang Bang You / Fits like a Glove / Crazy Crazy Nights / War Machine / Reason to Live / Heaven's On Fire / Tears Are Falling / I Love It Loud / Lick It Up / Shout It Out Loud / Rock And Roll All Nite / Detroit Rock City
Notes:
- An AUD recording circulates from this show.

April 2 - Thomas & Mack Center @ UNLV, Las Vegas, NV
Promoter: Evening Star Productions
Other act(s): Anthrax
Reported audience: (6,862 capacity)

Set list: Same as Apr. 1
Notes:
- Final date of the U.S. "Crazy Nights" tour, following which the band took a short break before heading for Japan.
- An AUD recording circulates from this show.

April 4 - Veterans Memorial Coliseum, Phoenix, AZ **TEMP HOLD DATE
Promoter: Evening Star Productions
Other act(s): Anthrax
Notes:
- A second date in the vicinity of a show at Compton Terrace, already a suburb of Phoenix on Mar. 25, was deemed pointless.

April 16 - Nagoya Public Hall, Nagoya, Japan
Promoter: Udo Artists, Inc.
Other act(s): None
Reported audience: (10,000 capacity)
Set list: Love Gun / Cold Gin / Bang Bang You / Fits like a Glove / Crazy Crazy Nights / War Machine / Reason to Live / Heaven's On Fire / Tears Are Falling / I Love It Loud / Lick It Up / Black Diamond / Shout It Out Loud / Rock And Roll All Nite / Detroit Rock City
Notes:
- There were no opening acts for the Japanese leg of the tour. The band arrived in Japan on Apr. 14.

April 18 - Castle Hall, Osaka, Japan
Promoter: Udo Artists, Inc.
Reported audience: (16,000 capacity)
Set list: Love Gun / Cold Gin / Bang Bang You / Fits like a Glove / Calling Dr. Love / Crazy Crazy Nights / No, No, No / Reason to Live / Heaven's On Fire / War Machine / Tears Are Falling / I Love It Loud / Lick It Up / Black Diamond / I Was Made For Lovin' You / Shout It Out Loud / Strutter / Rock And Roll All Nite / Detroit Rock City

Notes:
- Following the first night's show the set was expanded with "Calling Dr. Love," "No, No, No," "I Was Made for Lovin' You" and "Strutter" being performed.

April 20 - Bunka Gym, Yokohama, Japan
Promoter: Udo Artists, Inc.
Reported audience: (5,000 capacity)
Set list: Same as Apr. 18

April 21 - Budokan Hall, Tokyo, Japan
Promoter: Udo Artists, Inc.

Reported audience: (14,000 capacity)
Set list: Love Gun / Cold Gin / Bang Bang You / Calling Dr. Love / Fits Like A Glove / Crazy Crazy Nights / No, No, No / Reason To Live / Heaven's On Fire / War Machine / Tears Are Falling / I Love It Loud / Lick It Up / Black Diamond / I Was Made For Lovin' You / Shout It Out Loud / Strutter / Rock And Roll All Nite / Detroit Rock City
Notes:
- An excellent AUD recording circulates from this show.

April 22 - Budokan Hall, Tokyo, Japan
Promoter: Udo Artists, Inc.
Set list: Same as Apr. 21
Reported audience: (14,000 capacity)
Notes:
- This second night in Tokyo was professionally filmed and broadcast on Japanese TV. This show was partially released as the general bonus disk for "KISSology" Volume 2 in 2007. The heavily edited 38 minute DVD included: Love Gun / Cold Gin / Crazy Crazy Nights / Heaven's On Fire / War Machine / I Love It Loud / Lick It Up / I Was Made for Lovin' You / Detroit Rock City.

April 24 - Yoyogi Olympic Pool, Tokyo, Japan
Promoter: Udo Artists, Inc.
Set list: Same as Apr. 21
Reported audience: (12,500 capacity)
Notes:
- A decent AUD recording circulates from this show.

June 26 - Limelight, New York City, NY **FREHLEY'S COMET
Promoter: in-house / Hit Parader magazine
Other Act(s): Britny Fox
Reported audience: ~unknown
Set list(s): Rip It Out / Juvenile Delinquent / Something Moved / Cold Gin / Time Ain't Running Out / New York

Groove / Shock Me / Rock Soldiers / Breakout / Insane / Rocket Ride / Deuce

Notes:
- Gene and Paul jam with the band on "Deuce." The event was hardly spontaneous, since both bands had been rehearsing at SIR, and Gene, Paul, and Ace were getting along.

June 27 - SIR Studios, New York City, NY **REHEARSALS
June 28 - SIR Studios, New York City, NY **REHEARSALS
June 29 - SIR Studios, New York City, NY **REHEARSALS
June 30 - SIR Studios, New York City, NY **REHEARSALS
July 1 - SIR Studios, New York City, NY **REHEARSALS
July 2 - SIR Studios, New York City, NY **REHEARSALS

Notes:
- Prior to commencing rehearsals Gene and Paul made an appearance at a Frehley's Comet show at the Limelight Club and jammed "Deuce" with their former guitarist. Perhaps it's not too surprising that the song found itself back in a KISS set soon afterwards...

July 4 - Cheshire Fairgrounds, North Swanzey, NH
Promoter: Creative Productions
Other act(s): Dirty Looks, Balaam & the Angel, Mantis
Reported audience: ~4,000
Set list: Love Gun / Cold Gin / Bang Bang You / Calling Dr. Love / Crazy Crazy Nights / Fits Like A Glove / No, No, No / Reason To Love / Heaven's On Fire / War Machine / Tears Are Falling / I Love It Loud / Lick It Up / Black Diamond / Deuce / Shout It Out Loud / Strutter / Rock And Roll All Nite / Detroit Rock City

Notes:
- L.A. Guns were on the bill, but cancelled and were replaced by Dirty Looks. This show marked the band's first outdoors concert in the U.S. since 1978. Gene didn't breathe fire.
- This show circulates as an AUD recording.

July 8 - Forum, Halifax, NS, Canada **CANCELLED

August 12 - Ritz Club, New York City, NY
Promoter: John Scher Productions
Other act(s): Dirty Looks
Reported audience: 1,500 **SOLD-OUT
Set list: Deuce / Love Gun / Fits Like A Glove / Heaven's On Fire / Cold Gin / Black Diamond / Bang Bang You / No, No, No / Firehouse / Crazy Crazy Nights / Calling Dr. Love / War Machine / Reason To Live / Tears Are Falling / I Love It Loud / Strutter / Shout It Out Loud / Lick It Up / Rock And Roll All Nite / Detroit Rock City
Notes:
- After nearly 15 years KISS returned to the clubs for several special warm-up gigs for the European "Monsters of Rock" summer tour. During the break between shows leading to the club dates, Gene and Paul attended the Robert Plant / Cheap Trick concert at Madison Square Garden on July 29.
- From a mainstream mention: "KISS delighted its most hardcore New York fans Aug. 12-13 with two sellout shows at the Ritz club. In addition to playing songs from its more recent (non-makeup) albums, the group delved back into its very first album to deliver fan favorites like 'Deuce,' 'Black Diamond,' 'Firehouse,' and 'Strutter'" (Billboard, 8/27/88).
- This show was broadcast on radio via 102.7 WNEW-FM and as a result has been a popular bootlegger choice for various releases.

August 13 - Ritz Club, New York City, NY
Promoter: John Scher Productions
Other act(s): Dirty Looks
Reported audience: 1,500 **SOLD-OUT
Set list: Same as Aug. 12
Notes:
- Filmed by the band from the soundboard, this show was partially released as the "Best Buy" bonus disk for "KISSology" Volume 2 in 2007. The band flub the intro to "Firehouse" and

Paul comments that he's glad they're not broadcasting the show. The edited 46 minute DVD included: Deuce / Love Gun / Fits like a Glove / Heaven's On Fire / Cold Gin / Black Diamond / Firehouse / Crazy Crazy Nights / Calling Dr. Love / War Machine / Tears Are Falling

AIRWAVES Schedule 1

KISS EUROPEAN SCHEDULE 1988 AUG–OCT

Day	Date		Location
WED	AUGUST	17	LONDON, MARQUEE CLUB (provisional booking)
SAT	AUGUST	20	CASTLE DONINGTON – MONSTERS OF ROCK FESTIVAL
SAT	AUGUST	27	SCHWEINFURT, MAINWIESEN/UFERSTRASSE – MONSTERS OF ROCK FESTIVAL, WEST GERMANY
SUN	AUGUST	28	BOCHUM, RUHRSTADION – MONSTERS OF ROCK FESTIVAL, WEST GERMANY
SUN	SEPTEMBER	4	TILBURG, WILLEM II F.C., M.O.R. HOLLAND
SAT	SEPTEMBER	10	MODENA, ARENA NATIONAL FESTA DELL'UNITA – MONSTERS OF ROCK FESTIVAL, ITALY
SUN	SEPTEMBER	11	REHEARSALS PARIS, LE ZENITH
MON	SEPTEMBER	12	REHEARSALS PARIS, LE ZENITH
TUE	SEPTEMBER	13	PARIS, LE ZENITH
WED	SEPTEMBER	14	OFF
THUR	SEPTEMBER	15	COPENHAGEN, K.B. HALLEN
FRI	SEPTEMBER	16	GOTHENBURG, FROLUNDABORG
SAT	SEPTEMBER	17	STOCKHOLM, ISSTADION
SUN	SEPTEMBER	18	OFF
MON	SEPTEMBER	19	HELSINKI, ISHALLEN
TUE	SEPTEMBER	20	OFF
WED	SEPTEMBER	21	OSLO, SKEDSMOHALLEN
THUR	SEPTEMBER	22	OFF
FRI	SEPTEMBER	23	OFF
SAT	SEPTEMBER	24	WEMBLEY, ARENA
SUN	SEPTEMBER	25	WEMBLEY, ARENA
MON	SEPTEMBER	26	BIRMINGHAM, N.E.C. ARENA
TUE	SEPTEMBER	27	BIRMINGHAM, N.E.C. ARENA
WED	SEPTEMBER	28	OFF
THUR	SEPTEMBER	29	NEWCASTLE, CITY HALL
FRI	SEPTEMBER	30	EDINBURGH, PLAYHOUSE
SAT	OCTOBER	1	EDINBURGH, PLAYHOUSE
SUN	OCTOBER	2	OFF
MON	OCTOBER	3	BELFAST, KINGS HALL

August 16 - Marquee Club, London, England
Promoter: in-house
Other act(s): None
Reported audience: 500 **SOLD-OUT
Set list: Deuce / Love Gun / Fits like a Glove / Heaven's On Fire / Cold Gin / Black Diamond / Bang Bang You / No, No, No

/ Firehouse / Crazy Crazy Nights / Calling Dr. Love / War Machine / Reason To Live / Tears Are Falling / I Love It Loud / Strutter / Shout It Out Loud / Lick It Up / Rock And Roll All Nite / Detroit Rock City

Notes:
- KISS was the first band to play at the legendary Marquee Club's then new location at 105-107 Charring Cross at what was essentially a warm-up for the Donington show.
- A reasonable AUD recording from this show circulates.

August 20 - "Monsters of Rock", Donington Park, Derby, Leicestershire, England
Promoter: Aimcarve Ltd. / MCP
Other act(s): Iron Maiden (HL), David Lee Roth, Great White, Anthrax, Guns 'N' Roses, Helloween, The Bailey Brothers, Neal Kaye
Reported audience: 97,595 **SOLD-OUT
Reported gross: $2,739,090
Set list: Deuce / Love Gun / Fits Like A Glove / Heaven's On Fire / Cold Gin / Black Diamond / No, No, No / Firehouse / Crazy Crazy Nights / Calling Dr. Love / Tears Are Falling / I Love It Loud / Strutter / Shout It Out Loud / Lick It Up / Rock And Roll All Nite / Detroit Rock City

Notes:
- The most successful British MOR year, though two fans died during an audience crush while Guns 'N Roses' performed. Audience figures vary, some sources citing as many as 107,000 attendees. Megadeth were originally on the bill, but did not perform.
- 40 minutes' worth of the show, "Cold Gin" through "Shout It Out Loud," was broadcast on BBC Radio 1's "Friday Rock Show."
- From mainstream press: "Two heavy metal fans were apparently trampled to death at a recent Monsters Of Rock festival in the U.K., and a similar festival with the same name in West Germany led to large-scale rioting and more than 30 arrests. Neither of the festivals is related to the recently

concluded U.S. Monsters of Rock tour. U.K. officials are blaming a combination of slam dancing and slippery grounds for the deaths of two young heavy metal fans Aug. 20 during the annual open-air Monsters of Rock festival at Donington Park in the Midlands. The two were crushed to death as U.S. band Guns N' Roses took the stage.

Two other fans were hospitalized, and according to some reports as many as 250 more were slightly injured at the daylong event. The deceased are believed to have been knocked to the ground immediately in front of the stage and inadvertently trampled. The festival was not halted, and most of the estimated 90,000 audience members remained unaware of the tragedy. Organizers of the Reading Rock Festival, scheduled for the following week, subsequently banned slam dancing" (Billboard, 9/10/88).

August 27 - Mainweisen Gelände, Schweinfurt, Germany
Promoter: Shooter Promotions GmbH
Other act(s): Iron Maiden (HL), David Lee Roth (HL), Anthrax, Testament, Great White
Reported audience: ~40,000
Set list: Deuce / Love Gun / Fits Like A Glove / Heaven's On Fire / Cold Gin / Black Diamond / No, No, No / Firehouse / Crazy Crazy Nights / Tears Are Falling / I Love It Loud / Strutter / Shout It Out Loud / Lick It Up / Rock And Roll All Nite / Detroit Rock City
Notes:
- KISS were scheduled in the 4:20 - 5:20PM slot.
- Megadeth were scheduled to be one of the opening acts, but bassist David Ellefson had broken his arm. Treat, also scheduled, also didn't perform.
- From mainstream press: This show was marred by "serious outbreaks of violence and criminal damage by music fans started on the night before a similar Monsters of Rock concert package (minus Guns N' Roses and Helloween) was staged in that city Aug. 26. Thirty-five arrests were made, and

a critically injured U.S. soldier was rushed to the hospital as fans, many of whom had nowhere to stay, ran riot through the township streets. The fans' rampage went on all night. Streets were covered with broken glass from windows and bottles and rocks were hurled at local garbage-collection lorries that had attempted, under police protection, to clear the streets the following morning. Many fans, described as 'hooligans' by local police chiefs, camped out in the town center and, said one official, 'used the entire town as a toilet.' Though the festival itself was comparatively quiet and incident free, afterward gangs roamed the Schweinfurt streets, smashing shop windows and chanting" (Billboard, 9/10/88).
- Pro-shot VID circulates from this show, including footage of keyboard player Gary Corbett on the stage (rather than being more hidden). He had rejoined the touring entourage for this run of shows after being dispensed with earlier in the tour (prior to Japan).

August 28 - Ruhrstadion, Bochum, Germany
Promoter: Shooter Promotions GmbH
Other act(s): Iron Maiden (HL), David Lee Roth (HL), Anthrax, Testament, Great White
Reported audience: ~30,000
Set list: Deuce / Love Gun / Fits Like A Glove / Heaven's On Fire / Cold Gin / Black Diamond / No, No, No / Crazy Crazy Nights / Tears Are Falling / I Love It Loud / Strutter / Shout It Out Loud / Rock And Roll All Nite / Detroit Rock City
Notes:
- Testament replaced Megadeth on the bill which Treat cancelled.
- A couple of partial audience filmed videos circulate from this show.

August 30 - Reiðhöllin, Reykjavik, Iceland
Promoter: Split Promotions
Other act(s): Foringjarnir

Reported audience: ~5,000

September 2 - Kisstadion Lelàtò, Budapest, Hungary
Other act(s): Edda
Reported audience: (16,800 capacity)
Set list: Deuce / Love Gun / Fits Like A Glove / Heaven's On Fire / Cold Gin / Black Diamond / Bang Bang You / No, No, No / Crazy Crazy Nights / I Was Made For Lovin' You / War Machine / Reason To Live / Tears Are Falling / I Love It Loud / Strutter / Shout It Out Loud / Lick It Up / Rock And Roll All Nite / Detroit Rock City
Notes:
- Audience filmed video circulates from this show.

September 4 - Willem II Stadion, Tilburg, Holland
Promoter: Mojo Concerts / Stageco i.s.m. Norrderligt / Fair Warning Presents
Other act(s): Iron Maiden (HL), David Lee Roth (HL), Anthrax (opener), Helloween, Great White
Reported audience: (32,000 capacity)
Set list: Deuce / Love Gun / Fits Like A Glove / Heaven's On Fire / Cold Gin / Black Diamond / No, No, No / Crazy Crazy Nights / Tears Are Falling / I Love It Loud / Strutter / Shout It Out Loud / Rock And Roll All Nite / Detroit Rock City
Notes:
- The band were paid a $40,000 fee for this show and arrived in town the evening prior to the show. Amusingly, documents indicate Paul was booked at the Sonesta Hotel using "Mr. Spartacus" as his alias. Bruce used the cooler "Mr. Rockman."
- An AUD recording circulates from this show.

September 10 - Arena Festa De L'Unità, Modena, Italy
Promoter: Barley Arts / Warning Promotions
Other act(s): Iron Maiden (HL), Anthrax, Helloween, Kings of the Sun, Royal Air Force
Partial set list: Fits Like A Glove / Heaven's On Fire / Cold Gin / Black Diamond / No, No, No / Firehouse / Crazy Crazy Nights

/ I Was Made For Lovin' You / War Machine / Tears Are Falling / I Love It Loud / Shout It Out Loud / Lick It Up
Notes:
- Yngwie J. Malmsteen's Rising Force was scheduled to perform at this show, but were replaced at the last moment.
- Multiple AUD sources and VID circulate from this show.

September 11 - The Zenith, Paris, France **REHEARSALS
September 12 - The Zenith, Paris, France **REHEARSALS
Notes:
- Rehearsals were scheduled at this venue for the changes to the set resulting from the end of the Monsters of Rock leg.

September 13 - The Zenith, Paris, France
Promoter: SPS Presents
Other act(s): Kings of the Sun
Set list: Love Gun / Fits Like A Glove / Heaven's On Fire / Cold Gin / Black Diamond / Bang Bang You / No, No, No / Firehouse / Crazy Crazy Nights / I Was Made for Lovin' You / Deuce / Reason To Live / Tears Are Falling / I Love It Loud / Strutter / Shout it Out Loud / Lick It Up / Rock And Roll All Nite / Detroit Rock City
Notes:
- Yngwie J. Malmsteen was the scheduled opener for this show.
- An average AUD recording circulates from this show. A full VID also circulates.

September 15 - K.B. Hallen, Frederiksberg (Köpenhamn), Denmark
Promoter: E. T. Concerts ApS Presents
Other act(s): Kings of the Sun
Reported audience: (3,000 capacity)
Set list: Love Gun / Fits Like A Glove / Heaven's On Fire / Cold Gin / Black Diamond / Bang Bang You / No, No, No / Firehouse / Crazy Crazy Nights / I Was Made for Lovin' You / Deuce / Reason To Live / Tears Are Falling / I Love It Loud /

Strutter / Shout it Out Loud / Lick It Up / Rock And Roll All Nite / Detroit Rock City
Notes:
- This was the last show with Paul performing the show introduction.
- Partial audience filmed VID circulates from this show. A full AUD also circulates.

September 16 - Frölundaborg, Göteborg, Sweden
Promoter: EMA Telstar
Other act(s): Kings of the Sun
Reported audience: ~4,500 / 8,000 (56.25%)
Set list: Love Gun / Fits Like A Glove / Heaven's On Fire / Cold Gin / Black Diamond / Bang Bang You / No, No, No / Firehouse / Crazy Crazy Nights / I Was Made for Lovin' You / Deuce / Reason To Live / Tears Are Falling / I Love It Loud / Strutter / Shout it Out Loud / Lick It Up / Rock And Roll All Nite / Detroit Rock City
Notes:
- The return of the "you wanted the best..." intro. Yngwie J. Malmsteen's Rising Force were also scheduled to open both Swedish shows but were replaced by Kings of the Sun.
- Multiple AUD and VID sources circulate, one of which is commonly titled "Still Krazy" as a famed bootleg.

September 17 - Isstadion, Stockholm, Sweden
Promoter: EMA Telstar
Other act(s): Kings of the Sun
Reported audience: ~6,000 / 9,000 (66.7%)
Set list: Love Gun / Fits Like A Glove / Heaven's On Fire / Cold Gin / Black Diamond / Bang Bang You / No, No, No / Firehouse / Crazy Crazy Nights / I Was Made for Lovin' You / Deuce / Reason To Live / Tears Are Falling / I Love It Loud / Strutter / Shout it Out Loud / Lick It Up / Rock And Roll All Nite / Detroit Rock City
Notes:

- Pro-shot footage of "Love Gun" from the back of house was broadcast on TV Scandinavia's Nightflight special.
- A translation from a local review: "KISS is idling. The nearly 6,000 at the Ice Stadium last night were treated to a competent and certified rock show with both old and new hits. But KISS live resembles more and more a nostalgia trip for those already convinced. The myth surrounding them begins to be somewhat pathetic" (Aftonbladet, 9/18/88).

September 19 - Jäähalli, Helsinki, Finland
Other act(s): Kings of the Sun
Reported audience: (8,200 capacity)
Set list: Love Gun / Fits Like A Glove / Heaven's On Fire / Cold Gin / Black Diamond / Bang Bang You / No, No, No / Firehouse / Crazy Crazy Nights / I Was Made For Lovin' You / Deuce / Reason To Live / Tears Are Falling / I Love It Loud / Strutter / Shout it Out Loud / Lick It Up / Rock And Roll All Nite / Detroit Rock City
Notes:
- Gene and Paul were interviewed prior to the show.
- Partial AUD and VID recordings circulate, capturing the full show between them.

September 21 - Skedsmohallen, Lillestrøm, Norway
Other act(s): Kings of the Sun
Reported audience: (5,000 capacity)
Set list: Love Gun / Fits Like A Glove / Heaven's On Fire / Cold Gin / Black Diamond / Bang Bang You / No, No, No / Firehouse / Crazy Crazy Nights / I Was Made For Lovin' You / Deuce / Reason To Live / Tears Are Falling / I Love It Loud / Strutter / Shout it Out Loud / Lick It Up / Rock And Roll All Nite / Detroit Rock City
Notes:
- Lillestrøm is located approx. 10 miles northwest of Oslo.
- The full show circulates as an AUD recording.

September 24 - Wembley Arena, London, England
Promoter: Kennedy Street / MCP / Fair Warning
Other act(s): Kings of the Sun
Reported audience: (8,000 capacity)
Set list: Same as Sept. 21
Notes:
- From a mainstream review: "I grew up with the belief that the New Yorkers were a larger than life, outrageous spectacle on stage. The first night of their UK tour, at Wembley Arena, left that belief in tatters. Was this really what I'd come to see? No sparking KISS logos, virtually no pyro, just a wall of amps and a 'let's get this over with' attitude. Sure, Paul Stanley behaved like the rock star his is, all poses and leaps, but I feel it's all down to his commitment and enthusiasm that the band are still touring. I dunno, Gene Simmons just seems content to feast his eyes on the tastiest of female flesh he can find and doesn't come close to the focus of attention he was in the 'old' days. And he was wearing Adidas sneakers for God's sake! Also, while Eric Carr is certainly twice the drummer Peter Criss ever was, and Bruce Kulick is a more sober lead guitarist than his predecessors, they just seem to be there to make up the numbers" (Kerrang).
- Both AUD and VID circulate from this show, though the VID is incomplete.

September 25 - Wembley Arena, London, England
Promoter: Kennedy Street / MCP / Fair Warning
Other act(s): Kings of the Sun
Reported audience: (8,000 capacity)
Set list: Love Gun / Fits Like A Glove / Heaven's On Fire / Cold Gin / Black Diamond / Bang Bang You / No, No, No / Firehouse / Crazy Crazy Nights / Deuce / I Was Made For Lovin' You / Reason To Live / Tears Are Falling / I Love It Loud / Strutter / Shout it Out Loud / Lick It Up / Rock And Roll All Nite / Detroit Rock City
Notes:
- Audience filmed VID circulates from this show.

September 26 - NEC Arena, Birmingham, England
Promoter: Kennedy Street / MCP / Fair Warning
Other act(s): Kings of the Sun
Reported audience: (16,000 capacity)
Set list: Love Gun / Fits Like A Glove / Heaven's On Fire / Cold Gin / Black Diamond / Bang Bang You / No, No, No / Firehouse / Crazy Crazy Nights / Deuce / I Was Made For Lovin' You / Reason To Live / Tears Are Falling / I Love It Loud / Strutter / Shout It Out Loud / Lick It Up / Rock And Roll All Nite / Detroit Rock City
Notes:
- Reasonably acceptable audience filmed video circulates from this show.

September 27 - NEC Arena, Birmingham, England
Promoter: Kennedy Street / MCP / Fair Warning
Other act(s): Kings of the Sun
Reported audience: (16,000 capacity)

September 28 - St. George's Hall, Bradford, England
Promoter: Kennedy Street / MCP / Fair Warning
Other act(s): Kings of the Sun
Reported audience: 3,500 **SOLD-OUT
Set list: Love Gun / Fits Like A Glove / Heaven's On Fire / Cold Gin / Black Diamond / Bang Bang You / No, No, No / Firehouse / Crazy Crazy Nights / Deuce / I Was Made For Lovin' You / Oh Susannah/Medley / Reason To Live / Tears Are Falling / I Love It Loud / Strutter / Shout It Out Loud / Lick It Up / Rock And Roll All Nite / Detroit Rock City

September 29 - City Hall, Newcastle, England
Promoter: Kennedy Street / MCP / Fair Warning
Other act(s): Kings of the Sun
Reported audience: 2,135 **SOLD-OUT
Set list: Love Gun / Fits Like A Glove / Heaven's On Fire / Cold Gin / Black Diamond / Bang Bang You / No, No, No / Firehouse / Crazy Crazy Nights / Deuce / I Was Made For

Lovin' You / Reason To Live / Tears Are Falling / I Love It Loud / Strutter / Shout It Out Loud / Lick It Up / Rock And Roll All Nite / Detroit Rock City
Notes:
- This show circulates as an audience filmed VID.

October 1 - Playhouse Theatre, Edinburgh, Scotland
Promoter: Kennedy Street / MCP / Fair Warning
Other act(s): Kings of the Sun
Reported audience: 3,059 **SOLD-OUT

October 2 - Playhouse Theatre, Edinburgh, Scotland
Promoter: Kennedy Street / MCP / Fair Warning
Other act(s): Kings of the Sun
Reported audience: 3,059 **SOLD-OUT
Set list: Love Gun / Fits Like A Glove / Heaven's On Fire / Cold Gin / Black Diamond / Bang Bang You / No, No, No / Firehouse / Crazy Crazy Nights / Deuce / I Was Made For Lovin' You / Reason To Live / Tears Are Falling / I Love It Loud / Strutter / Shout It Out Loud / Oh Susannah/La Bamba/You Shook Me All Night Long/Good Times Bad Times / Lick It Up / Rock And Roll All Nite / Detroit Rock City
Notes:
- Roughly 50 minutes of the show was broadcast on Radio Clyde FM. A full AUD recording also exists.

October 3 - King's Hall, Belfast, Northern Ireland
Promoter: Wonderland Presents
Other act(s): Kings of the Sun
Reported audience: (28,000 capacity)
Set list: Love Gun / Fits Like A Glove / Heaven's On Fire / Cold Gin / Black Diamond / Bang Bang You / No, No, No / Firehouse / Crazy Crazy Nights / Deuce / I Was Made For Lovin' You / Reason To Live / Tears Are Falling / I Love It Loud / Strutter / Shout it Out Loud / Oh Susannah / La Bamba (partial) / Stairway To Heaven (partial) / Whole Lotta Love / Lick It Up / Rock And Roll All Nite / Detroit Rock City

Notes:
- Final show of the "Crazy Nights" tour. Towards the end of the show, Paul addresses the audience about the spitting that has covered the band with phlegm throughout the show: "Everybody here likes to spit, right? C'mon, I know you like it. Right? Now if you really wanna spit, when I count to three, why don't you spit up in the air and see if you can catch it on your nose."

- Kings of the Sun drummer, Clifford Hoad, recalled a purported Gene Simmons adventure during the visit to Belfast: "I can remember Gene Simmons having girl troubles in the motel; he would give them half hour each, down to the second. This all went astray when one of the girls decided she had fallen in love with him. I remember her screaming at him in a mixture of broken English and Hungarian, and him standing in the hallway sweating half naked with his bullet proof vest on signaling to me to get help!!!!. That gig was Belfast. When I asked him, 'what was with the bullet proof vest?' He said it gave him comfort, and for me not to worry about it. Quote 'You're not famous enough,' ha ha. He was right... Very funny guy" (Rock Radio NI, 10/16/10).

- A rather poor AUD recording (that starts out dreadfully but improves) has circulated from this show for many years, though it's representative of the poor sound quality of the venue. A complete video, with improved audio, also exists.

The Video

Details:
PolyGram Music Video 080-301-3 (U.S., 6/6/88)
Polygram Music Video 041-7072-2 (Australia, 1988)
Channel-5/PolyGram CFV-07782 (U.K., 1988)

Tracks:
01. Crazy Crazy Nights
Produced by Steven Brandman for The Company
Directed by Jean Pellerin & Doug Freel

02. Reason to Live
Produced by Doug Major for Cream Cheese Productions
Directed by Marty Callner

03. Turn on the Night
Produced by Bill Brigode for Cream Cheese Productions
Directed by Marty Callner

310 | Crazy Crazy Nights

Notes:
Produced by Eric Anderson and Len Epand. This video EP simply compiled the three videos issued in support of the "Crazy Nights" album. The original list price was $12.95.

Chart Action:
Chart Peak (USA): #15 (8/20/1988) with 6 weeks on charts. Other countries:

8/20/88	9/3/88	9/17/88	9/24/88
** 15 **	16	20	x

RIAA/Sales:
The "Crazy Nights" video was certified gold by the RIAA on Mar. 29, 1991.

The "Crazy" Reviews

A taste of the contemporaneous reviews the "Crazy Nights" album was anointed with...

"Run for the hills. They're back — this time without makeup and as loud and mindless as ever. This probably means a tour is in the works. The LP has 11 songs based on the same three themes: sex, partying and bad clothes. The word 'night' actually appears in the title of three of the songs, 'Crazy Crazy Nights,' 'Turn on the Night,' and 'Thief in the Night.' This is as close as the band will ever get to a concept album so buy yours now. You'll laugh, you'll cry, you'll KISS $10 goodbye" (Cleveland Plain Dealer, 10/2/87).

"With hit maker Nevison at the helm, group returns to the form it showed on 1985's 'Animalize'; 'Crazy Crazy Nights' has already debuted on the Hot 100. 'KISS Exposed' video has just gone platinum, ample proof that those awaiting a new KISS album are legion" (Billboard, 10/3/87).

"Going back to the last decade for a minute, I can recall seething at this group being pigeonholed into a band associated with the sub-munchkin or pre-teen crowd. Their makeup had a great deal to do with this, and the 'critics' often overlooked their music, particularly the guitar work of Ace Frehley. The KISS comic book in 1977 didn't help matters, either. I can recall of Gene Simmons saying that 'one of these days we will take off the makeup.' When the albums 'Unmasked' and 'The Elder' bombed in 1980 and 1981, it looked like the end for KISS. After all, they had outlasted their critics. It was announced that one more album would be released, and if it bombed, then KISS would disband. That

album was 'Creatures of the Night,' and it did well, in spite of the departure of Ace Frehley and Peter Criss. 'One more,' promised Simmons, and in 1983, off came the makeup with 'Lick it Up.' It went Platinum, as did the next two LPs, 'Animalize' and 'Asylum.'

That brings us up to 'Crazy Nights,' featuring new guitarist Bruce Kulick, who is already making a name for himself. The set is your basic KISS rock and roll album, with plenty of heavy guitar work. There is a cut called 'My Way,' but it is not Gene Simmons' tribute to Elvis (although Gene is an Elvis fan.) 'No, No, No' has shades of Van Halen, while 'When Your Walls Come Down' is your basic KISS rock and roll song. The group opted for Ron Nevison to produce this album, who has kept the basic KISS sound intact. This is the group's 21st album, and when I was reviewing new KISS albums in 1977, I did not think I would be doing the same in 1987" (Cumberland Sunday Times, 10/4/87).

"According to Paul Stanley of KISS, 'if you want bad news, read the papers. We're here to make you smile and forget all that.' To that end, the highly coiffed but naked-faced boys have released their 21st (honest) album, 'Crazy Nights,' hot on the heels of their platinum sellers 'Animalize' and 'Asylum.' A clue to the album's philosophy is this Stanley quite: 'Perspiration is, after all, the greatest inspiration.' 'Crazy Nights' has the KISS signature sexist material such as a couple of numbers with the imaginative titles 'Bang Bang You' and 'Good Girl Gone Bad' but, all things considered, it gets almost sentimental at times ('I'll Fight Hell to Hold You' and 'When Your Walls Come Down'). When they're not busy acting like overaged heavy metal rockers, the members of KISS are quite capable of turning out melodic, memorable tunes that are polished without taking on that tinny gleam so common in heavy metal" (Arkansas Gazette, 10/11/87).

"KISS was never as popular after the fans got to see what it really looked like. It became just another hard-rock band trying to slug it out. But the main factor that contributed to its downfall was not the unmasking. The decline had begun before, when the band started to get too slick. That took the outrage out of it. KISS has now recognized that. With 'Crazy Nights,' great strides are made to regain some of that original woolly edge. If there is anything fancy on this record, it is well camouflaged. Any synthesizer work is set back into the corners while sonic guitars occupy centre stage. KISS no longer wants to be a band that is spoken of in the past tense. The tunes here work at a frenetic pace as if to prove that the band is not licked yet" (Ottawa Citizen, 10/16/87).

"KISS keeps it simple, but without sounding all that stupid on 'Crazy Nights' (Mercury). As if to confirm the suspicion that there's more to KISS than cartoon makeup and the length of Gene Simmons's tongue, there's even less vaudeville and more music on the new album than there was on '85's comeback, 'Asylum.' There's little or nothing here that hasn't been done elsewhere by any number of other outfits. But with all of those years under its belt, and with producer Ron Nevison (Heart, Ozzy Osbourne) at the helm, KISS does it better and sharper than the competition — with a defter touch, less overkill, and a better knack for knocking off snappy melodies and for making the power chords fit the music. While the band probably squeezes just enough routine hormones, hedonism and escapism into these cuts to keep even the old fans happy, those same fans should be warned that most of those songs are also suspiciously melodic and good-spirited" (Winnipeg Free Press, 11/12/87).

"'They try to tell us we don't belong/that's all right, we're millions strong/this is my music, it makes me proud,' KISS says on the title cut. With that disclaimer, the group tries to

steal back its audience from Mötley Crüe. Give KISS credit. After 15 years it is still adept at writing authentic heavy metal that has some gut-level appeal. 'Crazy Crazy Nights' is already a hit, and 'I'll Fight Hell to Hold You' is as good as this genre gets. There is conviction in the vocals and the guitar playing is tough. Paul Stanley's 'My Way' is the group's sop to Van Halen. The keyboards are straight from 'Jump,' while the lead guitar is cribbed from Eddie Van Halen's work on Michael Jackson's 'Beat It.' Despite KISS musical contributions, what's truly astounding is how these 40-year-old men have remained in a state of arrested lyrical development. 'Liar, liar got your pants on fire,' begins 'When Your Walls Come Down.' KISS continues to display the social consciousness of cavemen and 12-year-old boys — although that is an insult to cavemen and 12-year-old boys" (Boston Globe, 11/19/87).

"Make-up and members may come and go, but the songs pretty much remain the same. This is competently executed but numbing metal-by-the-numbers, from the ode to head banging, 'Crazy, Crazy Nights,' to stoopid single-entendre exercises like 'Bang Bang You" (Los Angeles Times, 12/13/87).

"Twenty-one albums down the line and I'll be damned if those KISS fellas don't just keep getting better and better. Sedate all po-faced KISS kritiks, give the Washington wives a pacifying enema, and be sure to lock up all of your household pets... 'cause the original bad boyz are back and they're still hungry! We've all heard the rumours about 'keyboards' and 'wimping out,' but I'm here to reassure you that 'Crazy Nights' is quintessential KISS, a glorious amalgam of the very finest aspects of a glittering career, not so much a change in style, more a consolidation of the sophisticated Metal that the band have claimed as their own during the 1980s... Yet another triumph for the World's Greatest Metal Band, with Paul Stanley's work in particular reaching unparalleled levels of maturity, no doubt helped by his new writing partners" (Kerrang #156).

The "Crazy" Quotes

A taste of the contemporaneous quotes from the "Crazy Nights" era...

Gene: "Album number 21. Ironically, it's as exciting as the first one. When we started I remember thinking that if I had one LP out I'd be satisfied for the rest of my life... There's no new ground covered on this record, it's KISS as KISS should be — loud, f**king music! We've encountered a problem in that it seems far too sexual in content!! Maybe we should call it: 'Danger! Contains Too Much Sexual Content.' Hey, the politics of sex are important!!" (Kerrang #160).

Paul: "I think the songs and the overall feel of the band is pretty cocksure, very confident, and pretty unstoppable. It just feels like it's the right time and the right music... I somehow see it as a cross between 'Animalize' and 'Destroyer.' It's big and it's broad" (Rock Scene Spotlights #2).

Gene: "After meeting with Ron [Nevison], I came to the conclusion that though looking in the mirror you could see yourself, sometimes if you look too closely all you see are the same eyes staring back at you. In other words, if you hold your face too close to the mirror, you really see nothing. So this may be an interesting way to get a new perspective on the stuff. We certainly don't intend to bring out a Heart records, even though it was a wonderful kind of record, that's not what we're about. So I think it's gonna be an interesting collaboration" (Rock Scene Spotlights #2).

Gene: "It's a good album — a collection of rock 'n' roll songs in the tradition of 'Good Golly, Miss Molly.' We're not trying to go where no music has gone before. We're not dealing with the secret of life. We're talking about the facts of life" (Daily Oklahoman, 11/20/87).

Paul: "[Ron Nevison]'s someone I wanted to work with for a long time. There are a lot of guys around who consider themselves producers, but unlike doctors, there's no course, no license necessary. A record producer is something you wake up one morning and decide to be. So there's not that many people we respect enough to work with" (Toronto Star, 12/9/87).

Paul: "I was supposed to produce the new Poison album, which I very much wanted to do, but then it conflicted with the KISS schedule. I wasn't interested in doing it in any less than the best of circumstances. I'm interested in acting and producing, but I will only do either if I feel right about the projects. I don't want to ever apologize for anything I do, so the way to ensure that is not to do anything that I'm not sure of the quality" (Toronto Star, 12/9/87).

Paul: "Certainly there've been times when our career has been up or down, but you have to expect that when you've been around as long as us. I don't think any band, whether it's the Rolling Stones or anybody, is always on top. You can't, and be around this long. There's always this year's hula-hoop, and people are going to want to play with it, but when they get tired of it they go back to what was good" (Boston Herald, 12/11/87).

Dedicated to the memory of Eric Carr.

BOCA RATON PUBLIC LIBRARY, FLORIDA

3 3656 0700430 5

781.660922 Gil
Gill, Julian,
Danger Zone

DISCARDED

Made in the USA
Columbia, SC
27 July 2020

14858523R00176